If you want a mailman's shoes, don

Through snow, rain, sun and wind, Merrit takes us on one adventure after another.

You will also learn that while dog's get a lot of attention, future postal workers need to keep their eyes open for attackers with long ears.

JIM FERRETTI
Assistant News Director, FM News 101 KXL, Portland, Oregon.
Former kid on Mailman Mike's route
(you will meet Mike inside these pages)

Reading this book took me back to my carrying days. Through Merrit's words I was able to picture my first day on the job, and yes my first encounter with a not so friendly dog. This book was wonderfully written and worthy of all the praise coming to it.

MARSHA TATE
Manager customer service,
15 years with the PO, 3 years at Creston.

Merrit touches the heart of what a mail carrier is to a community and to our country. I laughed and cried at the stories while nodding my head in my own memories. This is what happens when you have a caring soul delivering your mail..

BILLY GANS
Manager Customer Service
35 years
Three month detail at Creston Station, 2012

Merrit Hearing was meant to be a letter carrier and "walk through the lives of his customers." I doubt anyone grew up dreaming of walking 12 miles a day, pushing paper into boxes and slots in all kinds of weather. But some of us, who, like Merrit, put on the blue suit and packed that mail bag, found their calling and embraced the job—even enjoyed it.

He has a down-to-earth way of telling the story of his career. From the uncertainty of a new job, to the realization the job was so much more than delivering mail and walking the miles, and all the way to retirement and beyond. Relationships were established—some for a lifetime others that faded away. But they all made an impact on Merrit.

His story will open the eyes of anyone not familiar with the daily trials and tribulations of a neighborhood mailman. Letter carriers will relate to all the things that can and do happen in this supposedly repetitive job.

Merrit does an excellent job of blending his personality into the story; his interactions with his customers over the years are what make this book hard to put down. He blends the different aspects of his personal life into the lives of the people on his route and also his fellow letter carriers.

JERRY G. FITZSIMMONS
Retired Letter Carrier
Retired Vice President of Br. 82 NALC

And Then the Rabbit Bit Me

WHY I LIKED BEING A MAILMAN

BY MERRIT H. HEARING

The adventures, encounters, and musings
of a Correspondence Distribution Engineer

TABLE OF CONTENTS

DEDICATION

These writings are dedicated to three individuals with whom I spent much more time with than I could have ever imagined. The four of us worked side-by-side-by-side-by-side on routes 54, 55, 56, and 57 at the Creston Station for 16 years. We loved like family. And we also argued and fought like family. We drove each other crazy. And we came alongside and helped one another out and picked each other up when those times of necessity arose. There was lots of laughter. Oh, was there an abundance of laughter. At each other, at ourselves, and at the occasional unintended machinations of our employer. But mostly, we labored together, working mightily to get the product of bills, letters, bulk business mail (don't call it junk mail, please), magazines, and packages into the waiting hands of our patrons. For those years of deeply remembered and mostly appreciated experiences, I lovingly dedicate this book to

Mailman Mike, Annie (Nabes), and Doug the Slug.

Thanks for putting up with this broken-down, grumpy old EX-mailman.

Chapter 1

YA GOTTA HAVE GOOD SHOES

"The privilege of sharing a lot of life"

"Tonight I feel a most fortunate man. Dang, I have been blessed. I was a mailman." It was the evening of Wednesday, April 29, 2015. These were the final words I typed on my social media post the night before my last day as a walking mailman of 30 years with the United States Postal Service.

I had been posting regularly for the past several months, updating my friends, coworkers, and customers of my thoughts and emotions as I made my way to the end of my career. Was it possible? Had I actually come to the end of the line? I had started my passage toward this ultimate day as a young man still in his 20s, and now I was a couple months short of being an "old" man near the age of 60.

When I started a first-class stamp was priced at 20 cents. When I walked out the door of my job for the final time, they cost you 49 cents each. I had worn (and worn out) five mailbags that had draped over my right shoulder day after day. I survived ten dog bites, 30 wet and occasionally cold Januarys (Mr. Winter), and 30 disgusting and sometimes sticky Augusts (Mr. Summer). The last 27 years of my career were spent on one route in southeast Portland, Oregon. So many days. So many miles. So many encounters. So many phone bills. Heck, so many SHOES!

Over my decades of delivering mail I had the privilege of sharing a lot of life with a lot of people, not only in the mail I brought, but also in moments shared with families. Kids growing. First days of school. Those same kids going off to college. Birthdays. Boyfriends and girlfriends. Graduations. Weddings. Divorces. Strokes. Cancer. Birth. Death.

So, come on along and walk some miles with me as I introduce you to some amazing folks, hard laboring coworkers, incredible kids, a few critters, and some memorable encounters with all of the above. You'll need some tasty and healthy snacks, plenty of H2O, and some supportive and comfy footwear. Now, about them folks.

Chapter 2

IT ALL COMES BACK TO PEOPLE, DOESN"T IT?

"Without my customers this book would not exist"

Even now—four plus years after my last day—it still feels quite bizarre that my career is complete. I started my postal journey in February of 1985 and spent my first two years working out of Multnomah Station located in southwest Portland. After a year and a couple of months employed at two other stations I finally made my way to Creston Post Office, landing on route 0655 and spending the remainder of my 27 years in the Postal Service on this same route, although with three small boundary changes over the course of the years.

Thirty years at the same job appears to be a bit unusual these days. In the Postal Service, 27 years on the same route is very unusual, especially on a walking route as opposed to a driving route. Most older carriers eventually choose to sit in a truck and drive the mail from stop to stop rather than walk. Having said that, when I retired there were two carriers still working at my station who had been on their routes longer than I had.

Over the years, as I told stories to my family and friends about my escapades, I was encouraged to first share them on social media and eventually to compile them into book form. I truly wish for my customers to recognize themselves in these stories, catching the appreciation that I feel and affection I hold for these moments and for them personally.

But at the same time it is imperative I still keep their identities private. For these reasons I have chosen to "hide" their real names, yet I will attach new names that keep the same cadence or style. For example, "David" might become "Daniel," and "Nancy" might be changed to "Naomi." You will also come across little ones described as "route kids" or "Route Kids." The capital "R" and "K" means those children were born while their family lived on my route. In other words, I had known them all their lives, and I was the only regular mailman they had known. Lower case "r" and "k" refer to any kids living on my route at any point in their life, just not from birth.

I have tried to be as accurate as possible with my memories. Fortunately, social media recorded most of my events and stories by date and time. When sharing these stories I will record the date next to the story, along with comments from others if germane.

In the interest of clarity I have made occasional edits to the original posts, but I have not strayed from the heart and spirit of what I originally wrote. What you will not read are any blastings from me at the United States Postal Service. Did I ever have issues with my employer? That sound you just heard was my hand clapping over my mouth. Sometimes I had serious problems with my bosses or the organization they represented. Hey, who doesn't? This is not the place for it. Three reasons.

First, the Post Office can afford much better attorneys than I can. (That's a joke, folks.) Second, you would only be hearing my version and idea of those moments. But third, and most importantly, I want these pages to be a celebration of the privilege I had to walk through people's lives. That phrase and idea—walking through people's lives— will come up again and again throughout these pages.

I also want to be honest in the sense of full disclosure. My career was not all lovely, and I went many years really not enjoying it at all. It was just what I did to bring home the money. There were many times when I regretted becoming a mailman and a couple of times I took significant looks elsewhere to see if I could possibly do anything else. Fortunately, I came around to realizing this is what I did and that I had to decide if I wanted to try to enjoy and appreciate what I was doing or just turn my life into a moping gripefest.

As the chapter heading says, it always comes back to people, doesn't it? It certainly did for me. How much? I will cite one simple long-lasting example. When our own children were still small enough to trick-or-treat on Halloween night, we took them around our neighborhood where we lived, of course. But what I couldn't wait for was to pile them into the car and drive them to MY neighborhood, to MY people, so MY customers could see them and talk with them and see how much they had grown over the previous year (uh, my kids, not my customers).

If you read the dedication to this book (and if you didn't, please go back and do so now), you saw three names listed—the three fellow letter carriers who I worked next to for so many years. But here's the deal. Without my customers, young and old alike, this book would not exist. So most of what you will read are my dealings with those folks, the ones who I met and chatted with day-by-day—some of them for well over two decades. I cannot thank them enough for the privilege and honor of walking through their lives for such a good portion of mine. Of course, if I had had my way, I would not have met any of them.

Chapter 3

BUT I DON'T WANNA BE A MAILMAN

"Fill out about 168 different forms"

I never intended to deliver mail for a living. Never entered my mind for a second. I was not one of those kids who wanted to be a fireman or policeman or astronaut . . . or a mailman when I grew up. In fact, even though I have memories of those other professions as a boy, either through firsthand experience (we attended church with the city Fire Marshal) or on television (I watched every rocket launch I could), I have but one shadow of a memory of our mailman. It is the vaguest imaginable memory of me being very young and playing in my sandbox. And a tall, swarthy-complexioned man in uniform walking by and saying "hello" as he passed by. That image looks very much like the cover of this book. But I truly could not tell you if this actually happened or if it has simply evolved in my imagined consciousness.

Although I certainly played outside, most people from my youth remember me as an indoor kind of kid. Humorously enough, at some of my reunions those who have not been in touch with me over the years were quite surprised to learn that I had become a mailman. I had more than one conversation that had this statement directed at me: "What, YOU work outside?!" Uh, yes.

What they remember is a kid who wanted to be a radio announcer from the age of eight. But that career did not work out and as I hit my adult years I found myself in various warehouse-type jobs. I boxed books, was a shipping clerk, and worked for an appliance parts company. I tried to make two different sales jobs work for me. I am not a salesman. As my uncle once told me, "You couldn't sell a dollar for 50 cents." I even studied to be an accountant for two years.

I don't remember that I took any interest in postal workers even as an adult – with one large exception. I worked as a shipping clerk for a Christian book warehouse in the mid-to-late 70's. The company was a middleman between publishers of Christian books and bookstores. Everyday we shipped hundreds of boxes of books all over the country via the postal service and also that company in brown. We had the same delightful postal truck driver pick up our parcels each day and we got to know him very well. Bill was always utterly cheerful, always had a kind word to share, and had a lovely uproarious laugh. Saying good-bye to Bill was one of my sorrows at leaving that job. Many years later after I had been working for the Post Office for several months, we sat down to dinner at a restaurant one night. I got situated at the table, looked across the aisle and was thrilled to see Bill sitting there having dessert with his wife. He was many years into his retirement. We had a nice little chat and he got a kick that I was now working for his former employer.

Then a few years after I got married to my first wife Cynthia, she was working as a waitress at a restaurant. I was not particularly happy with my current employment situation and one day she was serving lunch to some regular customers—a group of veteran mailmen. They suggested to her that I should take the postal civil service exam and go to work for the Post Office.

I was not the least bit interested. At least, not then. But after a couple more years spinning my wheels, I decided to give it a try. So in 1982 I took the United States Postal Service Exam for clerks and carriers.

The test consisted mainly of a piece of paper with three columns of fictional addresses. We had a few minutes to study these columns. Then the test went to another sheet of paper where these same addresses were listed, but not in columns. The assignment was that you had to remember what column any particular address had been listed in. I scored nearly 94%, which would normally garner an interview leading to a job in a short time. Normally. Because normally only a few hundred or maybe two or three thousand would take the exam at any one time. But in Portland in 1982, 18,000 folks took the test. So I had to wait nearly two and a half years for my first interview.

My interview went fabulously. I hit it off immediately with the woman who met with me. She liked the way I spoke of my current employer, Johnstone Supply, and I landed a job with the United States Postal Service. As a clerk. Excellent. That meant I could work inside. Except I didn't pass the physical. Don't ask. So now I had to have minor surgery, which shoved me back three months.

I got hired again, fortunately being interviewed by the same kind woman as before. She still wanted me to work for the Post Office, so I was "re-hired," so to speak. But this time it was as a city letter carrier, better known to the general public as a mailman. (Although I always preferred the moniker: Correspondence Distribution Engineer.) Sigh. Not what I wanted.

However, what I could do after delivering mail for a few months was become a supervisor, which meant I would not have to trudge all those miles.

My first day as an employee of the United States Postal Service was Saturday, February 2, 1985. Our group of new hirees spent three weeks at the downtown office of the Portland Post Office, learning how to drive postal vehicles, the rules and regulations of working for the Postal Service, how to case mail, and how to fill out about 168 different forms.

I am by nature not a competitive person. But I had waited a long time for this opportunity, and it became important to me to be the best in our "class." At each level of testing to see how we were doing at casing mail for speed and accuracy I had the top score among the trainees. If I was going to do this, I wanted to do it well. And that is how and why this all started and happened. But, first, there was the whole dog thing.

Chapter 4

HOW FLEXIBLE DO I HAVE TO BE?

"People walked out of that room"

On the day my postal career began I was 29 years old, married with one child, a little girl seven months old. I was in good health, ready to take on the United States Postal Service and show them how it is done. Well, maybe.

The very first item the Post Office wanted to test us new employees on was how well we followed directions. There were about 30 of us in a classroom sitting at desks. We were given sheets of paper that had a series of instructions on them.

The person giving the test got our attention and told us to read the paper carefully and do everything that was listed on it. I started to carefully read the directions. I have a tendency to hurry through tests, wanting to be one of the first to finish. I was no good as any kind of athlete so mental games were what I tried to excel at. So I wanted to get through this test as quickly as possible to impress my new employer.

But suddenly one of the other new hires stood up at his desk and began counting to ten . . . OUT LOUD! Then another one began to do the same thing. Then both of them began to clap quite loudly. What the—?

I looked at the instructions. It was a list of 25–30 very strange instructions. Standing up and counting to ten out loud. Clapping. Making owl sounds. Doing jumping jacks. (In all fairness, I do not actually remember the specific items, but they were at least this bizarre if not more so.)

However, I also have a tendency to read all the words on a page, so I carefully started at the top to see what was going on. There, in the middle of a phalanx of directions were these words: "Before you do any of the items on this list, read through the entire list and the directions at the bottom."

I carefully read through all the odd items and then found this instruction at the bottom of the paper: "Do not do any of these listed instructions, but simply turn this paper over and fold your hands to signal you have finished." Whew. Escaped. And let me tell you, these instructions got weirder and weirder as you got farther down the list.

About a dozen people were saying strange things and doing all types of curious things. Lesson taught. But this was not nearly as surprising as what came next.

———

They dimmed the lights and we watched "The Dog Movie." The Post Office wanted to make sure we knew what we were in for. Now, in those days no one had heard of a pit bull and even rottys were not common. The scary dog in those days was the infamous Doberman pinscher. So we proceeded to watch a dramatized set of dog attacks on mailmen.

No blood and guts but lots of growling and barking. And I kid you not, after waiting for nearly three years to get a job at the Post Office, five or six people walked out of that room during the film or immediately after. They wanted no part of the job. I was stunned! Wait . . . WHAT?! It's the

Post Office. Being a mailman. Did they really not make the connection about dogs and the job?

Eventually we were separated into two groups. Some went to driver training (learning how to drive right-hand vehicles of different sizes) while others learned how to case mail and fill out the forms. Then after a week or so the groups switched. Each group went through three weeks of training. The week of driver instruction (which included a video starring the iconic Jack Webb), one week of learning how to quickly and accurately case mail, and one week of studying rules, forms, and other miscellaneous items. My group had 12 people in it. I was very surprised to find out a few years later that out of those 12, I was the only one who continued on and had a career with the Post Office.

I survived my three weeks of training and was assigned to the Multnomah Post Office. I was hired as a Part-Time Flexible (PTF) City Letter Carrier. Flexible meaning they "owned" me. They would tell me where to work, what to do, and whatever hours they wanted me to show up. Alright, time to get this show on the road. Um . . . where's Multnomah?

Chapter 5

I REALLY NEED MY PANTS TODAY

"Was actually going to disrobe to get the mail delivered"

It turned out that Multnomah Post Office was located quite some distance from my home, way out in southwest Portland. It was an area of town I was not at all familiar with, which my supervisor found out one day about two weeks after I started.

"To get to the route you are doing today you need to head down Barbur Boulevard."

I looked at him with a completely blank look.

"Okay then, go out to Pacific Highway . . ."

Same look. "Sorry, boss, I don't know where either of those streets are."

Now, reader, you must understand if you are unfamiliar with the Portland metropolitan area, these are not little roads. They are huge with LOTS of traffic on them 24 hours a day. The look on my boss's face. Yikes.

Anyway, I found my way to Multnomah Station and walked in. Wow! There were real-life honest-to-goodness mailmen handling honest-to-goodness letters and magazines and packages. And I was there. Now this was exciting! But I also felt about six years old and about to attend my first day of school. I was beyond intimidated.

Better make a good first impression. The boss led me over to a grizzled old veteran of the Post Office who had been delivering mail for close to 30 years. Charlie. Nice guy. I wanted to let him know how delighted I was to be there. Now, you must remember at this point I saw working at the Post Office as an exceptionally glamorous career. I mean, delivering the mail! As I think back on this moment, I still want to face-palm myself.

I asked, "So, do you still get a big kick out of delivering the mail for the United States Post Office?" Yes, I really asked him this.

He was very kind and gently told me that, no, the sheen had kind of worn off on that a bit.

But I had actually stumbled into a perfect station to start off with. Nearly all the carriers there were extremely helpful and understanding of my overabundance of questions and comments. Which isn't to say they were not above giving us newbies a hard time occasionally.

I was still early in my career and thus had not been issued a uniform yet, so I was working in my regular civilian clothes. One Saturday a few weeks after I had started at Multnomah I was assigned a section on a business route that traveled along Barbur Boulevard. (Yes, I finally figured out where it was.)

Since it was a Saturday, many of the businesses were closed. I was given my keys and set out to deliver the section. The main key—called an Arrow key—that is assigned to carriers opens up all the blue collection boxes you see plus those doors in businesses and apartment buildings that open up to a series of mailboxes.

On this particular Saturday I let myself into an office building that was unoccupied for the day by first using the Arrow key to open a lockbox that holds the key to the office building. I stepped up to the mailbox unit that held the mail for multiple offices. It works with the large Arrow key being inserted into a lock and the entire door opens revealing all the mail receptacles to the mailman, but when locked and shut simply allows each individual business to withdraw its own mail. NORMALLY the key is attached to a clip-on device that is worn on the belt.

But this was not a normal situation. Since I was not wearing a uniform I was also not wearing a belt so the key chain itself was wrapped around a belt loop on my pants. The vets at the Post Office were not aware that I was not wearing a belt, which meant they did not know the Arrow key was attached to my pants.

I walked up to the wall of mailboxes that had the one main door and inserted my key. It would not turn the lock. I tried everything I could think of, but the lock would not budge. Well, I would just pull the key back out and find a phone and call my boss to explain.

Except the key would not come out of the lock. At all. I pushed, pulled, and twisted that key on its chain every which way I could. Nothing. It. Would. Not. Budge. As in, the door would not open. As in, I could not turn the key any further. As in, I could not turn the key back and start over. As in, I also could not remove the key from the lock. As in, I WAS NOW PERMANENTLY ATTACHED TO THIS MAILBOX!!

Remember, this is the mid-1980s, so there was no such thing as a cell phone. I called out for help, which went unanswered of course since it was a Saturday and there was no one in the building. I yanked on that sucker with all my might. It didn't budge at all. It is STUCK!

Now I began to panic. The key was stuck in the lock and the key chain was still attached to my pants. I looked around. There was no one there. I was stuck to this large mail receptacle. Now what?

I saw only one option—and it was terrifying. I would have to take off my shoes . . . and then . . . remove my pants. It was the only way I could extricate myself from the mailboxes. So I would have to strip to my undies, walk out of the building and find a phone, and call my boss to come rescue me. Not good—not good—not good. I mean it was a Saturday, but Barbur Boulevard was still quite busy with traffic. I had no choice. I took my shoes off. I took a deep breath and reached for the zipper on my pants.

"Can I help you?"

A female voice. I looked to my right and saw a woman in her 40s walking toward me. She had been down the hall putting in some extra hours of work on this Saturday and had noticed the postal vehicle pull up several minutes before. But she had also seen that it was still parked in front of the building, long after the time it should have taken to deliver the mail. So she had come to investigate. I explained my dilemma. She laughed and said, "Ah, they didn't tell you about the trick with the door, did they?"

"Uh, no."

The door had been damaged many months before and required two slight manual adjustments to open properly—the kind of adjustments that took three seconds to do if you knew how and where to do them.

I would have been left stranded there till my retirement 30 years later. Yeah, no, they must have "accidentally" forgotten to tell me that little tidbit of somewhat important information.

Oh, boy, did they have a hoot and a holler back at the station when I told them what had transpired. Apparently they had pulled this stunt on many beginners. But, of course, I was the first one who was actually going to disrobe to get the mail delivered. Yeah, hilarious . . . NOW.

⸻

But they were good folks at the station who never meant any real harm. And as I said, they trained me well.

There was Larry, a wonderful man who always wore cowboy boots to work and was extremely helpful and friendly and had the gift of being able to speak quickly in a kind of pigeon-English where he switched the beginning letters of words. "It's quite rainy" became "It's rite quainy."

His casing neighbor was a character named "Chessy-Fide." Or at least that's what Larry called him. His real name was Mel. After several months I learned that "Chessy-Fide" actually meant "Fessy-Chide" in Larry-talk, which stood for "Fessie-Child," which was a knockoff of Mel's last name. (You had to be there.)

Larry was so ridiculously charming that he could get away with saying just about anything and not offend anyone. And when he did say something questionable, his eyes would twinkle and he would declare—with just a hint of a southern drawl— "You can say it if it's true."

⸻

And there was dear old John. He had one of the driest wits I have ever come across. Old? Well, his career in the Post Office had started in the 1940s!

Dave had also been around for decades. He had a huge heart, but was very quiet. My vivid memory of him is during the Christmas season when he would come into work on his day off and stroll through the aisles of the station playing Christmas carols on his accordion.

Another veteran carrier was Don. I worked a few feet from him for about 18 months and I got a kick out of his low-key temperament and his love for many things sports the way I was back then. Don introduced me to Fantasy Football, which was a brand-new concept to me. I loved the idea of it and started up a Fantasy Football League with five other friends of mine. Our league—of which I was the commissioner (well, I was the one who started it!)— lasted 17 years. I have kept in touch with Don over the years. A good man.

Sannye was a huge help in showing me around the place, introducing me to folks, and generally being an unofficial tutor for me. She had started a mere three months before me but already knew enough to help steer me clear of trouble. Well, except with the whole key-stuck-to-the-mailbox fiasco.

Two other newbies made their way to our station in the next few months. Doug, who you read about in the dedication. I would eventually catch up with Doug again at Creston Station and we worked together for 29 of my 30 years in the Post Office. And Dwyn.

Dwyn was this sweet, tiny little gal who the station sort of adopted. She was as nice as could be and a bit shy at first. She would spend her entire career at Multnomah before retiring two years after me. We went to each other's retirement parties and have stayed in touch.

So back to my first days. I went out with Charley a few times to learn how to deliver mail from a half-ton vehicle (a large van) and a quarter-ton jeep. I was informed that a jeep was better known as a "tuna can on wheels." They were not the type of jeep you see advertised on television to go out four-wheeling. They were a rickety and battered conglomeration of right-hand drive vehicles that you would never want to depend on to get you somewhere in haste or comfort. Despite what you may think, understanding how to work a right-hand drive vehicle is not difficult. A bit weird at first, but you learn to adapt surprisingly fast.

Then I went out for a few days with another veteran letter carrier on what the Post Office calls a "Park & Loop route," where you drive to the route, walk a "loop" of about 15–30 homes and return to the vehicle to drive to the next loop. I learned how to "finger the mail," (hold a set of letters in your one hand while looking through them to get the next group ready for your next delivery stop. Just like you look through your bills at home, only with a full handful of letters).

Finally, I was ready to go out on my own. Prepare the mail at the station, load it into my tun . . . er . . . jeep, and go out and do a route by myself from start to finish. I had taken the postal exam. I had waited nearly three years. I had been delayed and finally hired. I had received training downtown on how to drive properly. I had received intensive training at the station on how to actually deliver the mail. Excellent! What could possibly go wrong?

Chapter 6

WAIT! COME BACK, COME BACK!!

"I ran through an arborvitae tree"

My first day solo. I had been waiting for this day for such a long time. I was anxious to make my mark. There was a lot of mail this particular day because it was the day after a holiday. So I got out of the office a bit late.

I was on a dismount route. A dismount route was sort of a combination of a driving route and a Park & Loop route. The mailboxes were not placed next to the street like they were on a driving route, but the houses were too far apart to do Park & Loops. So what you would do is drive up to a house, park and secure your vehicle, walk the mail up to the mailbox, then get back into the vehicle and drive to the next house.

It was not a fluid way to deliver the mail, but the only reasonable way it could be done in those types of neighborhoods. I loaded my jeep with the day's mail. Again, these jeeps were not exactly upscale vehicles. They were not made for off-roading adventures or driving over cliffs to some remote campsite. There was no air-conditioning (except a dusty five revolutions per minute, seven-inch wide fan) and a heater that would raise the cab temp from 40 degrees to either 42 or 112—depending on the faultiness of the coils.

And it felt like you WERE driving over a cliff if you hit a small pebble in the road.

But on this day I did not care. I was a mailman about to deliver the goods to several hundred homes without any help. I climbed into my tuna ca . . . er . . . jeep and drove off from the postal station at Multnomah, ready to be a real honest-to-goodness mailman! This is what I had been waiting for.

About a dozen houses into the route I pulled into a long, flat driveway. I would have to back out after delivering the mail, so I could turn around and head down the other side of the street. This driveway was very long and ran perpendicular to the house. I grabbed the mail, stepped out of the jeep, and walked up the sidewalk to put the mail in the box. The sidewalk was at a 90-degree angle from the driveway and then took a short left and up a few steps to the porch where the mailbox was.

I put the mail in the box, came down the steps, and came around the corner of the house to head back to my jeep—which was not there. Silly me, I must have parked farther down the driveway than I was remembering.

I took several more steps back and could now see a lot of the driveway in both directions. Gulp. No jeep. I raced the remaining distance to the driveway and looked to my right. There was my jeep . . . without me in it . . . rolling down the driveway . . . heading unhindered toward the open-doored garage of the house . . . and a BMW parked inside! (I must tell you that even now as I type this, over 30 years later, I still almost feel physically sick).

I had not only stepped out of the vehicle without the keys, without removing the keys from the ignition, I had not only left the jeep running, but I had also LEFT IT IN GEAR!!! If that jeep hit that car, my career would be over. If you had a vehicular accident during your first 90 days on the job (a postal employee's probation period), you were automatically terminated.

I saw my postal career rolling down that driveway into oblivion. And after waiting three years, a stupid mistake of monumental proportions was going to steal my hopes away. I ran as fast as I have ever run in my life. I ran THROUGH an arborvitae tree (I still don't know how I did that), caught up to the jeep, and slammed my foot on the brake about seven or eight feet before the jeep would have crashed into the BMW.

Three things saved my career that day. One, I had not shut the door of the jeep. Two, this was a very old jeep and even though it was still running and in gear, it was still rolling down that driveway at a snail's pace. Like a slow motion scene from a movie. But mostly, the reason I got to deliver mail for the next 30 years was a simple one: it was a right-hand drive vehicle. If the jeep had been left-hand drive, my career would have been toast.

My parents had raised me to be an honest person. But nothing had actually happened, so I saw no reason to call in and report this mishap. To this day, until this moment when they may be reading this account, I have never told anyone in postal management about this incident. I told my family, of course, and over the years we have had many a laugh about it. As a matter of fact, that year for my 30th birthday, my mother— who had been a champion cake decorator back in the day—made a cake and decorated the top with a drawing of a mailman chasing a jeep down the street yelling after it, "Wait, come back, come back!"

But I made it through the remainder of that day without further mishap.

As the days and weeks passed, the job of being a mailman took on a familiar pattern, which allowed me to begin noticing my surroundings, so to speak. I made it through my 90 days without incident and was able to relax a bit.

After I had been at my job for 99 days, my supervisor came up to me one morning and offered me a "congratulations" and informed me that I was no longer a PTF—that I had achieved the status of being a "Regular Carrier." What I did know was that now I was much more protected within the job if I had an accident or illness—and more importantly, I was now guaranteed at least 40 hours of work per week.

What I did not know was how extraordinarily quick this was. I found out later that almost everyone hired in the past at the Post Office had been PTFs for months and sometimes years before they made regular.

As the years progressed and hundreds of newbies came along after me, virtually all of them had to wait many years to achieve the status of regular carrier. There was just the briefest of windows in the mid-80s where new carriers made regular in such a short time. (It all has to do with a mathematical formula comparing the number of new hires to the number of current employees.)

So you may be wondering if over the length of my career I tended to let folks know how quickly I became a regular carrier as they waited month after interminable month to reach that status themselves. Hey, would I do that?

Time continued to march on and the idea of doing this job for 30 years became more and more plausible. So I started to ask myself some questions. How tough is this job going to be on me physically? What are the varying personalities of my workmates? How do I deal with the weather? (My first Mr. Summer came along. You will read much more about him and me in later chapters). But I did make it through the first spring, summer, and fall fairly unscathed. Then Mr. Winter hit. A whole new set of problems to deal with.

My first winter in the Post Office was a cold one. This led to two moments that caught my attention forthwith. One was funny, the other quite scary. I was delivering on another dismount route one Saturday afternoon. It was bright and sunny, but there was snow and ice in patches everywhere. I had to drop off mail at a house that had a two-length car driveway that was steep and frozen over. Fortunately, at the far end of the driveway there was a stairway that had been cleared off that led up to the walkway and porch. I made the delivery safely and headed back. One step before I safely reached the stairs I hit a patch of ice at the top of the driveway. My left foot went out from under me and I found myself barreling down the driveway balanced wobbily on one foot and in a sitting position.

I slid down the entire length of the driveway, hit a dry spot at the bottom, popped up into a standing position directly in front of my postal van and calmly stepped up and into my car as if I entered it this way every day of my life. I would have paid serious money to have seen video footage of this maneuver.

On another bitingly cold afternoon I was sent out to help someone else finish their route. I had not been on this route before so I was unfamiliar with the roads. It was late in the day and had gotten quite dark. I was trying to find my way along the route and took a right turn onto an unknown street that was very steep—and covered in slick, worn-down snow.

I tried unsuccessfully to avert the right-hand drive truck from descending, but it was too late. And then the truck slid a bit and I found myself sliding down the street— sideways. What made it worse was that I had my window down because I had been delivering mail out of it on this driving route. I looked out the window at the length and steepness of the street and I remember silently wishing with my whole heart, "Please don't tip over; please don't tip over!" I could imagine that big old van tipping and the street rising up to crash into my open window with me laying on it. But, I just took a nice and surprisingly slow slide down to the bottom of the grade into the next street. Unscathed again.

———

One day that fall I witnessed something that cracked me up and that I again I wish I had video of. I was subbing on a route along Barbur Boulevard. Hey, now that I knew where it was, they were not afraid to put me out there anytime. I came up to a weird duplex, with the second apartment on the top. It was a very steep staircase to the upper level. I'd estimate the porch was at least 15 feet high, and probably closer to 17–22 feet above street level.

On that porch was a lady relaxing and reading . . . and a sleeping cat. Just as I got to the top of the stairs the cat suddenly noticed me and was totally startled. The cat darted its eyes right and left, and then . . . LEAPED FROM THAT HIGH BALCONY PORCH!! She looked like a Superman-wannabe in fur. She hit the ground running and dashed to the back of the house. I was astonished. To this day I have never seen a cat jump from such a height. I don't know who was laughing more, me or the owner. Hysterical. What a weird cat. But nothing like the canine that was going to cross my path.

Chapter 7

GETTING CLOSER, FINDING MY WAY, AND ONE LEGENDARY DOG

"You're a real mailman now"

While at Multnomah Station I got my first taste of what it felt like to have my own route, although not on a permanent basis. One of the regular veteran carriers needed to take an extended leave of absence. No one with more seniority wanted to take over his route since it had a high volume of mail, so I volunteered. The leave of absence took considerably longer than expected and I ended up doing the route for more than a year.

I loved the aspect of having the same route every day. And although it was for the most part a driving route, I got to know several patrons along the way. The route was in an affluent part of the zip code, so I delivered to some incredibly gorgeous homes.

One of those homes belonged to an actual British lord and lady, although I did not get to know them at all. However, during the Christmas season their very British maid offered me an amazingly tasty and light English pastry. The scene in their kitchen with this young lady felt very Dickensian and I kept wondering if Tiny Tim might be hiding in the next room.

While on that route I also got to be friends with a player from the National Football League to the point of being on a first-name basis with him and his wife. At the time I was involved with the fantasy football league I mentioned earlier and I had the delight of telling him that I had drafted him for my team. He thought that was cool, but when I told him I drafted him to be a substitute and not a starter he rolled his eyes and laughed.

I kept in contact with a few of these customers for several years after I left the station and am still in contact with one of them all this time later.

That would be Karen, a very sweet and beautiful woman a couple years older than me. She worked at a firm on my route in southwest Portland and I'd visit her there over the years, bringing my kids along with me so they could get to know her and vice versa. She brought a small board with her to her workplace one day and attached it to the wall in her office with the intent that when I brought the kids in to visit she would measure their height to watch their growth over the years. They got a kick out of it. Karen and I lost contact for a bit, but when I located her again years later I was deeply touched to know that when she had left that company she took the board with her and still had it in her possession. How cool is that?

One other significant thing happened for me at Multnomah. As I said, virtually all of the carriers there were considerably helpful to us new hires. But it was also never far from anyone's mind that we WERE the newbies. The Christmas season arrived and with it the station Christmas party. It was my first in the Post Office.

This particular year the organizers decided to have a talent show put on by the carriers. We had vocal performances, a magician, a violinist, and others. I had been part of the puppet ministry at church for ten years, so wrote a script as a solo act around the idea of "Night Before Christmas." I inserted many of the carriers by name into the poem, describing some of the events that had transpired at the station over the year. When I finished, I was stunned to have everybody erupt in cheering and clapping. It brought the house down.

One of the veteran mailmen came up to me after I returned to my seat, clapped me on the shoulder, and exclaimed, "Merrit, you're a real mailman now!" I was beaming the rest of the evening (and most of the next week as many of my coworkers kept coming up to me to tell me how much they enjoyed my performance) and never again felt like a rookie. I was officially accepted. I was going to be a mailman.

Oh, I did mention before that my goal was to eventually get into management and become a supervisor so I could work indoors. Wellllll, I came home from my third day on the job, walked into the house and told Cynthia, "Not for DOUBLE the money would I want to be a supervisor." I had seen immediately it was not to my liking. Incredibly, I had decided I was going to work outdoors for my career. Also while at Multnomah we had our second child, another little girl.

After two years at Multnomah I got transferred to Forest Park Station where I was given a "Utility" assignment. A utility carrier (or ute) is the person who subs for the regular carrier on his day off, plus also for four other regular routes. You do the same five routes every week, a different route each day. I lasted an entire . . . month.

Many of the routes out of this station were located in downtown Portland. A whole different way to do the job. Frankly, I was overwhelmed. Some of the routes I had done at Multnomah were only 250–400 stops. (On some of the driving routes, homes were located far apart, plus they received much more mail because of the wealthiness of the neighborhoods.)

My first day at Forest Park I stepped up to case mail on a route that had . . . 996 stops! What?! Some of these routes were on the outskirts of downtown Portland in huge apartment buildings that had dozens and dozens of names and specific addresses located at a central mailbox in the lobby. You might stand there for half an hour (or, rather I stood there for that long) sorting through the mail.

Some of the mailboxes had large and heavy brass doors that needed to be constantly lifted up and down to reach any particular mail slot. And I do mean heavy. You are holding a large handful of letters in your left hand as you sort them with your right. Then you realize the mail you have ready to put into the box belonged on the lower section of mailboxes. So you had to lift this several-pound heavy brass door, hold it in place with your shoulder, put the mail in the box, let the door slide back down, and prepare the next batch of mail, possibly having to repeat the entire process. For several minutes. It was a disaster.

During my four weeks at Forest Park I did have one pretty cool moment, however. I was in the mail room of a large apartment building in the northwest section of downtown Portland. The mail room was located in the dark but clean basement of the complex. I was doing the usual tossing of letters in these big old brass mailboxes when I came across a name that looked very familiar. It was a cousin of mine who I had not seen in 20 years. I didn't even know he lived in the Portland area. I finished putting the mail in the other address slots, walked to his apartment, and knocked on the door. The door opened and there stood my cousin. He of course had no idea who I was.

"Yes?"

"Are you Byron [his last name]?"

"Yes. Why?"

"Do you recognize me?" I was hiding my name tag.

"You're the mailman, but, no."

"You have no idea who I am to you personally?" Again, remember he had not seen me since I was 13.

"Not a clue."

"My brother was one of your closest friends when you were a kid." He and my brother are much older than me and had frequently hung out together when the families visited each other. Now he looked confused. I think he thought he should know me but still had no idea.

I said, "You and I had the same grandfather." At this point his eyes got really wide.

"You're not Merrit?!"

I laughed and we embraced and had a lovely visit for about 15 minutes. I went on my way, never to deliver mail to that apartment building again ---- nor to ever see my cousin again. He died a few years later. I am very thankful we had those few moments together.

But I left that assignment as soon as I could and landed at Sellwood Station as a "Reserve." Not as bad as a PTF. Guaranteed 40 hours, but moved from route to route as necessary.

I was at Sellwood for a year and met a few more interesting mail carriers. One in particular was memorable. "Cruiser." A play-on-words from his name. But also, he may have been the most impressive walking mailman I ever saw. You could watch him walk his route and he seemed to just slowly meander his way. But he was so smooth and seemed to glide down the street. He would finish his route LONG before the rest of us finished ours.

Letter carrier uniforms for the most part are not what you would designate as fashion statements. But "Cruiser" always looked like he'd had his made by a tailor.

One day, while on an unfamiliar route, I came across an interesting name as I was delivering. This will be an exception to my not sharing names, but you will understand why. I am changing the first name but suffice it to say that it was very common.

Anyway, I came up to a house, and as I got the mail ready, I noticed that the tenant's name was Tom Hearing. Same last name as mine. My father had always told me that if I ran into someone with our last name, they were almost certainly related, since our last name was so unusual.

I knocked on the door and met Tom and we chatted for a few minutes about the uncommonness of our name. After a bit we came to the conclusion that we were probably distant cousins since both of our dads had grown up in the same area of eastern Oregon. It was a nice chat, and as I got ready to leave, I fingered through the letters in my hand to give him the rest of his mail.

I was stunned and startled to come across another name. I showed it to him and asked if that person lived there. He told me it was the prior tenant. This was weird. The name was Tom Merrit. How weird that two consecutive tenants at the same address had the same first name and the last name of "Merrit" and "Hearing." And in that order. "X-Files" theme music time.

It was a rainy morning on a route that ran along a main street in the Sellwood District. I had done this route a handful of times so was fairly knowledgeable about where to go. On this particular day my vehicle was a Ford Pinto. Yeah, I know, but there it is.

I pulled to the curb to deliver a loop. I got everything

ready from the driver's seat that I could then started to climb out and shut the door. With my keys still in the car. Sort of. My Arrow key chain was longer than normal and also had my car keys attached. The key chain was attached to me, so the keys were inside the car and I was outside with the chain stuck in the locked door. But I didn't panic. This was not like last time when I was attached to the mailbox door and almost removed my pants.

Oh, no. I had gotten much smarter. For one thing, I was now wearing a regulation uniform. And I was wearing a belt and had the keys attached to a clip that was on the belt. Also, the doors on this Pinto had a fairly wide crack between the door and the frame so I should be able to withdraw the key. Piece of cake.

I slipped the keys off the clip and got down on my knees and went to work. It was raining and the street was wet, but I was not to be deterred. Finally after about 20 minutes I was able to first slip the key chain and then the key through the crack between the door and frame. Success! Okay, now on to delivering the mail.

I walked around the back of the car to withdraw the mail and my mailbag from the front seat of the car. It was at this very moment—and much to my chagrin—that I remembered that before I had gotten out of the car I had reached over . . . and not only UNLOCKED the door . . . but had actually swung the door . . . OPEN! As I always did when driving a Pinto. Yes, it's true. I had spent 20 wet minutes wily removing the key from the inside of the locked car . . . while the door was open on the other side. Sigh.

———— ⤬ ————

One day I was substituting on a route I had never done before. It seemed like a nice neighborhood and the mail volume was reasonable. It turned out to be one of my most miserable days as a mailman. What I had failed to realize was this particular route was just a few blocks from the Willamette River. It was summer. So besides the weather being uncomfortable to begin with, I also had to fight off thousands of awful flying gnats all day. They were everywhere—and all day long. Ugh. I just scratched after I typed that sentence. Really.

While at Sellwood I took another step toward becoming a "real" mailman by receiving my first of ten dog bites. It was just a little dog, nothing serious.

———

But it was another dog that forever planted himself into my postal memory. The legendary Bona (pronounced bone-uh).

It was a warm day in the summer of 1987. I was assigned to a route in the well-to-do area of Eastmoreland in southeast Portland. The route was very confusing for first-timers. The streets tended to wind this way and that rather than being laid out block by block.

But what could be even more baffling were the locations of most of the mailboxes. Because it was an area of affluence, many of the patrons had their mailboxes in hidden, hard-to-see, or out-of-the way places. It could be mailman's nightmare. As I prepared to head out the door a couple of the regular carriers who had delivered the route in the past told me to "just follow the dog."

"Say what?"

"No, really. He will show you where to walk."

"Uh huh." How dumb do these people think I am? Okay, granted, I had given them reasons to wonder in the past, but still.

I drove to the beginning of the route and was a few homes into the first section when I saw a woman in her front yard with a very large, but obviously calm canine.

"Is this your first time on the route?"

"Uh, yes."

"This is Bona. He would be happy to walk with you today to show you where to go. This can be a confusing route to deliver the first time."

"Sure."

I smiled to myself and thought, "Whatever." Bona was a big dog, about the size of a collie but thicker. Not fat, just bigger through the shoulders and torso. He was easygoing and somewhat lethargic. I started off and he came along a bit behind me. When I got back to my car after the first loop he walked off down the street.

"Okay, well so much for the helping dog," I thought. I drove to the next section and there he was waiting for me. A few houses into this section I was completely flummoxed and could not figure out where the mailbox was. I looked to my left and there was Bona, seemingly waiting for me. I walked to where he was. Sure enough. There was the mailbox hidden around the corner and the pathway to the next stop. Well, I'll be.

And so it kept on. Time after time as I struggled to figure out where to go next, Bona would be looking at me, patiently waiting to guide me on my rounds. It was truly uncanny and amazing. When I finished a loop I'd get in the car to drive to the next section and there he would be waiting when I arrived.

There were many times I knew right where to go, yet could not find the mail receptacle. I'd look around and there he would be, waiting at the exact right place. I would stubbornly think I could figure out where a mailbox might be hidden. And every time there would be Bona, with a knowing look on his face.

After several instances of this I just started following him without question. Occasionally, on an easier section of the route, he would go off and play with the neighborhood kids. But he would always return to see if I was doing okay.

During my lunch break he once again went off to play with the children. But he walked with me the whole day and through and around the ENTIRE ROUTE. At the end of the day, I walked back to my postal car and he turned around and headed for home.

I did the route many times over the next few months. It was a terrific route. (All mail routes are created equal. But some routes are more equal than others.) About 85% of this route was in the shade during the hot summer months. A big plus. I would always look for Bona. But now that he knew that I knew my way around the route he'd spend more time with the kids and less time with me. He was incredible. Good ol' legendary Bona. Would that all canines be like him in temperament and intelligence. I will never, ever forget that day. If I had not lived it, I would not believe it. What a great dog!

The P.S. to this story is it also became my favorite route to deliver during my year at Sellwood. That summer was a particularly warm one in the Portland area. And I ended up doing this route many times, which was fabulous because of how much of the route was in the shade. It turned those overbearing days from being searing hot to just warm. Of all the routes at all the stations during all those years I was a mailman, this route was my favorite to deliver, other than the one I ended up with at Creston.

But I was longing to settle down with my own route close to home. So month by month I checked out the available routes in the Portland area. Finally, one came up that looked like a decent possibility. I wasn't looking for someplace to land for years and years, just a starting point in my neck of the woods. But this route was at a station much closer to home. And after enjoying those 18 consecutive months while on the same route at Multnomah, I really felt as if I wanted to just have my own route.

Chapter 8

BECOMING ONE WITH THE ROUTE

"We fought like brothers"

It is always fascinating to me the simple moments in life that lead to extraordinary circumstances. I had now been in the Post Office three years. I wanted to be closer to my home and I finally had attained enough seniority to bid to get a route of my own. Regular hours. Regular scheduled days off. Working in the same place inside and outside each day.

The monthly sheet was posted that showed what routes around the city had been vacated, thus becoming open to bids. Anyone and everyone could bid on a route. Whoever had the highest seniority was awarded the assignment.

A route was available at Creston Post Office. The station itself was located about five minutes from my house, and the route was in an area in southeast Portland I was familiar with; in fact, I had lived on this route for two years about a decade earlier. I did not want to step into a route that would be a nightmare because of location, length, or dogs, so I stopped at a gas station one day while delivering out of Sellwood and called Sannye, the carrier friend of mine who had helped show me the ropes when I worked at Multnomah and who had now been at Creston herself for about a year.

I asked her about the route. She told me it was a bit long but in a nice neighborhood. But mainly she told me that having my own route was a great step in the door. If I didn't like it, I could always bid on another route later. So I sent my bid in and was surprised when I got the route assignment. Little did I know how my life would change and be affected by that simple phone call.

———✦———

My first day at Creston Post Office I walked in still quite fresh-faced and naïve. The date was May 7, 1988. I was coming up on my 33rd birthday and now had two children. I would stay on that same route—0655—till the day I retired 27 years later. The idea of being on that same route for that long was the furthest thing from my mind.

Over those years I progressed from being a relative newbie in the Post Office to a veteran, to a grizzled old-timer, to a legend (well, in my own mind anyway). Doug from Multnomah was already there (and still is as I write this). Other than him and Sannye, I didn't know anyone else at the station.

———✦———

The route I had bid for and landed on was 0655. The 06 refers to the last two numbers of the local zip code, the 55 was arbitrary, though usually it meant it was near routes 54 and 56. Fortunately for me, route 0655 was located next to route 54 and the mailman on it. He was already a grizzled veteran. Mike. Or as my kids grew to affectionately call him, Mailman Mike.

Mike already had 18 years in the Post Office and had been on his route for a few years. Mike and I would work next to each other for the next 22 years. We fought like brothers.

We laughed like hyenas. We griped about our employer in unity. We told each other stories (frequently the same ones again and again). We had a delightful time together.

We were nothing alike. He had been to Vietnam, was beyond passionate about sturgeon fishing, never got overly emotional, and was just a big old character with a thousand stories. He never thought I would make it as a mailman because I was such a wuss. He told me this many times over the years and still can't believe I actually made it. He loved my kids. He brought me to work every day for several years when our family had only one car and would not accept dollar one in gas money.

"Hey," he gruffly told me more than once, "I just want to make sure you get to work so I don't have to carry part of your route." But he also enjoyed it when he brought me home from work and my four little ones ran down the driveway squealing, "Daddy's home! Daddy's home!" Then they would all pile into his little red Toyota pickup and crawl all over everything. (Oh, did I say "four little ones"? During my first three years at Creston we added two more kids, another girl then our only son.)

Mike acted overtly brusque but you would be hard pressed to find a nicer man. I used to tease him all the time (and still do) that he worked with me longer than he ever worked with anyone else. "Don't say that!" he would bellow. I learned a lot about being a mailman from Mike. His first lesson was the most important. "Look bud, this ain't no sprint. It's a marathon." He was referring both to the length of doing a route daily, but also to the idea of walking and carrying mail for decades.

I settled into the routine of being the regular mailman on one route. I loved that aspect of it. Knowing what you will be doing day to day. Knowing when your days off would be and being able to plan them. Having the same car to drive every day. In fact, for my 27 years on the route I drove only two postal vehicles. I had a K-car for the first nine years and then for the final 18 had a van. Except for when they were in for maintenance, these two carried me and all the mail I delivered for the rest of my career. Oh, a quick aside. That van I drove was and still is the most comfortable ride I have ever experienced as a driver. Not just for a postal vehicle. For any automobile I have ever driven. The seat fit me perfectly and the ride was very smooth.

———— ∞∞ ————

I soon discovered a principle for myself that I passed on to the new hires who came after me. The "2/2/2/2" principle for those who grab onto a route and stay on it for extended years. These are all approximations, of course. But generally it takes two days on a route to have a bit of a grasp on where you are going and how to get it done. It takes two weeks on a route to become comfortable on the route so that you know where to park for each section and where the mailboxes and dogs are. You know many of the names of the patrons on the route, although not personally. It takes two months to become proficient. You know exactly what to do, where to go, and what it will take. You are starting to get to know some of the customers fairly well. The route no longer seems at all new and you acquire a certain level of confidence. And then I always said it took two years to become in my words "one with the route." The route became ingrained in your thinking and routine.

You know who gets what magazines, and who pays their bills consistently late. You know most of your customers by name, and perhaps some of them have become friends. You even have a very good grasp of who used to live on the route before you became the mailman, so it is rare if you deliver mail to someone who has moved off the route.

—⟨⟩—

But I was starting to have my first health issue and it needed to be addressed or I was going to be in a world of hurt—literally. My feet were causing me real problems. I was in pain every day and by the end of a long week I was seriously struggling. They were swollen and terribly tender much of the time I was working. And if I was going to be a walking mailman . . . well, we got big problems.

I was wearing fairly good shoes, but it didn't seem to make much difference. Then my mother-in-law Grace suggested one day that I buy an extra pair of shoes and rotate them on a daily basis. She explained that my shoes were not getting the chance to dry out completely after a day of delivering mail and that dampness was accumulating into a plethora of foot problems.

It seemed too silly to help, but I was desperate. So I bought another pair of shoes and began rotating the two pairs every other day. And my foot issues went away. For good. Other than some pain from fallen arches and the expected fatigue from the daily/weekly/yearly grind (especially in hot weather), I had fairly comfortable feet for the remainder of my career. That fabulous advice I received from Grace I passed onto dozens of newbie letter carriers over the decades.

Also from this experience, I realized the necessity of getting very high-quality shoes. That became clearer and clearer as my feet, ankles, knees, and back became older and older. The Post Office gives carriers an annual uniform allotment for purchasing their postal clothes. As the years passed I'd spend nearly all of this money on shoes and tended to ignore till the last possible moment of replacing my well-worn shirts and pants. Which became a characteristic I was known for and teased about. I frequently looked threadbare—or worse. It was not unusual to find me arriving for duty with small holes in my clothes or a shirt so thin you could read a book through the material. I didn't care. I wanted my feet comfortable! Everything else was a luxury.

I also got to experience and enjoy my first Christmas season as a regular mailman on a route. A sweet woman on my route gave me a baggie of Chex mix as a gift. It meant a lot to me. Over the years I received many gifts and tips. But for 27 Christmases this dear lady never failed to give me her homemade treat. More on Christmas and packages and people later. I will tell you now that it was my favorite time of year to work. Despite the potential weather issues. Yeah, we better spend some time talking about the weather. Not that we can do anything about it.

Chapter 9

NEITHER SNOW, NOR RAIN,
NOR HEAT—BUT ALL ON THE SAME DAY?

"Suddenly I heard a "BANG" to my right"

"How can you stand to be outside and deliver the mail when it is so cold/hot/wet/windy?" I was asked that question innumerable times in my career. Oh, here is a piece of advice I will give you for free. Under no circumstances when your mailman approaches with the mail should you ever ask, "Is it cold/hot/wet/windy enough for you?" Nothing irritates mailmen more. Except maybe, "You can keep the bills," followed by a big laugh as though you are the first person to ever say it. Believe me, after hearing that phrase 10,617 times, not so funny. That and "Oh, my dog doesn't bite."

Uh huh. But I digress. Why and how do we deliver mail in adverse and punishing weather? Because we have gotten used to eating and having electricity and phones. It's your job. Here is another way to look at it that settled it for me. I figure everybody's job has "stuff." You know, that "stuff" that you wish you didn't have to deal with but it is simply part of the job. You either learn to deal with the stuff" or you go into another line of work. I was a mailman. Weather and dogs were my "stuff." That is what it boils down to. As this very short post from late in my career points out:

March 9, 2011

I'm thinking: rain, snow, sleet, hail, sunshine—in a span of 25 MINUTES!

Like my compatriots in blue I have delivered in all types of weather: blistering heat, blizzards, heavy snow, torrential downpours, ice storms, high winds, hail (you've never heard such a cacophonous racket as the sound of heavy hail pounding down on your head while you are wearing one of those hard-shell pith helmets), thunder and lightning, and the worst that occurs with some regularity, windy sleet.

My first severe test with weather came in my first winter on route 0655. Luckily for me, it also turned out to be the worst weather experience I ever had to deal with. It was January, 1989. For three straight days the cold was beyond brutal. The temperature hovered around 10 degrees. Now, that in itself for Portland, Oregon is VERY cold. We usually have a few days in the 20s and rarely in the teens.

But beyond that, for these three days the wind was howling. Sustained winds in the 25–35 mph range with gusts (which were frequent) up to 40+. The wind chill crept down to nearly 15 BELOW zero.

I wore three pairs of socks, regular shoes, rubber pullover shoes, regular underwear, long underwear, sweat pants, postal pants, rain pants, T-shirt, long-sleeved shirt, postal shirt, sweater, heavy winter coat, gloves, scarf, ski mask, and a Russian-style winter hat—26 items of clothing. I also learned to keep my left hand—the one holding the letter mail—behind my back as I walked, keeping it out of the wind as much as possible. A dreadful three days.

Some of my fellow carriers suffered frostbite during those dreadful days. I escaped that malady. But those three days were agonizing. My age was only 33, but for the first time in my life I felt old. I cannot express to you my gratitude that I never had to face weather like that again.

Oh, there were some miserably cold and windy days, but nothing ever approached that infamous January of 1989. I have often wondered how I would have coped in my later days as a mailman. I have come up with three scenarios. One, I would have retired on the spot. Two, lay down and weep. Three, die in the effort. I don't know. I just don't know.

As I said, I delivered in every type of weather over my 30 years. However, for the first 27 years of my career I had never delivered in thunder and lightning. Granted, we don't get a lot of that in Portland. But every time we did, it was either my day off, I was on vacation, I was recovering from an injury, or it was during off hours. Then we got a pretty wicked one on a late afternoon in 2012. I mean it really flashed and rumbled. I loved it.

What I didn't love was hot weather. I hated Mr. Summer. And everybody knew I hated hot weather. My customers. My coworkers. My family. Everyone. The reason I hated delivering in hot weather more than cold weather was twofold. First, you can dress for the cold and wet. You put more layers on or put your rain gear on and head out. Might it be a miserable day? Sure. But at least you can prepare.

Hot weather? Once you get down to short sleeves and short pants, that's about it. Unless you want to get arrested. Second, on a cold day, once you are done, you drive home in your heated car to your heated home. But on a hot day you may very well be climbing into a car without A/C and going home to a house without it as well.

But beyond that, the hot weather just zaps the energy out of you. It can feel relentless and it is not just the day that drags—you do as well. Sticky. Sweaty. A heavy bag draped over your shoulder. Trudging along as the perspiration drips down into your eyes. You can either not wear sunglasses and squint yourself into a headache, or wear them and walk yourself into a spiderweb the size of a minivan.

Looking back, my first crystal clear memory of really disgustingly hot weather was the summer of 1986. I was on the route I had been "temporarily" assigned to and was driving one of those jeeps I mentioned earlier. Fortunately that 'tuna can' was equipped with the most state-of-the-art cooling technology imaginable. Well, it was a six-inch fan that whirled about 12 revolutions per minute, showering the driver (if you could actually get it to point towards yourself and stay in that direction) with more dust than cool air. They were miserable. Since I was driving the mail from box to box and my customer contact was minimal, I rolled up my pant legs and shirt sleeves as far as possible and only buttoned one button on my shirt. (The polo style shirt for letter carriers was still a few years away). It was just 'ugh' in that jeep. But I also received a lesson that summer that there is always someone worse off. One blistering hot day I was getting close to the end of the route. I was hot, sticky, and really done with the stupid hot weather. I drove around a corner and spotted a scene that made me shudder. There – upon a roof -- was a group of guys laying down asphalt. I could not imagine the sheer misery of doing that job on that day. I have always wondered what the temp was on the surface of that roof. Maybe I don't want to know.

For me, those hot summer days were just simply dreadful. An image that will stick with me always is shuffling along on those blistering days and feeling just the whisper of a breeze. I would stick my arms straight out from me like airplane wings just to catch the slightest waft of cool air along and under my arms. Now I acknowledge and appreciate that summers in Portland pale on the "dreadful" chart compared to Houston or St. Louis or Miami. I can only comment and attest to the summers I experienced while delivering the mail.

But maybe even worse (during working hours anyway) had to be cold sleet on a windy day. Man, those icy needles just pummeled you, and with the wind there was no place to escape it. And that wicked east wind howling out of the Columbia Gorge. "The Hawk" is what Mailman Mike used to call that infernal wind. What made this especially difficult was that it would cling to your fingers and get in between the letters and down your neck and up your sleeves and . . . well, you get the idea.

———

Although I preferred cold weather over hot weather, there was one aspect of the chilly stuff that was worse. My hands. The cold can be just dreadful on your hands as you try to use your fingers to work through the mail. I discovered a trick a few years in that worked for me. My route started out with a short residential section. After being inside a building or warm car for a few hours that cold weather could be a highly unpleasant change on the ol' phalanges. But I found that if I took just a minute or two after I finished my initial section and re-warmed my hands inside the car before continuing, I was probably okay after that.

The next section on my route was my business section. This was the next unpleasantness in dealing with the extreme temperatures. If the weather was the above mentioned cold, naturally all the businesses had their heat on, and usually fairly high. If the weather was hot, most of those same businesses had their air conditioning on. Going in and out of all those buildings to drop off the mail was brutal on the system. Cold-hot-cold-hot-cold-hot. (Or hot-cold-hot-cold ...)

The worst weather to get around in are ice storms. Driving is very difficult. Walking? My back hurts just thinking about it. But one ice storm brought a much remembered incident that even now brings a smile to my face. As per usual, we were told to be extremely careful as we walked and not to attempt any delivery that appeared unsafe, particularly stairs.

I was gently trekking my way near the halfway point of my route on Woodstock Boulevard. I came up to a house where a Mr. Kralick lived, an elderly man. I didn't hesitate for a moment. It was a long, steep staircase to the porch and there was no way I was even going to consider attempting delivery. I would just have to bring his mail back the next day. I began to band up his mail to toss into my pouch for the next day's delivery.

As I started to walk past the steps, suddenly I heard a BANG to my right. There was a bucket, with a rope attached to it. I looked up and at the top of the stairs on the porch sat Mr. Kralick holding the other end of the rope with a smile on his face. He had seen me on the other side and waited for me. I tossed his mail into the bucket, smiled, and shot him a little wave. Then he reeled it in. It was the highlight of a very difficult day. He has been gone many years now, but I still smilingly remember that moment. What a hoot.

Many years earlier I had witnessed the dramatic effects of a howling windstorm. And something happened that day that I never experienced before, nor did I after. I first mentioned this on social media on the 20th anniversary of the day, which fell about eight months after I retired.

December 12, 2015

It was 20 years ago today that I witnessed the most ferocious windstorm of my postal career. The weather forecasters had warned it was coming. It was about 2 o'clock in the afternoon. I had delivered about 60% of my route when the air changed from absolutely perfectly still to a fierce gust nearly instantly. It was beyond calm. No movement. Then, literally, within a span of maybe five seconds, it was gale force winds. It was nutzoid out there. You had to hang on to the letters with an ironclad grip and keep alert for flying debris.

About an hour later our supervisors came out and told us to halt delivery and come back to the station for safety reasons. In my 30 years as a walking mailman, it was the only time we were pulled off the streets due to weather. It was a wise decision because the wind that day was crazy-nuts-scary. There was a lot of tree and other damage in the area. But seeing as how no one was injured, I consider this a good memory because of its uniqueness. Two decades later I can still picture the stunning abruptness of wind speed going from 0 mph to probably 45+ mph in mere seconds. The sound, the fury, the vision of the trees blowing turbulently—all resonate within my memory with such crisp clarity that even now I could take you to the exact spot where it happened. It was a day.

By the way, despite all the high winds I worked in over 30 years, I only lost one piece of mail in all that time. Well, two actually, but I got one of them back. One brutally cold and windy day I was putting a first-class letter into a mailbox when a gust of wind whipped it right out of my hands. It was 50 feet away and still hastily flying down the street in mere seconds. No way was I ever going to get it. I was severely disappointed because I had never lost a piece of mail before.

Twenty minutes or so later I was two blocks farther along the route when I spotted the letter stuck in a thick bush. Saved! My record was still intact. Many years later I did lose a piece of mail as it was ripped from my grasp by strong wind. But it was only an advert so I didn't lose any sleep over it. Yes, all mail is important, but some mail is more important than others. I was just glad it was not a birthday card from someone's Aunt Helen.

———◦◦◦———

Working in the Portland area, rain was a frequent companion. If you can't deal with rain then PDX is not the place to be a walking mailman. On sprinkly days, you can probably get through the day without much discomfort. But no matter how good your rain gear is, if it is RAINING, you are going to get wet. Rain slides down your sleeve as you reach up to open a mailbox. Rain sneaks into your collar as you stand under the edge of a porch. It just happens. You deal.

That being said, there were a handful of days that it was Noah's Arking out there. You get soaked. But there was one day I distinctly remember. Two reasons. It was toward the end of my career. And also I thought I had outsmarted the weather, only to ruefully discover that was not so.

It was the Monday before Thanksgiving in 2012. It didn't just rain this day. It wasn't even a Noah's Ark day. No, it DRENCHED all day long. Notice, I did not say I got drenched. No, what I mean is the sky was drenched. You've heard of sheets of water. Uh-uh. These were blankets of water. Constant and all day. I had been in harder rain for short bursts of maybe an hour or so. But this was a constant, unending, vicious downpour all day long. The kind of day where you get totally wet and then it gets worse.

But I had weathered many rainstorms by this point. I carried spare clothes in the car with me every day. After sloshing around for a few hours I'd had enough. I grabbed some dry garments and a towel and headed back to one of my businesses to get a fresh start. I was not going to be miserable the rest of the day. I was too old for this nonsense. I used up my lunch break to thoroughly dry off and change. Let's do this.

Now I must reiterate that it had been pouring all morning. As hard as I had ever worked in. I headed back out. And it rained even HARDER. I got through two more sections. I was already soaked to the skin. The kind of wet where every item of clothing is soaked. Water running down your legs. Every step resonates with a big squish. I stopped on a porch of one of my favorite customers and looked at the rain from the comfort of that covered respite. I could not believe it could rain that hard for that long. Surely it would let up. Nope. Not for the entire day. The wettest day I ever experienced.

An oddity. The customer's porch I was standing on. I never understood this, but she was the last house in a string of seven homes that produced a rain anomaly ON ME. I posted about it three months before I retired.

January 16, 2015

I am going to use two numbers in this story. The first is a very close approximation, the second is exact. Because that is how my mind works. In all the years I have been on my route in my postal career as a walking mailman I have been caught in a rainy downpour WITHOUT my rain gear about 26 or 27 times. Here is the oddity: 19 of those times was within the same span of seven houses at a corner where two of my streets meet and I make a turn. Believe me when I tell you, when I start that section of delivery, I make SURE it looks like there is ZERO chance of rain before I leave my vehicle without the rain gear.

I cannot imagine why this happened so much. I guess I will never know. I have friends from my delivery days that I still occasionally go visit within those seven houses. I think

I will start tossing my rain pith helmet into the car when I head over there.

Without a doubt my favorite times of the year to work were the spring and fall. Mostly for the milder weather. But also for the foliage.

April 19, 2013

The fragrance of lilacs is my fave smell in the world. Last spring because of my ankle injury I missed the lilac season. I am totally immersing myself in it this year. Today I was downwind about seven feet from a thick lilac tree as a slight breeze began. Dang, it was positively heavenly.

October 19, 2013

Why do I like being a mailman? Because sometimes you get weeks like this past one to walk around in. I cannot recall a more spectacular week of weather WITH such vibrant and tapestry-like colors.

April 17, 2014

Because there is not a more magnificent olfactory experience than standing downwind from a huge lilac tree in a breeze.

Portland is ill-equipped to handle heavy snow. Fortunately it is rare when it interferes with our mail delivery. But, oh, the Christmas of 2008. We got buried. Deep drifts of snow for days. Our vehicles out of Creston Post Office were chained up, of course. But we could not handle the depth of the snow. Some of the trucks even high-centered on the built-up snow in the streets.

So for three days all we could do was pair up with the carrier from a neighboring route and go out to only deliver parcels. Two of us would put all of our packages into the truck and drive out to the route(s). Parking in those drifts was completely out of the question. So we'd pull onto a street that was somewhat passable. Park the car in the middle of the street and leave it. Hey, there was no other traffic, either. We would grab some parcels and off we'd go.

At the end of the day we would have to take all the mail that had been computer-generated into the correct delivery order and case it by hand along with the other mail that is already cased by hand. On the 22nd and 23rd of December we worked from 7:30 in the morning till 8:00 in the evening, give or take 15 minutes. Again, all I could think was "I am too old for this." There are so many fans of snow out there; I cannot help but wonder how they would feel dealing with it as we had to. I expressed my "frustration" about this during this horrific snowpocalypse.

December 15, 2008

Sorry, but I am wishing terrible thoughts on all those folks who wanted the snow but are spending all day inside.

Those are pretty much the same thoughts I had toward those who prayed for the hot weather to come.

June 30, 2011

And thus endeth what was FOR ME the greatest June WEATHER-WISE in my entire career. It was delightful. But I suppose you silly "sun folks" gotta have some time, too. Alright, but I won't be happy about it.

Nothing bugs a mailman more than the "Oh, it must be a marvelous day to walk your route today!" sentiments when the thermometer is pushing past 85 degrees. You want to say, "No, ma'am. Actually it is disgusting. Why don't you slip this mailbag on for the next nine miles and we will broach the topic again when you are finished."

But, alas, you just smile (hopefully) and mumble you would prefer 52 and breezy. You will hear more of my unfriendly thoughts about summer weather in later chapters.

But as I said, if you are going to be a letter carrier, you simply have to decide that you will deal with the weather as best as you can. It is all part of the job of being a regular day-to-day walking mailman.

Chapter 10

I'M ALL FOR REGULARITY

"I watched their children grow up"

The years at Creston began to add up. A man who retired a few years before me gave a nice speech on his final day at work. He made this sensational and very accurate statement: "The days drag, the years fly." They did, and they did.

We had those two more kids I mentioned earlier. In February of 2000 I reached the 15-year mark, which was the halfway point of my career. It was also about this time that my wife and I split up.

I was also beginning to have my first severe health issues. I'd had back problems for years. But now with my job those problems were becoming unmanageable. For the first time in my life I was starting to have "panic" pain, where the pain became so intense I felt as if I could not function as a person, let alone a mailman carrying a bag over his shoulder.

In the summer of 2001 I finally had surgery to remove and replace two discs in my back. Before the surgery I had missed a cumulative total of six months of work. I never missed another hour after the surgery because of my back.

Older folks from my route began to die and newer families started moving in. When I first started my route in May, 1988, an elderly woman lived on a corner lot. She passed away just a few weeks after I began. Her son moved in and eventually his daughter and granddaughter. I had four generations of that family at one time or another. And the fourth generation, a little girl, became my oldest Route Kid, with me being her only regular mailman from birth.

When I retired, she was still living in the same house, now 23 years old. Somewhere in a box in storage I still have pictures she drew for me when she was a tot that she left for me in her mailbox. Another girl, who lived just down the street, was my second oldest Route Kid. She was 18 when I retired. Krista and Nancy became first two special little girls, and then young women in my life. Like many on my route, they became my friends.

These families, like so many others, I would get to know and love over the next 27 years. And they provided most of my mailman stories. These were the families where I took my kids for Halloween. I watched their children grow up and they watched mine. I would not trade those stories and people and experiences for anything. I became part of their neighborhoods and they became a part of me. Delightful symbiosis.

Another thing that became apparent to me during my first couple of years at Creston and on my own route day after day was that I was no longer feeling like a young man. There was not a specific day or incident (although those three days of frigid weather certainly didn't help), but sometime before I turned 34 I began to feel my age. I did not recover from tough days as quickly. Sprained ankles caused more disruption, happened more frequently, and took longer to recover from.

The idea of "routine" starts to become, well, a routine. If you do not like your job, delivering mail can become an extremely dull stream of never-ending days of severe routine.

I had some years like that. But I guess any job can get that way, no matter how "'glamorous.'"

A sometime running gag at Creston was that we as letter carriers should behave in the same manner as professional athletes do at their job. A defensive lineman "sacks" the quarterback and does a dance. A running back scores a touchdown and spikes the ball or carries on with some other celebration. They go crazy for doing precisely what their job descriptions call for while being paid exorbitant amounts of money.

We used to laugh at the idea of us behaving in the same manner when we delivered a certified letter properly or got an express package to the customer on time. Can you picture a mailman doing a little jig or spiking his dog spray on your porch after he has presented you with your mail in a timely and correct fashion? I always said that would have added a little sparkle to our jobs. Couldn't seem to get the bosses to sign off on it though.

The most senior of the carriers began to retire and a new generation of younger mailmen (okay, let's be clear about this: when I say "mailman/men," I am also including women; just saying) came in and I could see myself becoming a "veteran" mailman. Now from time to time the youngsters would ask me for tips on how to do their job. Mailman Mike was still there but he had moved to a new house a few miles away so now a quiet and very kind gentleman named Dave began to give me rides to and from work. Like Mike, he did this for several years and refused to take a nickel in gas money. I truly worked with many fabulous folks. But fabulous dogs—other than Bona—not so much. Everybody always wants to know about mailmen and dogs. So let's get to it.

AND THEN THE RABBIT BIT ME

Chapter 11

THE BIG BARK IN THE DARK

"The deepest, fullest, most terrible bark"

I mentioned earlier about the "stuff" that all of us must face in our jobs. Early on, my brother once remarked to me, "There is no way I could do your job because of the dogs." I had many folks say to me over the years they would have to do another job the first time they got bit by a dog or had one charge them. I get it—and would truly understand a few months before I retired.

So just what is it with mailmen and dogs, anyway? Is it even a thing? Yes, most definitely. The two most prevailing theories that I cling two are these. The first is obvious. The mailman comes on the dog's property. He approaches the house. He leaves something unidentifiable at the house. And sometimes – if the tenants have left mail out to be picked up - he takes something away (horror of horrors to the canine!). The second idea is not so obvious nor is it clear if it is even authentic. When a mailman walks with a bag slung over his shoulder it changes his gait. The footfalls do not hit the pavement with the same regularity and evenness because of the extra weight, however small it might be. This puts the dog on a higher state of alertness and edginess. "Something is not right! I must investigate with all vigor and viciousness!"

Or something along those lines. Then add on to this tense uneasiness the former situation and the sum total ends up as: "You aren't walking properly! Hey, get off my lawn! Don't touch my house! Stop leaving those paper products in that little box! Hey, bring those letters back where they belong! Alright, I must do what I can to prevent this madman from murdering my family!" I am certain scores of canines had this exact conversation take place in their minds as I meandered along minding my own business.

———

Unfortunately, I never had another dog like Bona. Dogs are part of the job. Period. Especially on a walking route. Some of the encounters were pleasant or even funny. Many, not so much.

During my first few months at Multnomah I was delivering on a route I was unfamiliar with late in the afternoon of a fall day. It was just starting to get dusky. I was on a dismount route and came upon a large paved semi-circular area. It was not so much a driveway but more a place to turn the truck around after the delivery. I parked the car and walked the 25 or so feet to the mailbox, which was surrounded by shrubbery on a concrete block wall. Between the time of day, all the shrubbery, and the shadowy area, it was somewhat darkish. I put the mail inside the large mailbox, closed the door, and had just barely started to turn around when I heard the deepest, fullest, most terrifying bark I had ever heard in my life. To this point I had not as yet had my first dog bite. I froze in my tracks. There had been no dog there before. I looked up at the bushes. There it was! The biggest head on a creature I had ever seen. Apparently it was a dog. I hoped. It was actually a huge (even for them) Malamute, a breed I had never encountered before. And he was as friendly as could be. He was behind a fence and he and I had a little chat. Obviously he was a very gentle dog. But even now, I can close my eyes and still hear that deep, rolling, "ROLF!!"

Besides receiving my first dog bite at Sellwood Station, two other dog moments happened during my time there. One funny, one not. One to me, one to someone else. I was delivering in an unfamiliar neighborhood one warm afternoon when I suddenly found myself surrounded by three large and aggressive dogs, two of which were German shepherds.

This harrowing encounter lasted several minutes. It almost seemed as if the dogs were working together. When I say surrounded, I mean it. They took up a triangular position around me and when I moved they moved in tandem, barking at me and seemingly at each other. I was finally able to nimbly squirm my way behind a gate and wait for them to disperse. I waited about four or five minutes before I slunk my way carefully back to the truck so as to make my way to the next loop. To this day I am still not sure why they let me "escape."

While at Sellwood Station I became good friends with a carrier named Lenny. We had much in common and had about the same amount of seniority. He told me a story about what had happened to him one day—it still makes me laugh. He was on a route he did not know, but it was one that had a well-earned reputation of having dog problems. So he was understandably jittery as he made his way around. He was putting the mail in a box when out of the corner of his eye he noticed a huge gray dog looming over him. He whirled around, and with the utmost skill whipped out his can of dog spray. (Mailmen are not allowed to carry pepper spray because it is classified as a weapon. What we carry is a sort of ammonia based concoction.) He soaked that thing. I mean he showered that gray beast with a LOT of dog spray. Well, let me tell you, neither Lenny nor any other mailmen was ever bothered by that huge menacing . . . statue . . . of a dog ever again. Don't mess with letter carriers!

—⋙⋘—

Even though these situations can be highly unpleasant, most mailmen understand there are going to be those unexpected encounters (uh, not with statues, but actual dogs). What is incredibly irritating and tiring are those dogs you must deal with again and again. In my first weeks after I landed my own route I had a lovely almost daily run-in with a dog on one of my first stops. He was a Doberman. He was demon-posse—er . . . very aggressive and I hated approaching the porch.

The dog was always indoors (responsible owner), but would fly into the door viciously. It was a wooden door, one of those older kind with 12 small, rectangular window panes that were about 4 by 6 inches in size, separated by strips of wood. I wasn't worried about the dog coming through the door, obviously. But, maybe I should have been.

One day he came flying at the door . . . and smashed through three or four of the panes of glass and split the wood between the glass panes. There was broken and cut glass everywhere, splintered wood, and one snarling brown face still trying to make his way through the door.

I leaped off the porch. He continued to lunge for me. I wasn't sure what was going to happen first. Would the dog get through the door and nail me? Would he lunge and slice his throat on the shards of glass? Or some combination of those two awful outcomes? The owner arrived very quickly from the back of the house and was horrified. He made sure I was alright and took the dog back into the house. That one shook me up. The door was replaced and I never saw the dog again. The owner took him out to a home in the country.

———— ∞ ————

Some dogs were just annoying, not dangerous. There was a little irascible rascal that didn't come out often but was a pain when he did. He'd come at me and I'd step toward him and then he would run to the side and replant himself for his next charge. One day as he was charging and yipping, I had just had enough. I saw what was coming up behind him and made an executive decision to get him away from me, at least for this day. We kept doing our tango together until I maneuvered him right where I wanted him. I made a fake rush at him and he responded by turning slightly to the side and starting to run . . . smack dab into a telephone pole. He wasn't hurt (I don't like dogs but I'm not THAT guy), but he was definitely dazed a bit and lost his balance. He looked around uncertainly, did a slight stumble, and went home. Was that laughing you heard from the local letter carrier? Could be.

There was another dog I had issues with toward the end of my route. He was sometimes aggressive and sometimes not. He was a large . . . something-or-other. I was across the street from his place of residence. He chose this moment to be his most aggressive. Suddenly he came flying out from the backyard, making a beeline for me. I was in my late 30s at the time. I saw him coming, and when he hit the street it was obvious he was coming all the way over to get me. I acted instinctively, took a few steps, and grabbed the four-foot-high chain-link fence at the house where I was and leaped over it—mailbag and all—ala Jason Bourne. And I swear to you that dog was starting to step up onto and over that fence like a person until the owner yelled at him from across the street. About that moment one of my coworkers drove up who had witnessed my daring-do and asked if I was alright. I assured her I was fine, although I was still shaken up and more than a bit ticked off. I am not known for my athletic prowess (read that: clumsy and unskilled), so she asked me, "How did you do that?" I didn't know then and I still don't know now. You just do what you have to do.

Another time I had to climb up onto the roof of my car to avoid a dog that came flying down the street at me. But there was no athletic prowess involved here. I simply crawled onto the hood and then quickly surmised that was not going to be high enough, so I clambered as high as I could go, which fortunately was higher than the canine could jump.

A few blocks away lived Mr. Wolf. He owned four Shelties who came out every day to greet me at their fence. Mr. Wolf was a wonderful man and terrific dog owner. Those four dogs and I got to know each other very well over nine years. After they announced my arrival, Mr. Wolf would come out and we would chat for a couple minutes.

This was the first time I had been around a "family" of dogs. It was fascinating to see their various personalities and temperaments. There was the alpha dog who usually noticed me first and issued the initial warning barks to the rest of the pack. He'd trot over to the fence to inspect the situation. He was not unfriendly, just business-like.

The youngster of the bunch was always too involved with other goings-on to make the initial discovery of my appearance. But then he would bound over, behaving as if he was wholly responsible for letting the rest of creation know of my coming.

Mama dog was probably the most consistently friendly, jauntily running over and taking in the occurrence with aplomb.

Then finally would come the Old One, moseying over partly because he saw no need to hurry and partly because he had arrived at the time of his life where that was normal or even top speed for him. He seemed to be uncaring whether I was there or not. He never became friendly, and despite his advancing years, Mr. Wolf told me that if I should ever venture into the yard, it would be the Old One who would cause me the most trouble.

As the years went by it was interesting to watch the dogs take on different roles. Mr. Wolf would come out with the dogs and chat with me probably nine days out of ten. After the boundaries on my route were moved a bit south, I no longer delivered to the house but I would from time to time stop by for a visit (outside the fence) and have a chat with him or his wife. They were one of the first couples I got to know during the early days of being on my route. Mr. Wolf and his Shelties. I always looked forward to that part of the day.

But it goes with the job that most encounters with canines were not for the best. One of my worst, and one that still causes me trouble today happened the day after Thanksgiving in 2009. Which meant there was no school that day. Which is what I believe led to the accident. I was working a couple sections on another route before I headed off to do mine. I came up to a house and pushed the mail through the slot in the front door.

About one second later I heard a huge thump and much loud and violent-sounding barking. I remember thinking I was glad I didn't have to face whatever monster lived behind that barrier. I started walking back out of the yard to head to the next stop. Suddenly I heard the door open. I wheeled around and saw a pit bull hurtling toward me at breathtaking speed. He did not want to make friends.

As he got to me I did a quick olé and managed to barely avoid getting bit. He was going so fast that he ran quite a bit past me. The adrenaline was coursing through me. He charged me again. I slid out of his path again as he flew by. I knew it was only a matter of time before he got me because I was already spent from the extreme tension.

I was yelling at the house the entire time, screaming at them to come get their dog. I started quickly back-pedaling, trying to figure out a flight plan to safety. Suddenly and totally unexpectedly I was airborne. My feet had hit a deadly combination of wet, slickery leaves plus some oil smeared on the driveway. Involuntarily I did a Three Stooges pratfall. My legs went out from underneath me and I came down from a height of about four and a half feet to land solely and squarely on my . . . elbows. They took my entire weight and the full brunt of the fall.

I can't even describe the pain shooting down my arms. But that was not my first worry. I was now lying prone on the driveway, unable to move because of the shock of the fall and the slipperiness of the driveway . . . and the dog was about seven feet from me, now with nothing to prevent him from attacking me with all his fury.

The last thing I remember thinking was I needed to cover my neck in case this went the worst way. That is what they train us to do as a last resort of protection. Get the neck protected as much as possible to try to limit the extent of the damage. I was just starting to bring my hands up and resigning myself that I was going to get badly nailed by this out-of-control dog.

Through the fog of terror I heard the door open, a voice call the dog's name, and I watched the dog run back into the house. I laid there for a few seconds, trying very hard not to vomit. Then I got tremendously angry. I started screaming at the house and its occupants. I was furious at their irresponsibility and that I was needing assistance. What I got was nothing.

Looking back, I can only guess that the kids were home by themselves, there being no school because of the previous day's holiday. The parents were probably not home. And I was most likely delivering the mail much earlier than normal which startled the kids and the dog. They probably (I'm hoping) merely opened the door to see what was going on, not knowing the dog would come barreling out. I never did find out. I got myself to my postal vehicle and called my boss to tell him what had happened.

I was going to bring the mail back from that section, take a break, and head out to my own route. I was in pain, but I didn't think I had done any damage. I drove back to the station. As I pulled into the parking lot, there was another carrier there with his wife to pick up his paycheck on his day off. I got out of the car. And almost passed out.

They helped me up the ramp into the station. I must have looked pretty haggard and unsteady because they wanted to take me to the hospital to check me out. I wasn't sure but was thinking it might be a good idea.

My fellow carrier assisted me into the men's room and helped me peel off my jacket. He took one look at my elbows and quickly ushered me back out to my supervisor. They looked quite disgusting. Very bloody and bruised. And I was starting to feel really ill. To the hospital we go.

But there was a slight problem. My left leg was starting to become very sore and I couldn't seem to bend it in order to get into my boss's car. We managed.

At the hospital the nurse wanted to clean up my elbows so they could see how much damage there was. My left elbow was really chewed up from landing so hard on the asphalt. My right was not as bad. She wanted to give me a shot in the elbows to deaden them before she started to clean them. I did not want shots in my elbows, so I suggested they start on the right one and see how it went.

She squirted a saline solution on my right elbow and I wanted to jump out of the chair. "Um, I'll take those shots now, thank you."

There was a humorous moment as she was cleaning them up. She asked the obligatory question of what had happened. I told her the story and mentioned at the end that I was glad I was wearing a lined jacket when I landed or my elbows might have looked worse. She sat bolt upright and pushed herself back a foot or so on the stool she was sitting on. She was incredulous that I was wearing a jacket and my elbows still looked that bad.

I asked her what they looked like and she said there was a small hole on the surface that she could look down a long way. Cool! My elbows were very tender for weeks, and if anything even brushed up against them it could make me wince. But no permanent damage.

However, to my quad and left hip—well, that was another story. I had torn something in my left quad when I'd slipped on the oily leaves and apparently my left leg had jutted out to the side as I slipped. I spent the next several weeks going to nearly 50 physical therapy sessions. It never fully healed, and from time to time it will still cause me a bit of discomfort. The damage to my hip showed itself later. It still causes me problems to the point that occasionally I need to take some mild pain meds to be able to sleep. Driving a stick-shift car is very uncomfortable and will cause me extreme discomfort for several days and sometimes even longer. But the dog had not gotten me. I was lucky. This time.

One day on my route I came up to a porch. Perched there was the ugliest cat I had ever seen. And I am not making this up. The cat looked up at me . . . and barked! Speaking of which—

Chapter 12

IT AIN'T JUST THE DOGS, FOLKS

"Still breathing fast and my heart was racing"

There be other critters that are also the bane of mailmen. Dogs are certainly and consistently the worst. So much so that we have these thin cardboard placards called "Dog Warning" cards so that if a person unfamiliar with a route is delivering, he can place these cards in the mail stream as a, well, warning of an impending and potential dog situation.

I have been fortunate because I have never had to worry about turkeys, chickens, geese, or other creatures to "fowl" (sorry) up the safety of delivering my route.

There was this cat once. Seriously. I had a cat on my route that was positively vicious and aggressive. To the point that I had to insert a "Dangerous Cat" warning card in my route case. This cat would whip its paw at you if you came even remotely close to his whereabouts when approaching the mailbox. Fangs showing, hissing, the whole "'kitten and kaboodle" (sorry, again).

———✎———

I also had rare encounters with flying birds (as opposed to the fowls). Both times came AFTER I was thinking about the famous Hitchcock movie. The first time was simply one of those days where nothing of significance was happening. Just a regular day of delivering the mail. After you've been a mailman for a couple of decades—like any other job—sometimes you just go into rote mode. I was walking along on autopilot.

My mind began to wander, and for no reason whatsoever, I began thinking about the movie "The Birds." For the next 10 to 15 minutes I replayed scenes from the film, remembering the horror of it. I was suddenly aware that the same two crows had been following me up and down the street, hopping along the wires or taking short flights from place to place. I felt as if they were aware of me because they were staying even with me as I walked along.

It was kind of funny—at first. I got in my car and drove to the next section a block away. They were there again. And again they followed me down the street on the wires. Now it was creepy. You know, this seemed like a good time to drive to a restroom for a quick break. They were gone when I returned. If I had not been just thinking about the movie right before I noticed them, perhaps the creep factor would have been lower.

The second time was wayyyy more unnerving. At the beginning of the residential part of my route I started my first section down by a park. It was one of those times that happens about twice a year when the crows were making a huge racket in the trees. It usually means there are babies or possibly an injured crow. I mean, they were big-time noisy. A real racket. Which got me to thinking about the movie. About how my son loved the film. The birds attacking the kids. People's eyes pecked out. The tension of the movie, etc.

At THAT moment—LITERALLY—and for the first time in my life, a bird flew across my face. All I saw was a dark brown blur. From his size I would guess a sparrow. How close? I can still feel the spot on my cheek where his wing grazed me and I felt AND heard the airflow from his wings flapping. Scared the dickens out of me. Thirty minutes later I was still breathing fast and my heart was racing like a madman.

There is another creature that mailmen hate dealing with. But first, a warning.

When we brush up against a spiderweb we all tend to shudder and quickly and crazily brush off the creepy stuff. But you haven't seen moves like that of a mailman who has walked fully and completely into a huge web. It is the mailman dance. And if you aren't the one dancing, it is a riot to watch. The problem is that a walking mailman is busy looking down at the mail in his hands or in his mailbag to prepare it for the next delivery stop.

Much of the walking that is done is in this position, not looking ahead at what is directly in your path at eye level. It is nearly unavoidable and happens to every mail carrier a few times every summer. It is never pleasant and sometimes leads to unusual moments.

In the very early days of being on my route I was coming up to a house where the mailbox was attached to the house. This was reached by ascending a few steps leading to a porch. The folks living at this address were very nice and I had been there many times. I came to the steps and was still looking down at the mail in my hand as I climbed the stairs.

Just as I got to the top step I suddenly and defiantly stopped. No reason. Just my gut telling me to stop right THEN. I brought my eyes up and looked straight ahead. My face was just inches from the biggest and most expansively thick spiderweb I have ever seen.

And in the very middle of that web—two inches from my nose—was the biggest spider I had ever seen. A behemoth. He was staring at me with intense malice. (I know, but it sure SEEMED like it!) I caught my breath and slowly backed away. It has been more than 25 years since that moment so I honestly do not remember what I did next. But I can also still see that octo-legged ogre daring me to pass.

———— ✺ ————

My other vivid memory dealing with spiders is worse. One warm summer day (one more reason I hate summer) I was in the last five minutes of my route. I had my head down and was quickly prepping the mail for my next delivery at a four-plex, looking forward to the end of the day. I was not paying attention and suddenly felt that horrid feeling that I had walked face first into a huge spiderweb. Instinctively, I had shut my eyes. I madly did the aforementioned wild mailman-walking-into-a-spiderweb dance and thought I had everything off me.

I opened my eyes only to be met with the hideous reality that I still had some web caked across my left eye. And in the middle of that web—directly across my field of vision—was a multi-legged beast. How big you ask? He stretched far enough across my orbital area that I could not see the ends of his legs . . . in either direction!

He was actually attached to my eye socket and was across my eye like a pirate's patch. Now, I am not terrified of spiders, but you ain't never seen an old man flail so spasmodically in your life. (I just shuddered typing that.) Nothing more came of it so I cannot claim it as one of my worst moments as a mailman, but for those 30 seconds, that was about as unpleasant a time as I had. Ewwww.

Over the course of my career there were dozens of spider moments, but those two pretty much encapsulate the issue. As I said at the outset of this chapter, I was lucky in that I didn't have to face too many other types of creatures other than canines. Well, there was that one time with one critter in particular . . .

Chapter 13

OPENING A GATE INTO INFAMY

"I kicked at him again and again"

As I mentioned before, frequently the biggest moments in our life occur by sheer happenstance. A seemingly innocuous and routine spot in time blossoms and blooms into a remarkable and long-remembered instance. Such was the case that became my most famous—and infamous— encounter. A regular delivery at a regular home on a regular day during a regular week. Incredibly, I cannot recall the exact YEAR this happened, although the details are burned into my conscience like a searing brand. My best guess is 2003.

It was springtime. Early in the week leading up to Easter. About 40% of the way into my route I had a lovely and well-cared for duplex. I entered the property on the southeast side through a gate in the chain-link fence and delivered the first half of the plex like I always did. I rounded the corner of the building and began the walk to the other half, facing the same direction as the other part, but set back farther from the fence.

There sitting on the porch were two white rabbits. The mailbox rested on the wall of the home, just above the opened-door cage with the cute little bunnies. They were sitting there calmly. I was maybe 20–30 feet from the cage.

Suddenly, without any warning from them or provocation from me, one of the rabbits made a mad and frenzied dash—right at . . . ME! What the . . . ? He came flying across the yard with a determined look in his eyes, headed right for my feet. He was not slowing down. I kicked at him to try to dissuade his rush. He came at me again!

And . . . AND THEN THE RABBIT BIT ME!!! And again. I couldn't believe it! Those teeth were like sharp little needles puncturing my leg. He would not be deterred! I kicked at him again and again while crossing the yard and making my way over to the other gate. I was taking side-steps while backpedaling in the direction of the gate. I could not stop him. He bit me three or four times. And still would not desist from his attack. What's going on?!!? I am actually being attacked by a RABBIT!

He would not stop! He would not slow! He would not back down! I could not get away from this beast. Finally realizing my only recourse was to retreat and remove myself from the "danger," I slung my mailbag from off my right shoulder, and taking the action we had been trained to do in attacks of this nature, I forcefully tossed it on top of the mad hare. This is what we have been trained to do with small dogs that we cannot get away from. I then stepped back out of the gate and quickly latched it shut.

Okay, a couple things. First, I was never actually scared at any moment during this "battle." I was just caught so by surprise that I just wanted to get out of there. Second, I don't care what anyone may tell you, those teeth are SHARP!! We see these cute little pictures of sweet little bunnies gently nibbling on a carrot. HAH! Vicious little varmint.

I wasn't injured (except my pride), nor was I any longer in duress. The problem was, my ankle WAS tender and I was thoroughly ticked off. But worse, my mailbag was now inside the yard on the wrong side of the gate. The rabbit was still there, pressing up against the fence, still trying to get to me. I mean, REALLY? About this time the owner of the home came out and asked me if I was alright.

"NO, I'm not alright! Your stupid rabbit just bit me!"

"What? Oh no. I'm so sorry. What can I do?"

"Get him back in the cage and then hand me my mailbag."

He felt really bad about what had happened, and I calmed down fairly quickly. As I said, I wasn't actually hurt and could certainly continue my rounds. He apologized again and I headed off. And if I had just left it at that, nothing more would have come of the occurrence and no one would have been the wiser—nor would I be remembered for this incident lo these many years later. But I had been trained to report all incidents with animals, so I felt obligated to report it to my supervisor, which was my first mistake.

I called my boss:

"Hey, this is Merrit on route 55. I need to report an animal accident."

"Okay, what happened?"

"I was just attacked and bitten by a rabbit."

Silence, followed by: "I'm sorry, what was that?"

"I was just bit by a rabbit."

More silence. Very loud silence.

"You're telling me you just got attacked by a rabbit?"

I could hear a bit of chuckling in the background over the phone.

"Yes, that is what I said."

"I just want to make sure I heard you correctly. You got attacked by a rabbit?"

More chuckling.

"Yes, I was attacked and bitten by a rabbit."

"Uh, where did the rabbit bite you?"

Definite laughter in the background.

"On my right ankle."

"The rabbit bit your ankle?"

The laughter increases. It was getting louder, and there was definitely a growing audience to the conversation. I could picture a small group of postal workers listening in to this ridiculous report.

I proceeded to lay out the incident in as much detail as I could. With each line of description my boss would repeat my words out loud which brought more and more hilarity in the background, especially as he was trying not to laugh as he took down my statements.

I finally finished giving him my verbal report and continued on with my day, falsely assuming that THAT would be the end of it.

When I returned to the station at the end of my day and walked into the mail area I was met with a roomful of amused faces and guffawing. I mean it was ridiculously funny. But they weren't done with me yet. My boss called me over and I had to look over his written report of my phone call while he and other mailmen looked over my shoulder with big dopey grins.

Yes, yes, it was all fine, can I go home now? I drove home, walked in the door and made my second mistake, which has had far longer and lasting implications. I told my family. My children thought it was hysterical and over the years this story has grown and they make sure EVERYONE hears it.

We had a sweet lady mail clerk at Creston for many, many years named Brenda. She is one of only two people I ever worked with at the Post Office that EVERYBODY liked. They don't come any nicer or more caring than Brenda. In the main room at our postal station next to the time clock is a wall that has posters of safety warnings and rules as issued by management that are changed from time to time.

The morning after the rabbit incident, as I came through the door Brenda came over to say good morning and we chatted a bit as we normally did at the beginning of the day. Her shift started in the wee hours around dark o'30, so I always made it a point to greet here as I entered the building.

As I started to make my way to my case she innocently remarked, "Oh, by the way, there's a new warning poster up on the wall of some new dog problems in our area. You should probably take a look at it."

Sounded like a good idea to take a look before I clocked into work. I found the poster and started scanning it. There was a picture of a pit bull, a rottweiler, a German shepherd—and a chocolate Easter bunny. As I looked at it and shook my head I became aware of several of my coworkers observing me. Everybody busted up laughing. Brenda? BRENDA?! Oh, man.

But it WAS funny and grew into one of my favorite stories about my career that I have re-told countless times. Two postscripts to the story. Several years later I was bit by a dog. Not seriously, but it left a bit of a bruise on my thigh. I texted my daughters to let them know. Almost immediately I got a response back from my eldest. Oh, she is worried about her dear old dad. Uh, no. It read, "Was it a rabbit again?"

But the best part of this story from my point of view is what happened a couple weeks later. I never saw the rabbits after the day I was bitten. About a week after the Easter holiday had passed, the owner of the home came out to check up on me and say hello.

"Hey, how are you doing? Are you alright?"

"Yeah, there was no harm done. It's kind of funny now."

"Well, I just wanted to let you know that it wasn't only you. That rabbit was mean to the entire family. It came after us and our kids. It was terrible. He scurried all over the house trying to get at us."

"Oh, no. I'm sorry to hear that. Is everyone okay?"

"Oh, yes. In fact, what I really wanted to tell you was that the rabbit, which we had bought as an Easter gift for our kids, actually ended up being our Easter dinner. I thought you would want to know that."

Over the years, as I have related this story, I have always finished this story of my encounter with the mad bunny the way I am going to tell you now:

MAILMAN: 1
RABBIT: 0

Fortunately I have never had to deliver a rabbit to someone's house. But there have been other, ahem, interesting items.

Chapter 14

HAVE YOU EVER DELIVERED A . . . ?

"It creeped me out big-time"

Like any job, most days as a letter carrier are basically routine. You deliver bills, jun . . . er . . . bulk-business mail, catalogs, magazines, newspapers, letters, advertising, other correspondence, and parcels of all types, shapes and sizes. Those parcels can be gifts, boxed fruit, books, CDs, medicine, clothes, photographs, and, well, pretty near anything. As I have found out. And occasionally those parcels become anything but routine. At least not routine in the sense that regular folks handle the contents on a regular basis.

I got my first example of that early on. On the route that I landed on out of Multnomah Station when the regular carrier was gone for over a year, I had a business right at the beginning of the route. The folks who worked there were very kind and friendly.

I noticed after a few weeks that I kept delivering the same size and weight of box to them two or three times a week. The dimensions were a bit larger than a shoe box but it was heavier than I would normally attribute to a parcel of that size. Same size and weight every time. The odd thing was that it was sent by Registered Mail.

A piece of Registered Mail carries with it the

implication of monetary value. Every person handling it—from the one who initially takes it at the Post Office on through each and every employee who transfers it—has to sign for it, taking responsibility for its security until it is handed off to the next person right up until delivery where the person receiving it has to also sign off.

We guard those articles of mail with extreme care because if it is lost, the Post Office will follow it to the person who last signed for it. Anyway, every one of these parcels came Registered Mail. After delivering a dozen or more of these over several weeks my curiosity got the better of me so I asked the employees at this business establishment if they could tell me what I had been delivering. They gave me a look that told me I should have already known, but they told me anyway. Perhaps this would be a good time to tell you that the business was a mortuary and mausoleum. It is kind of funny now, but at the time I was dumbfounded that I was actually transporting cremated human remains! I was so glad that I had not been simply tossing these packages around in my postal vehicle. I can tell you that from that point on I certainly made sure I handled them with care (and maybe just a bit of trepidation).

There are two kinds of parcels that mailmen will deliver as soon as possible to get them out of the truck. Baby chicks. Oh my stars, but do they make a racket! Oh, sure, ONE baby chick is cute to listen to. Not a dozen. And sometimes we deliver food. No, not from your local market. From overseas. There were many times I delivered some type of seafood to a family who still had relatives across the world. You tend to want to get those out of your truck quickly because of the assault on your olfactory senses.

I have delivered a few coconuts. Not in boxes. Just as "themselves." Yes, you can send a coconut through the mail. Now, wait! Before you do, (or put anything else "interesting" in the mail stream) check with your local Post Office to find out restrictions and rules. One coconut delivery was extra special. I posted about it.

June 7, 2014

Today I delivered a coconut. Not in a box, just a coconut. It is not the first time I have done this. This was my third. But my first in probably over 15 years. It was sent from Hawaii. What made this one cool is that instead of the address being written by a magic marker, the writing on this one was carved on. Really cool.

I also delivered an apple once. But never an egg. The old-timers used to tell us that way back in the day occasionally a person would want to challenge the Postal Service and would take an egg in to be delivered. The Post Office would take a certain pride in getting it delivered unharmed. Raw or cooked? Not sure. You can't do it anymore, however, so close your refrigerator door.

Twice in my life I had the "pleasure" of delivering many heavy packages to the same house over several days as someone "moved by mail." Seriously. I'm not talking beds and couches and appliances. But they would send large boxes of books, lamps, clothes, linens, bedding, pictures and other wall-hangings, etc.

But as I think back to unusual deliveries my mind catches on five stories in particular. I will share these from worst to best.

———⊂∞⊃———

In the early days of being on Route 55 I entered a business toward the beginning of my route. The lady who ran the shop was coming up to the end of her career. She was extremely nice and I always enjoyed chatting with her when I came in. But not this day.

As I walked through the door I noticed she was quite upset about something. That was the second thing I noticed. The first thing that grabbed my attention were the multiple law enforcement officers gathered in her small office.

They looked at me as I stepped in and they said, "Oh, good, we have been wanting to talk to you." Not a good start to the conversation. It was about to get worse. Not for me, but for what had happened. When I had delivered her mail the day before, along with the usual magazines and bills and junk mail had been an envelope that contained a death threat to her.

She was clearly and understandably quite upset. The officers wanted to know if I knew any details about the letter. Where it had come from and how it had come into my possession. They were investigating to the best of their ability to find out who had sent it and if it had entered the mail stream in an unusual way. I knew nothing about it and had no specific memory of delivering it. Nothing ever came of it, thankfully.

She was never bothered or threatened by anyone again and they were never able to figure out who sent it. It creeped me out big-time that I had actually handled a letter like that.

There is a multinational company that I hate. Okay, I don't hate THEM. Just their catalogs. It became a running joke among my friends how much I hated delivering their catalogs. Which always came out in the hot month of August. And which every customer received. I posted about them every year.

August 3, 2011

I hate . . . Hate . . . HATE . . . H.A.T.E (blank) catalogs!!!!!!!!!

Everyone in my life who knew I was a mailman (which, actually IS everyone in my life) also knew how much I despised the dreaded things. Here are two comments I received from this posting:

We got ours today, and were chatting about you in the kitchen.

We got ours today. My husband actually mentioned you and how much you hate them when he brought it in from the mail box.

Which brought some funny and unexpected comments to drop into my life. In August of 2012 we watched the opening ceremonies of the Summer Olympics from London. I was especially moved by the dropping of 7 billion pieces of confetti representing every person on the planet. I commented on social media about this and even jokingly remarked that I had spotted "my" piece of paper falling. One of my high school buddies responded with: "Perhaps the confetti came from shredded copies of this year's (blank) catalogs!" His words positively cracked me up. In August of the next year he messaged me.

August 8, 2013

Thought about you when "that" catalog came in today's mail.

The catalogs were horrible. I actually considered trying to choose my vacation one year so as to avoid having to deliver them. They arrived every year for about a decade. For the record, I have nothing against the store, just the catalogs. (Although, on principle and solidarity I will never shop there). The first August after I retired a dear friend sent me this via social media:

August 7, 2015

Thought of you when my (blank) catalog came in the mail. Knew you were not missing the joy of delivering those things at all. :-)

True that!

Two years later my wife's niece got hers in the mail.

August 3, 2017

I thought of you today as I opened my mailbox to find an (blank) magazine. Sure bet you are happy you weren't delivering those today in the 100+ degree weather?. Every time I get one of those magazines it reminds me of you.

———

The other consistently beyond miserable item we deliver is election mail. Ugh, yikes, and arggh. Four things you need to know about election mail.

One, it tends to be ultra-thin and hard to handle. And if it is made out of card stock, it is a huge trap for severe paper cuts.

Two, it is not unusual to receive at your case four or more specific mailers on any one day, which means a dreadful time of casing the mail and handling it on the street. You will just have to take my word for it.

Three, nearly everyone gets a copy of each mailing.

And four, nearly everyone who receives a copy has no interest in reading it.

Every four years during national election time it becomes a ghastly and abundant overload of horrible mailings to handle. Late in my career I made it a habit during those years to plan two of my vacation weeks during the final half-month before the election just to miss this miserable time.

One year, after the election and when I returned to work, one of my junior coworkers walked up to me and exclaimed, "Merrit, you are a genius!" It had been an especially unbearable two weeks of continuous mailers and he was lamenting the unpleasantness of it all and that I had missed it.

———— ∞ ————

Delayed mail stories. I only had one significant one happen to me during my career, but it was a doozy. This happened in late winter or early spring in 2007. Ralph and Gabe, father and son, lived next door to each other right at the beginning of the first residential section on my route. At the time, Ralph was in his early 80s and Gabe was about 60. One particular morning as I was walking up Ralph's driveway to deliver the mail into his box, they pulled up in their car. Verbal pleasantries were shared as I flipped through the letters to pull out first Ralph's and then Gabe's mail to hand to them. My eye caught a new name I did not recognize.

"Who is Shirley Johnson?" I asked. The two men looked at one another.

GABE: "Shirley?!?"

RALPH: "Shirley was my mother."

I told him I had a piece of mail for her. Now, remember, he was in his 80s.

ME: "Well, that's strange."

It flashed through my head that it was probably a piece of junk mail from a company with an out-of-date mailing list. (That can happen from time to time.) But in one glance I noticed two things. It was a postcard, so therefore first class mail, with a postmark. The postcard was handwritten and the postmark had been hand-stamped. It had been specifically dropped in the mail with the intention of reaching Shirley.

GABE: "Uh, my grandmother has been dead for over 30 years."

Well, now this was getting really weird.

ME: "Well, this postcard is addressed to her. The postmark is from Barrow, Alaska."

RALPH: "Well, my mother was in Alaska with my sister Marge about 35 years ago."

He then told me that Marge had also passed away several years ago. About this time I noticed the postmark looked odd. I read it more carefully.

ME: "Oh my goodness. The postmark on this is dated September 1976!"

THIRTY-ONE YEARS AGO!!! We all just stared at each other.

"Do you have any idea what's going on here?" I asked and handed the postcard to Gabe so he could read it.

He chuckled, and dumbfoundedly said, "Well, it appears this was sent from Alaska by my Aunt Kathy, my dad's sister, to her mom, my grandmother, when she had gone to Alaska for a short time."

It turned out that Gabe's Aunt Marge, Ralph's sister, had written the letter to Gabe's grandmother—Ralph and Marge's mother—31 years earlier after the mom had returned from Alaska where she had been living for a short time with her daughter.

The card was the daughter/sister/aunt letting her mom know that things were going well and she missed everyone, etc. The mom had died the next year. The postcard was in remarkably good condition and perfectly readable. And the postmark was clear.

And it had been canceled in Alaska 31 years previously. My best guess is that it had gone through the Alaskan Post Office, been postmarked, and then who knows what happened . . . ? It most likely either at that point slipped under a machine or desk or something there, was finally found 31 years later, and put back into the regular mail stream.

But it had not landed in the cogs or gears of some grimy, greasy machine because it was in near pristine condition. It had not been handled by a person, because the way it arrived to me was in my computer-generated letter mail, which is in itself really unusual.

The three of us were stunned at the history of this letter. It was so strange that the card had come through the postal system without being noticed by anyone. Had it been seen, it would have arrived to me in a completely different manner and this magical moment would not have happened. And that I had in my hands a piece of mail that had been sent from Alaska during the first months of the bicentennial year of our country, and after 31 years had arrived on THIS DAY on MY ROUTE at the PRECISE TIME they pulled up to the house and the PRECISE TIME I was delivering the mail. And I would have never noticed the date if the conversation between us had not occurred.

If they had moved at any time during those three decades, the whole thing would have remained a mystery and the letter would have gone to the dead letter office because I would not have recognized the name. The next day Gabe graciously gave me photocopies of both sides of the postcard as a keepsake, which I still possess. Over the years he and I would again shake our heads at the memory and idea of what had transpired. Without a doubt, one of the greatest stories of my 30-year career.

———

Another one of my favorite delivery moments was not so much what I delivered—although that was integral to the story—but the reaction of the customer. Express packages must be attempted before noon. In 2009 I had an Express package to deliver to a young couple who lived about four-fifths of the way through my route. So I had to deviate from my normal delivery pattern to schedule an attempt of the delivery of this package before the deadline.

They were not at home, and since most Express packages require a signature I left a written notice in the mailbox. I returned to their house on my normal rounds later in the day. It was about 4:00 in the afternoon. I knocked on the door. Still no answer. So I continued on down the street.

About five minutes later when I was three houses farther along my route, the man to whom the Express parcel was addressed came casually down the sidewalk and hailed me, coming up to me to collect his small package. He calmly walked up to me, very nonchalant.

Again, it was 4:00 in the afternoon. He said he was glad he had caught me. I knew him well enough to ask what was in the package.

"Oh, those are our wedding rings."

"Oh, cool. So when is the wedding?"

With total aplomb he replied, "This afternoon at 5:00."

I didn't say anything, but my brain was going "!!!!!?????!!!!!" You could have pushed me over with a feather. I immediately got agitated and told him to quickly sign the form. I still cannot believe how calm he was about not having his wedding rings in his possession ONE HOUR BEFORE HE WAS TO BE MARRIED. I am so glad I was not too late with his parcel.

Late parcels? Oh, sounds like we should talk about Christmas.

Chapter 15

GET YOUR CARDS AND PACKAGES IN THE MAIL EARLY

"A sense of community"

I love Christmas. Hardly headline-worthy, that statement, eh? But many postal employees don't like the holiday season, and understandably so. It can be so ridiculously overwhelming. Besides all the family obligations that everybody else also has, postal workers have jobs that can "split the seams" of a person's endurance over several weeks.

First, in the weeks leading up to December the catalog and other advertising mail increases dramatically as retailers push their wares onto the public in hopes of bringing in the bucks. Then, as Christmas month hits, there are the packages and cards and more packages and more cards and more . . . well, you get the idea.

I came up with a theory that the condition of the economy does not affect the busyness of the season for the Post Office. Picture in your mind a "typical" Christmas season in America, however that may look to you. A certain number of folks travel to other destinations across the country to visit family. There are many people who do not travel but buy scads of gifts and send them through the mail to those family members elsewhere. Folks with less disposable cash send a few gifts to cities around the country. And innumerable people send Christmas cards.

If the economy is robust, then more cards get sent and some others send a few more gifts through the mail system than they might normally. The more well-off people are now traveling, but they still probably send the gifts by mail rather than hauling them by plane, train, or car.

If the economy is in a tighter time, some of the people who in the first scenario were traveling, now may be purchasing and sending many gifts through the mail. Those who may have been in the bunch that sent gifts are now sending cards instead—still through the mail. The ones who only sent cards in the first example? They are almost certainly still sending those cards. All this to say that year-to-year the United States Postal Service is bombarded during the Christmas holidays. And me? I LOVED IT!!

Yes, there were times the weather could be challenging. (See previous chapter on weather and Christmas 2008.) But in the Portland area, while November can be a big, cold drippy mess and January can be horrendous, it is not unusual for December to be only mildly wet, and there are many days that are no more than cold and crisp. If there is snow it is usually just a dusting or maybe up to two inches. Once you can get past that, for me, the month was filled with wonder and delight.

I loved handling and delivering Christmas cards. I loved the myriad of colors of the rows of letter mail waiting to be sorted or delivered. And a card has a certain feel to it that just feels pleasant to the touch. It is not wispy thin, usually not slippery, and is easy to hold and slip into a mailbox. Grasping a handful of Christmas cards is a real treat. And as opposed to bills or adverts, a Christmas card is an item that the sender has enjoyed sending and the receiver will enjoy receiving. I'm sorry, I just really loved looking at, handling, and delivering Christmas cards. Loved it!

Every year without fail there was always a little flux in the flow of Christmas cards. Not coming in. Going out. I found it humorous and a wonderful example of human conditioning. One year I posted about it:

December 20, 2012

As a mailman I am about to experience a yearly tradition on my route the next couple days. Picking up Christmas cards from some of my customers to put in the mail stream for delivery. What is so special about this? These are not normal Christmas cards. These are folks sending late Christmas cards. These are people sending Christmas cards to people they got Christmas cards from but did not send Christmas cards to. It happens every year around these closing days before THE day.

The junk mail stops. There is about a two-week stretch in mid-December where there is virtually no junk mail. The retailers know there is not enough time to send out a mailer, allow the customer to spend the time to peruse the advert, mail in the order, and have the retailer get it shipped back to the customer in time for Christmas. I suspect as more overnight deliveries take place from businesses, this may change. But it didn't in my postal lifetime.

Seeing the excitement of my route kids as they anticipated the big day. Or chatting with the older kids as they counted the days till Christmas break from school. Little ones and Christmas? What could be better? Speaking of which . . .

As a mailman, there is nothing better—NOTHING!—than coming up the walkway to a house a few days before Christmas while carrying a large parcel and seeing a little shining face or two in the window. Those faces sparkle with anticipation, and YOU are the one bringing gifts from Grandpa and Grandma!

When a parent lets a four-year-old out the door to greet you when you have a package like that, it is off-the-charts fabulous. For a minute, you are part of the family as the little one hops around you, asking "Whooz-it-fwum, whooz-it-fwum?!" Man, it doesn't get better than that!

I also loved seeing the "old kids." Ah. It didn't happen every year, but occasionally this scenario played out. I had watched kids grow up while I was their family's mailman. Maybe when I started on the route they were 5 or 8 or 10 years old. They have now grown up and moved away and have families of their own. They come back to visit for Christmas. Perhaps I haven't seen them in a couple years or more. Maybe one of their parents has passed on and they are there to be with the remaining parent. They are outside the home with THEIR kids hanging lights or doing yard work or they just see me from inside the house. As I hit the porch the door opens and there is my grown-up route kid, maybe with his or her little one at the side. And I hear this: "Mr. Merrit, are you still the mailman here for Mom?" Hugs. Laughter. Meeting the kids. Questions back and forth about our respective families. Is someone cutting onions? My eyes seem moist as I remember these precious moments.

<hr />

There is something about working Christmas Eve. Oh, it was fantastic if your day off for Christmas week happened to fall on Christmas Eve. More time with your family and all that means. It was great, and when it fell that way every few years or so it was celebrated with gusto. But most years I worked Christmas Eve. It meant a day where there were treats at work. The bosses (well, most bosses) would bring in a terrific spread of meats and cheeses and maybe other coworkers brought in cookies and such.

But as I walked my route there were greetings of "Merry Christmas" throughout the day. Maybe some last-minute treats and gifts and tips from customers. More on that in a minute. People would come out and give hugs and thank me for my service and ask what my plans were and how was my family. As the day waned I would begin to see the celebrations beginning in the homes and the anticipation of being with my family would grow.

Lots of waves back and forth from folks in those homes. Back to the station to pick up the very last parcels of the season. Back to the route to deliver those parcels with some final holiday greetings. Back to the station again. As the carriers trickled out to head home there were hugs and greetings and warmth. And a sense of pride amongst us that we did it. We survived and successfully navigated another Christmas season.

———— ∞ ————

As we all know, the Christmas season can also be a time of emotional difficulty, depending on our circumstances, family situations, etc. A time such as this led to one of my most tender moments as a mailman during the Christmas season of 2011.

But you need to know about two of the biggest events in my life previous to that. In the summer of 2007 my son Elliott, just 16 years old, drowned in the Pacific Ocean when he was caught in a sneaker wave. As you can imagine it was the most devastating thing to happen in my life.

Everyone in the Post Office and those of my customers who knew of it were incredibly supportive. I won't get too much into it now, but if you're interested in the particulars I have written a book about my journey of losing my son. It is titled *Lessons from a Son's Life . . . and Death*. Then two years later I re-met and began dating a woman I had known during my college years. Jill and I got married in the summer of 2011. As that holiday season arrived I was hugely emotional, it being just the fifth Christmas since Elliott had died and also being my first with Jill as my wife, after having been single for more than 11 years.

So my sensitivity meter was running wild and ultra-sensitive. A nice young woman named Trena had moved onto my route six or seven years previously. I did not see her very often, but our encounters were always pleasant and friendly. One day just before Christmas I delivered a huge package for this woman early in the day, putting it in what I thought would be a safe place on her porch but out of view from the street.

What I did not know was that an individual had been sneakily hiding and then following letter carriers in the area and stealing parcels almost immediately after delivery. Late the next day I came by to make sure she had gotten the package. She had not. It had been stolen. I felt terrible, and then felt worse when I found out it was a Christmas package from her father who lived on the east coast. Graciously, although she was frustrated with what had happened, she was not angry with me, although we were both furious about what had transpired. For several minutes we just spent some time together talking about Christmas and families and memories. And then suddenly we were hanging onto each other, both weeping at what we were missing but also at the blessings we both had in our lives. It was one of the tenderest moments I ever experienced as a mailman and cemented the two of us as dear friends. My last three Christmases as her mailman we always took a moment to remember that day. On my last day before I retired, we spoke once more about that moment three and a half years previously and also shared tears again at a friendship born of sorrow and togetherness.

———— ∞ ————

Treats, gifts, and tips. Yes, I got them. I felt awkward about taking them and probably shouldn't have. HAH!!! Not a chance. I loved it! I liked getting stuff. But not for the reason you may think. A mailman walks the rounds day after day. Rain. Heat. Days of weariness. Then for a couple of weeks or so many of your customers say, "Hey, I'm aware and appreciative of the effort you've put in. Thanks so much!" Man, that'll do it!

Whether it be with a card, cash, or candy. I treasured every gift, and even now the remembrance of those efforts of appreciation for me brings a deep glow. But one homemade gift, or rather the simple homemade card that came with it, remains the most prized ornament of my career. This family had lived on my route for several years. Ironically, they lived in the downstairs part of a two-story duplex where I had lived in the upstairs apartment several years before I started working for the Post Office. It was actually our residence during the time when I took the postal exam back in 1982.

This family had moved to this address in the late 1980s. One of their kids became my second oldest Route Kid. They had given me homemade fudge in the past for Christmas. But during this particular Christmas season there was a card attached. It also was homemade, written on thin cardboard stock with a red marker. The card started with a customary greeting: "Merry Christmas Merrit! Here is some fudge Bonnie made." Then I was stunned with the following words:

Knowing you, our "mailman" and friend
has helped to give me
a sense of community
I never felt before.
I so cherish that.
Thank you.
Your influence on our neighborhood is very positive.
Love to your family from ours. Jason

At the end of my days when I will perhaps have forgotten everything else about my career, I will still remember this. The card is framed and hangs in my study even today.

———— ∞ ————

As the years passed the bag of memories I captured during my years of delivering mail in the holiday season grew. The idea of that aspect of my job coming to an end became difficult to grasp.

December 21, 2012

Today was my heaviest Christmas card delivery day this season. I LOVE it. This is my favorite time of year to work. It is my 28th Christmas in the Post Office and 25th on the same route. I love bringing packages to a house and seeing a little face or two in the window that is glowing. I love the feel and color of the cards. Though it doesn't happen often, I LOVE when someone's grown children arrive for the holidays, and I was their mailman when they were still kids, and they remember me. As I was ruminating on these treasured times over the past few days, I was struck with a sad thought. If all goes according to plan, I only have two more Christmas seasons left as a mailman. I am sooo looking forward to retirement, but I will miss this part of the job.

December 24, 2013

Another Christmas season at the ol' PO is over. I didn't get to participate as much as I wanted, but I totally enjoyed what I did. I only have one to go. Which makes me sad. It is my fave time to do my job. Something tells me a year from this moment I will be quite melancholy.

Melancholy? That doesn't even come close. More on that later. Right now, let's get away from wistfulness and enjoy some interesting folks.

Chapter 16

THERE'S SOMETHING ABOUT A MAN (OR WOMAN) IN UNIFORM

"The place went nuts"

I never thought about that axiom much until one evening at my church. There was some sort of service being held that day in the late afternoon. I did not have time to change out of my uniform into my "civilian" clothes, so I went against my usual practice and attended while still in my blues. I came across a very dear friend of mine, a much younger woman who I saw on a regular basis at church. We had known each other for several years and had a very deep but completely platonic friendship. She had never before seen me in my postal uniform.

We sat down to have a chat and I was suddenly aware that she was patting and touching my postal coat and shirt nearly continuously as we talked. Not in any sort of inappropriate way, but just in a manner totally foreign to our relationship. I looked at her, chuckled, and asked her what in the world she was doing?

She looked at me, obviously a bit startled, and realized that she had been "caressing my uniform." She hesitated a moment and told me she had not been aware what she had been doing and said I looked really good in my uniform.

We laughed about it and continued our conversation, sans the pawing. Did I tease her about it for months after? Now, would I do that?

Believe me, at the Post Office a uniform attracts zero attention. They are not flattering (except for the carrier at Sellwood I mentioned earlier) but I must admit the first time I put on those blue-striped pants and light blue shirt, it was SOMETHING! But after the first day or so—

I was employed with hundreds of folks over the years who wore that blue regalia. Boy, howdy, did I work with some CHARACTERS! I wish you could have spent some time with them in the work environment of the United States Postal Service. What a hoot!

Oh, don't get me wrong. I didn't like everyone I worked with. And certainly many did not like me. And there were lots of days when there was bickering and whining and anger. But there were very few I actually disliked. And truthfully, when I think back on the images that flood my memories about my workmates, what I remember the most is working together to accomplish our task, with teasing and much laughter.

I will obviously use only their first names, but I want to introduce you to some of my favorites and tell you a bit about why they were such a delight to work with. Actually, I won't just use their proper first names. After I became one of the veterans at Creston I started hanging nicknames on some of my fellow letter carriers. I'm not completely sure why. After a while almost all of them ended up with nicknames from me.

I never initially intended for most of them to have nicknames, but it got to the point where I hardly called anyone by their given name or with a regular voice. This may have all started when I first hit the Creston Station in May of 1988. At the time there were five men named Bill who were letter carriers there. So they had all "earned" nicknames so we could distinguish them in conversation. "Big Bill," "Willie," "Quiet Bill," to name a few.

In my early days at Creston most of the carriers and clerks were older than me. The station was in the process of "turning over" a generation of mailmen. Many of the old-timers were fast approaching retirement. Quite frankly, I remember little about them. I was a newbie still trying to find my way and figure out what the Post Office was all about. There was still so much information and instruction to take in. The first person I met was Mailman Mike who I have already talked about and will get back to in a bit.

Another good man was Steve, who I had worked with at Sellwood. We lost him much too soon due to illness. But he was an interesting fellow. He wore several big rings on his fingers, most with a large blue stone in them. He was very quiet but had a limit to how much nonsense he would take. One afternoon another carrier just would not stop yammering at him about something and Steve, who was not a big man, warned the culprit that he would take action if the guy didn't shut it. The guy kept yakking. Steve walked over to him and simply picked him up off the floor and deposited him in a large parcel hamper (about the size of a hotel laundry basket). The only thing injured was pride, but the guy never bothered Steve again. How we missed him over the years.

We also missed dear Kelly, one of our union stewards. She was my family's mailman for several years. As nice a woman as you would want to know. She spoke some very eloquent words at my son's memorial. She grappled with cancer for a few years before finally succumbing. Her death hit us hard.

Donzie was a very nice man who was considerably older than I was but looked five years younger than me. It drove me crazy how a guy working outside like he did could stay so young looking. We are both retired now and I still see him every few weeks and he no longer looks five years younger than me. More like 15. Sigh.

During my first years at Creston I was an avid fan of basketball. Pete and I would spend many hours debating several aspects of sports, but especially our mutual disdain for Shaq and our admiration of the impeccable outside shooting skills of Reggie Miller and Geoff Petrie.

Tamara was a tall, slender, auburn-haired beauty who became a fast friend. She only worked at Creston a short time, but I saw her often on her own route out of a different station as I drove through the neighborhood where I lived. There were always catch-up chats and words of encouragement for each other when we saw one another. When my son died, she went out of her way to drop off a personal note for me at work.

Big Bill (one of the five "Bills" mentioned earlier) was a gentle giant who had been the carrier of my route a few years previously. We loved to chat about our passion for baseball. For many years after he left Creston I'd call him the evening before the Opening Day of the Major League baseball season, wait for him to say "hello," and then bellow into the phone: "BASEBALL!" He always laughed and then we would discuss our predictions and hopes for the coming season.

The other big baseball fan at the station in my early days was dear Royce. He was an older gentleman who regaled me with delightful stories of his baseball fandom from when he was a kid. He spun lovely tales of watching some of my baseball heroes on television that I only knew from afar through books. We spent many an hour discussing the finer points of the great game we both loved avidly. I am not sure who, but someone at the station came up with a fantastically inspired idea of how to send Royce off to his retirement years. At the time Portland had a minor league baseball team. A trove of us went to a game together the evening of his last day of work and arranged with the club to have Royce throw out the first pitch. He had no idea and was deeply touched. When they announced his name and why he was there over the public address system we went wild in the stands. It was a grand moment.

Doug the Slug from Multnomah was there, of course, and we took up right where we left off. For the next 27 years we worked just a few feet from each other, sharing the trials and joys of life in and out of the Post Office. About that nickname. Two reasons. First, well, it . . . uh . . . rhymes with Doug! But, secondly, Doug was most definitely not a slug. He was moving fast from his first initial steps inside a postal building, and 30 years later he still moves faster than I ever did, including when I was in my youth.

There was Donna-Do, my first utility carrier, the person who regularly did my route on my day off. Donna was a hoot, with a generous heart and a boisterous personality. If you meet her, you must be sure to ask her to sing "The Christmas Song," especially the line what wonders if reindeer really know how to fly. It became a holiday tradition between the two of us.

After Donna-Do left, another utility carrier took her place. One of the most character-y characters who ever graced our station. And with one of the wildest nicknames I have ever heard. This one did not come from me. The person who hung it on him and the reason why have been lost to me through the passing of the years. Geno Fat-Wallet. His real name was Jeff but I don't honestly remember anyone ever calling him that. He was a hoot and a half. Never serious about anything and always with a smart-mouth comment about anyone for any reason whatsoever. Over time he became a good friend and someone I trusted implicitly. And an avid Detroit Tigers fan which led to some terrific trash talking between the two of us. He worked with us for just a few years before moving to a different station.

Everyone needs at least one friend in their life like Linda is to me. For years Linda was a fierce union warrior for us in our battles against management. When I had questions regarding my rights during many issues I faced in my career, she always had the answer or knew what direction to point me in to find it myself. But more importantly, she was and is a good friend. Why do I say everyone needs a friend like Linda? Linda and I disagreed on virtually everything. Politics, social issues, religion. You name it, we were frequently at odds. But only in our opinions, not in our spirit. We never fought but always listened to each other with respect and dignity. In this age of people being furious with the prospect that anyone could dare disagree with them, our friendship was and is refreshing. She is appreciated by me.

Without question my closest friend during my first decade at Creston was Willie (yet another of the five "Bills"). We hit if off right away. Over the years we spent a lot of time together, attending many concerts together. Our mutual passion for music cemented a treasured friendship, and although he has lived several hours away for the past 20 years, we stay in regular contact. We both celebrated new daughters into our homes the same week. We fiercely rag on each other, trying to outdo the other in our insults of each other's intelligence, looks, personalities, and anything else we can think of. Nothing is off limits. A dear man to me, he is.

Another person who had a child around the same time as Willie and me was Mary Jo. She didn't work at the Post Office very long, but I loved working with her. She was fiercely delightful.

Dave was a very quiet man of the highest integrity. I didn't know him very well until he offered to be my regular ride to work for several years. Over that time we got to know each other quite well. We had countless conversations over our frustrations about work and bosses and weather and . . . . I cannot count how many times one or the other of us would remark that we still had so many years left before we could retire and wondered whether we would make it. He put in more years than I did, and on his last day I drove out to his route and walked a section with him, reminiscing about our careers and sharing the wonderment that we had indeed both made it to retirement.

July 22, 2016

Today I also got to say fare thee well to my old mailman buddy, Dave W. He is retiring after 33 years in the USPS, the last 30 on the same route. Both of those numbers are more than I compiled. And everyone likes him! A big thank you to Terri P. for the heads-up about this. He was my ride to work for over eight years way back in the day. We used to wonder what it would be like to finally be able to retire from delivering mail. That was 20 years ago. Now we both have made it. A good man.

But it was Mailman Mike who I worked right next to at the beginning and right up until his last day, a few years ahead of me. Mike should write his own book! Man, the stories he threw my way. He was sure I would never make it as a mailman. I didn't seem to have the passion nor the health to withstand 30 years of this very physical job.

The physical demands on a letter carrier's body are insidious. You don't notice the damage until years and years later. He used to always say delivering the mail was like picking strawberries, which he had done as a kid. "Merrit," he would say, "You have to get to the end of the row."

As I said earlier, Mike and I fought, laughed, cajoled, complained, and worked together for 22 years. I cannot imagine what my career would have been without him. But he will be ticked off if I say much more about him, so I will move along.

—— ∞ ——

As the older generation of carriers vacated the premises, a new group of youngsters came along. And suddenly, I was viewed as a veteran letter carrier. Now I was being asked the questions of how to do the job and survive.

J. Lee became my new utility carrier and over the years earned the title of "Best Utility Carrier in the Universe." More importantly, she became a very dear friend who was always there for me. She took very good care of my route when I had a day off and is also a highly talented photographer. I appreciate her more than I can say.

There was Johnny, an avid and long-suffering Chicago Cubs fan. (By definition, aren't all Cubs fans 'long-suffering'?) Over the years we had many baseball discussions. I regretted that when his beloved Cubbies won their first World Series in 108 years in 2016, I was no longer at the station to experience that amazing joy with him.

There was "Cheddar," a quiet unassuming man everyone liked. He worked directly across the aisle from me for many years and then one day he decided he'd had enough, gave his notice, and walked away from his postal job. A lot of us envied him for being able to make that decision.

TP (in Da House) is a fierce warrior, the toughest person I have ever met . . . and as dear and tender of a friend as I have ever had. Over the years she and I swapped story after story and laughed to the point of tears. I seemed to have a knack to really hit her funny bone. More than once she would be bent over at the waist, holding on to her stomach, begging me to stop talking before she peed her pants from laughing so hard. She never did, of course. But oh how we laughed! TP is highly opinionated, at times very loud, and a complete delight to have a conversation with about football, family, delivering mail, and a myriad of other topics. If you are her true friend, she will do anything to help you—with no thought of recompense.

Another tough lady was Barb. I admired her willingness to take no nonsense from anyone, including management. My favorite moment with her came about halfway through my career. Creston was going through a tough time. (This will be one of those rare times in the book where I gripe about postal management.) Middle management had decided we were performing as a miserable station and getting poor results, so they sent out a team of toughies to put us in our place.

The chief lecturer was giving us the what-for, telling us what a lousy postal station we were and had just let us know in no uncertain terms how things were going to be, finishing with some specific instructions of how we were going to be carrying out a particular new task in a way that we had not done before. Barb spoke up.

"Well, that is all fine and good, sir, and I am sure we are all thrilled with how things are going to be, but just how do you expect us to accomplish this task?"

The manager said, "I will tell you. What route are you?"

Barb took a couple steps forward and proudly and fiercely spat out, "I am NOT a route! I'm a person! My name is Barbara, and if you wish to explain to me what you mean, then please address me as such."

You could have heard a stamp hit the ground. Dead silence. He then proceeded to address her by her name and explain what he meant. In all my days, I don't think I have ever been more proud of a fellow worker nor more proud to be a mailman. Dang, woman!

<hr />

KARL(!) was a fun person to work next to for a few years, almost always able to make me laugh. At his case he had a photograph of an outing with his children. It is one of my favorite "Daddy with his kids" pictures I have ever seen. He developed his nickname from me by the way that one of our supervisors used to address him.

He was eventually replaced by (Helloooo) Arlen. I loved working next to Arlen. You never met a more pessimistic, woe-is-me, Eeyore-like person in your life. And he would be the second to admit that. The first would be his wife, uproariously laughing in agreement. He doesn't want anyone to know it, but he is also a very caring person who became one of my closest friends at work.

Murray and I worked at Creston for several years together but it was not till he transferred routes and ended up across the aisle from me that I got to know him and his delightful idiosyncrasies. He and I share an affinity for two things. We both love puns. And the badder the better. We also find dates interesting. When November 11, 2011 came around (11/11/11) it was a race to see who would tell the other first. And the same with December 11, 2010 (12/11/10) or February 4, 2006 (I will leave this one for you to figure out) and the like. But one precious memory with Murray stands out from the rest. When my son died Murray was on vacation and unable to attend the memorial. During the time I was off work I went out and walked to keep my legs in shape for when I returned. One day I was out walking with my daughter about three miles from home.

Our journey took us through Murray's route. As she and I headed back home Murray and I spotted one another. We approached each other and without a word being spoken he lovingly embraced me with a hug borne of sorrow and care. This memory is firmly impressed on my soul and also on his. We stepped back and both continued on our way, with nary a word uttered. None were needed.

Donny became a good friend. He was from New York City, and his father and I attended the same church. He has a lovely wife and together they raised eight kids, four girls and then four boys. He is an ex-Marine (although I have been told "once a Marine . . ."). Not sure how it started or who started it, but we used to regularly go through a routine where we would pretend to punch each other. It might happen while we were in line at the time clock to start our shift, or possibly just as one of us happened to walk around the other's mail case. A shot to the gut would be offered (along with accompanying sound effects that only the male of the species seems to bother with and refine to an art form) and the other would double over in feigned injury (you know, the way most men soccer players behave). As the "injured" person crumpled in a heap, an additional crashing blow to the head would commence. It was great fun and led to a delightful moment for me on my last day of work before I retired.

In my 30 years working for the Post Office, I only met two employees that EVERYONE liked. One was Brenda, my chocolate Easter bunny pal. The other was Sweet Virginia. Her name was Ginger but I deemed her Sweet Virginia because, well, she WAS sweet. We worked together for several years and I never heard anyone ever say a bad word about her as a person or a worker. When her retirement day arrived I wrote about her.

April 29, 2014

It is my day off tomorrow, so I will say it now, my fondest farewell to one of my fave coworkers EVER, Sweet Virginia, known to the rest of y'all as Ginger. I have worked with hundreds of folks in my 29 years in the Post Office. Only two were liked by everybody, Ginger and Brenda. Brenda retired a couple years back and Ginger's last day is tomorrow. I will miss her terribly. Best of retirements, Sweet Virginia. I am hopefully not too far behind you. Blessings.

One of her coworkers commented on my post that Ginger was one of the most genuine and nicest people they had ever known. I heartily agree. She and I still remain very good friends. What I did not know at the time was that I would retire exactly a year to the day after she did.

Marilyn would often bring us all cold water out to our respective routes on those brutal hot days in the summer. At first she would gift us on her days off, and then even after her early retirement, she would make the sweet purchase and deliveries to us. Always appreciated.

———∞———

Tyra was fun. She was frequently the object of teasing because she would say whatever happened to be on her mind. And she would take that teasing with a smile of resignation and her eyes would dance at the realization she had done it again.

Not everyone is gracious about being the object of teasing, but Tyra would usually laugh right along with us. It's one of the reasons she came to be such a good friend. There came to be one classic Tyra moment that stood head and shoulders (literally) above the others. I was in my late 40s or early 50s and still at a point in my life where I was fairly physically fit. Tyra is about a dozen years younger than me.

During one of my vacations I was out getting some walking in before I returned to work in order to build up my legs for the daily haul. I was a couple miles from home and it was a very warm day. So I did something that I never do, especially at my age, and doubly-especially in public. I slipped off my T-shirt to try to cool off. I wadded up my shirt in my hands and continued on my way. My location put me within the confines of Tyra's route. Unbeknownst to me, Tyra drove by me and noticed me walking. I did not notice her and she did not have time to stop. When she returned to the station she made the same fatal mistake I had made with the rabbit incident. She opened her mouth and shared her experience. She was in a group of other coworkers and said this: "Hey, I saw Merrit out doing some walking on my route. He had his shirt off."

And then she made her error with these words: "He didn't look too bad!"

Oh. My. Word. The other carriers hooped and hollered and lost their minds. They razzed her unmercifully. When I returned from vacation I think I had been in the building all of 27 seconds before more than one of my coworkers was regaling me with the tale. Poor Tyra was mortified, but as time went by she took the entire incident with complete grace and good humor, laughing at herself as quickly as we did.

The story was one of those stories that became a tale as the years went on. And always Tyra was teased and always she responded with "You guys!" But with that ever-present twinkle in her eye. Three years after I retired I was driving in southeast Portland very late one afternoon and spotted a postal vehicle returning to Creston Station. I only caught a quick glance at the driver and thought it was Tyra but was not sure. I contacted her that evening via social media.

July 30, 2018

M: Did I see you driving back to the station on 52nd tonight about 6:15?

T: That was me! Dang, I didn't see you. You must have been wearing a shirt."

When I read her words I positively howled in laughter. What a good sport. One year at the station Christmas party Tyra and I were sitting together and just visiting. Someone said they wanted to get a picture of the two of us together so we obliged. I don't remember which of the three of us came up with the idea, but eventually a photo was taken of Tyra sitting on my lap. (I don't think it was my idea [even though I was single at the time] but I certainly did not mind!) It became a yearly tradition for the two of us.

———

Three other ladies came along during these days who became very dear friends and who to this day are important colors on my canvas. Annie was able to get route 0656. Although this route is not literally next to mine out in the streets, our cases were right next to each other. We worked next to each other for 21 years, sharing life, laughter, and sometimes the ludicrousness of the job.

She rarely called me by name, but rather "Nabes," short for "neighbor." I tagged her with "Annie-May." She is a blond fireball with fiery eyes and a strong work ethic. I cannot even start to express my delight at having her as my work neighbor for over two decades. We got along beautifully.

One of Annie's closest friends is V-Toria, a brown-haired woman with a ridiculously engaging smile. The two of them together can turn into a fierce, shopping, gigglefest. V-Toria has a heart of gold and was always there for a quiet chat about life and family and work. She became and is one of the dearest postal friends I have.

When my son died, these two women went out of their way to keep me smiling and feeling cared for. I am very grateful to and for both of them. When Mailman Mike finally retired, V-Toria was able to bid and capture his route, 0654, just on the other side of me. So I had V-Toria to my left and Annie to my right. For the last five years of my career I called them my blond and brunette sandwich.

My Christine. Oh, My Christine. As personal a friend as I ever had in the Post Office. A petite little blond with a dynamo inside. Not sure when or why I gave her the moniker of My Christine, but she was. We became fast friends and our friendship only became closer and closer as the years passed. When my son died, she was the first of my coworkers to contact me to see how I was doing. No fault to the other employees. They had been instructed by a professional counselor to not contact me, but My Christine would have none of it. She was going to check up on Her Merrit no matter what anyone said.

More layers of new employees kept coming along. More friendships were forged.

A-Lan was one of the hardest working people I've ever met. He seemed to have a perpetual smile on his face and if he wasn't smiling he was tossing out a laugh, frequently at the more than occasional absurdities of our jobs.

Kimmy was a plain-speaking auburn-haired delight. She and I took some getting used to but did become very good friends. I so appreciate her honesty and openness. She is exactly one day younger than my wife Jill, so there is another connection there.

Dear Tin-Man. He came along and worked on the other side of first Mailman Mike and then V-Toria. He came to us from Vietnam with the most splendorous smile you have ever seen. His name was Tin but of course we all added "Man" for obvious reasons.

One time he won a drawing at work to get an extra day off and someone asked him if they could have it instead. When he said "no," the response was, "But I thought you had a heart." Tin-Man and I used to tease each other all the time.

He has a delightfully thick accent, and I used to give him a hard time about it. He would laugh at me and tell me, "But, Merrit, I'm speaking English!" Then we would both crack up. Such a dear man. Our routes bumped up against each other in southeast Portland and once or twice a week we would see each other from across the street. We started singing the song "Heartaches by the Number" to each other. I have no idea why. But it is one of my treasured postal memories.

CHUCK-AY! came along during my final few years. He was brash (in the best sense of that word), loud, and a delight. My last few months he was able to capture a route of his own whose case was located in the same aisle as mine. We got to know each other fairly well at the end. Such a character.

Gordon. Well, I called Gordon "Bozo" for a few years because he was such a goof and always had a big smile and hearty laugh blazing forth. But I dropped that particular moniker and he became one of the rarities in my work life without a nickname, although everyone else called him "G-Man." Gordon did pick up on something that had been a part of me and my routine for years at Creston Station.

A letter carrier handles three types of mail: letters, flats (magazines, catalogs, newspapers, etc.), and parcels. There are three main classifications of mail incorporated within letters and flats. First class is personal and business (banks, insurance, etc.). Second class is mostly magazines. Third class is business bulk mail, or what the public calls "junk mail." On any given day the first and second class mail must be delivered that day. If mail volume is high or the weather is bad or there is a shortage of workers on any particular day then the third class mail can be left till the next day. It is left on the floor at each carrier's case.

As I got older it became more of a challenge to take all the mail every day. One day about halfway through my career someone asked me if I was taking all the mail that day or leaving some of it on the floor at my case. I responded that there was nothing on the floor but the tile. I started making this declaration every day that I took all the mail at my case (whether anyone asked me or not).

As the years passed, it got shortened to "Nothin' but tile, baby!" and became a well-known rallying cry for me. The older I got the louder I yelled it. A bit obnoxious, maybe? What's your point? Anyway, Gordon liked it and sometimes when I yelled it out he would mimic me in his charming Vietnamese accent. This popped up in a lovely way on my last day of work.

Aaron also came along toward the end of my career. A true gentleman and very hard worker who for reasons that completely escape me I dubbed "the worst carrier in the station." He was not, of course, but he was a terrific sport about it and at my retirement party I awarded him with a sincere gift of thanks. More on that much later.

I called Pam "Happy Pam" because she always seemed so bubbly. She worked across the aisle and directly behind me the last few years of my career. She is a lovely lady with a big smile, lots of giggles, and much talking to herself. I am so "happy" about that because it was hard to stay in a bad mood if you were working close to her. During my final week of work she presented me with a gift of a clock. A 'retirement clock.' How so? The numbers have been placed willy-nilly all over the face of the clock and the heading at the top reads: "WHATEVER." It sits on my desk everyday.

Pam's retirement clock she gave to me.

One of the young men who came along my last few years became one of my closest friends and ended up with my favorite nickname. We just hit if off immediately, originally because one of his children had the same first name as one of mine. But we just got along famously from day one.

He has given me permission to share his entire name because of the story with it. Jason Bonnett. As I have already shared, over time I seemed to bestow nicknames on most of the folks I worked with. And every morning when I saw them I greeted them with that name, whether it be KARL!, or Helloooo, Arlen, or Happy Pam. But I did not greet Jason in this same way.

He worked on the other side of the station from me. And nearly every day, a few minutes after we clocked on and began our shift, I'd wait for a quiet break in the general hubbub of chatter and call out in my best sonorous voice: "JAY-son bo-NAY!!!!!" And he would respond in a faux bored response: "Merrit Hearing." It became possibly the vocalization I became the most known for. It certainly became very dear to my heart. I continue to meet him for lunch from time to time and greet him the same way when I see him.

During my postal career I used and went through five over-the-shoulder mailbags. I kept one when I retired. I gave one to each of my daughters. And I gave Jason the one that would have gone to my son. That is how dear he is to me.

———— ⤜∞⤛ ————

One of the last youngsters who came along during the final few years of my career was Dear Elizabeth, a young woman with a spitfire personality and a heart of gold. We also stay in touch and my only regret is that I only got to work with her for a short time. Like many others I have mentioned, she is a total hoot and was a delight to work with.

I have left many folks off this list. Obviously I cannot list them all. There is not room to tell you about Kipper and Hobber and Ricardo and Petticrew and Mr. Sloan and Mike T. and Roger and ..... dozens of others. And there were times at Creston when the turnover rate was faster than others, so there are many I simply can no longer remember. But I was most fortunate. The vast majority of people I worked with were high-quality people with good work ethics who wanted to enjoy their jobs and try to enjoy each other.

Yes, there were a handful of unpleasant folks. What job doesn't have? But when I think back over my career, especially the 27 years at Creston, the image that flashes through my mind and heart is one of camaraderie and togetherness. Do I perhaps see things with more pleasantness and with rose-colored glasses now that I am retired? Maybe. But not too much, I believe. So many of these folks are still friends and I keep in touch with a lot of them. Simply put, they were there for me.

They were there for me when my son Elliott died. They raised a large sum of cash for me to help with expenses and so I wouldn't need to worry about money while I was off work. A couple dozen of them came to Elliott's memorial. The comfort and concern they showed in the following months was so very tender and welcomed.

They were there for me with all my kids. Let me tell you, I was the most obnoxious daddy you ever met. I always had a story or a picture to share about my children. A quiet joke at work was to tell new employees "Don't ask Merrit about his kids!" Ha!

They were there for me with my health issues. I missed more than my fair share of work with back problems during the first years and with falls and injuries during my last years. These folks picked up the slack when I was not able to carry my route.

They were there for me in my weirdness. I am by nature very picky and persnickety—my dad's word for me. I like things done in a certain way and with definite orderliness. The Post O has "helper cards," which are letter-sized card-stock paper for writing instructions on for things like where a mailbox is located, who has moved out of a house, etc., or bright neon cards to warn of possible dangerous dogs or other hazards. Well, I had more than anybody. I became "legendary" for my helper cards. Because despite whatever "help" they may give, they also have to be handled individually, which causes more work for the substitute letter carrier.

———— ∞∞∞ ————

    They were there for me when Jill came along in my life. I had been single for a decade and it was widely known that I had not dated—nor had any interest in it—in that entire time. So many of my coworkers were thrilled for me when Jill entered my life. A certain amount of that happiness for me was undoubtedly because of my son's death, the fact that I now had someone to spend life with who would love me and make me happy.

    When I realized I wanted to marry Jill, I could think of no other group of people I would rather share that joyous experience with than them. Over the first months that we dated she had the opportunity to meet many, but not all, of my fellow mailmen. Things became more serious between us, and more of them became aware of my relationship with her. So I began to formulate a plan.

    It was time for our annual station Christmas party. I had started up and organized these parties for several years, but in December of 2010 Tyra and V-Toria put it together. At one point during the festivities I stood up, clanked my glass and called for attention. I then gave this speech:

    "I just wanted to thank Tyra and V-Toria for putting this party together. They did a great job (applause). As you know I have been coming to these parties all these years by myself. But not this year. This year I have brought my girlfriend. Everyone, this is Jill (applause). Jill, many of these are my nearest and dearest friends—some, not so much (laughter). So this just seemed like the right place and time to do this."

With that, I got down on one knee and took out the ring and asked her to marry me in front of all of my coworkers. The place went nuts. It was the best moment I ever had with my fellow United States Postal Service workers. I was proud and happy, and they were proud and happy for me.

Jill and I got married the following August. Before the day arrived, two hilarious moments occurred at the station regarding our relationship. Both happened late in the afternoon after most carriers had finished their routes and were either getting ready to head home or else were getting a head start on preparing the next day's mail.

First, you need to know that when Jill and I got married I was in my mid-50s and Jill was a few years younger. Also, I had helped raise four children and Jill was a mother of three. So we had both been . . . ahem . . . well . . . by choice, we had both become unable to have any more children.

You also must remember that I had not dated anyone for nearly ten years before I met her. One afternoon one of the carriers yelled across the station: "So, Merrit, are you and Jill going to have any more kids?"

I kind of chuckled and said, "No, that would require TWO miracles."

Immediately, Doug the Slug popped his head out from his case and replied: "Well, you found a woman. Wouldn't that constitute as one miracle?"

Everybody completely lost it. I was bent over in tears laughing so hard I thought I would be sick. Oh, my gosh. Simply way too funny!

Our wedding day was scheduled for a Saturday. Two days before, on Thursday, was my final day of work before I took two weeks off for the wedding and honeymoon. Same scenario. An afternoon winding down with a few carriers in the station. And again, someone bellowed from across the room: "Hey, Merrit, what are you and Jill going to be doing on your honeymoon?"

Before I could answer, JAY-son piped up with: "He's going on his honeymoon. What the heck do you think he will be doing?!" Again, I almost fell over with laughter. Good people. I miss them. Jill and I had a small wedding but a huge reception a week later. Many of my coworkers (and several of my customers from my route) came to the celebration. It was fabulous.

One more tip of the cap. Many of my co-workers were brave servicemen and women of the United States military. I am ever so grateful to them for their dedicated service. It is because of what they have done with their lives that I am able to do with mine what I have.

———— ∞ ————

If you talk to a postal worker for very long about their job, you'll almost certainly hear the horror stories of terrible bosses. I definitely had my share of them. Some were dreadful. But this book is about me holding up my career as a good thing so we will dispense with remarks about them.

But let me finish this chapter by briefly showing my thanks for the handful of really good bosses I had. I appreciated my time working for Matt (my last supervisor who made things unstressful at the end); Lance (tough, but completely fair); and Sandy W. (a supervisor during my first year at Multnomah). She wasn't there long but we got along famously, no doubt helped by our mutual passion for the music of Neil Diamond.

Then there is Brian, a character who I thought had a wicked sense of humor. He became infamous for getting his tie caught in the station paper shredder. He also showed his integrity by trusting in mine when I made a dreadful but innocent slip-of-the-tongue. And finally Kary (very easy-going). He made the months following my son's death as non-burdensome as he could. But I offer special thanks to five.

Jim D. My first supervisor at Multnomah. Just a plain nice guy who displayed a large amount of patience with my constant talking and questions.

Billy. He might have become my favorite boss ever if given the chance and time to stay at Creston longer than he did. Of all my postal bosses, he was the one who seemed to understand the plight of our jobs in dealing with weather and high mail volume and being consistently understaffed and the one who stood up to middle management the fiercest for us.

Rhonda. A beautiful woman with a beautiful smile and a kind heart to me. She was at the station when I was having my biggest health issues with my back and missing so much work. She was encouraging and yet also was honest in assessing my situation with my time off work and rehabilitation.

Marsha. A statuesque lady who went from being just my boss to becoming my friend. She was the manager at Creston my last two years and made that time for me comfortable and was understanding as my work injuries began to take a toll on my performance. I have a fabulous photo of me taken in her office on my next-to-last day of work with my feet up on her desk.

Ed. I am proud to call Ed my friend. He was my supervisor over two different periods of my time at Creston. He very possibly saved my career with some very timely and pointed advice at a time when I needed to hear it. He knows the details and that is enough. (Don't go there; I wasn't doing anything shady or illegal, LOL). He attended my retirement party (as did Marsha and Matt), and I was privileged to attend his a year later.

Again, when I think of my time at Creston I obviously think about weather and hard work and walking many miles. But what I think of first are these folks. They helped make the job way more enjoyable than it could or even should have been. When I think back on my 30-year career the word that always comes to my mind first is "people." I worked with a very special bunch of folks and I consider it an honor that they were and are a part of my life. They are the first part of my "people." Now let me tell you about the other part.

Chapter 17

HAVE YOU MET THE LADY WHO LIVES AT . . . ?

"Became a highlight of my mornings"

Whenever I ponder my 30 years as a walking mailman, it staggers me the quality, quantity, and differences of the folks I delivered mail to. Mailman Mike always told me that I was not just delivering their mail, but that I was walking through their lives. Incredibly, most of these folks allowed me to do just that.

Many, many of these people brought me into their lives and let me become more than just their mailman. I consider so many of my ex-customers as my friends, and some of them are extraordinarily close to me . . . and I feel honored that they feel the same way to me. I have been invited to neighborhood block parties. At one of these one of the hosts told me that of course I was invited. After all, I had been in the neighborhood longer than any of them except for one family.

I was invited to birthday parties, anniversaries, over to watch ballgames, and into homes to welcome a new baby or to offer my condolences to someone who had lost a family member. Even now, as I write this, I am shaking my head at the idea of all of this and what my career with these dear folks meant to me. And because of all of that, this will easily be the longest chapter in this book. Because a lot of fabulous folks came across my path in those 27 years.

I have trimmed the list down considerably, but these people brightened my job beyond what I can express, and I must celebrate them. So tighten up your shoes, grab a swig of water and come on out to route 0655 in southeast Portland with your ol' broken-down, grumpy mailman and meet some folks.

The first character is the best, most trustworthy auto mechanic you will ever meet. I was Leonard's mailman for more than 20 years. He is loud, obnoxious, rude . . . and a very dear friend. Oh, don't mind the description. He would use much worse words to talk about himself. Or anybody else for that matter. Leonard curses a blue storm . . . AT you . . . IF he likes you. I love the guy. I can still remember when my oldest daughter Maria called me on the phone, nearly in tears with happiness, because she knew Leonard must really like her because he had sworn at her with vigilance.

Across the street from Leonard's place of business are some apartments. Mr. Lawrence lived there for several years before he passed. Every day he greeted me with the same three words. It didn't matter if it was 98 degrees, pouring down rain, or blustery and cold. Each and every day when he came out to say hello and grab the mail he would lean over his balcony at the top of the stairs and call out to me, "Where's your coat?!" I mean, even if I was wearing one! Also at these apartments was James, tall and slender with a wonderfully sonorous voice. We usually talked about our kids. He only lived on my route for a few years (and almost always wore black). But I can close my eyes and still hear that rich, deep voice of his. And on the upper floor lived one of my 27 year customers, Mitchell. Of the two dozen or so customers that I had for the entire 27 years, I knew Mitchell the least well.

Our schedules just did not coincide conveniently for us to have many chats.

Down the street was a retirement center. It was one of my favorite places to stop. It had a good restroom break spot and was a good building to drive to if I needed to stop to change into dry clothes on those monsoon days. The complex has 50 apartments. Over the years I got to be good friends with many of the tenants. Unfortunately, because of the nature and age of the tenants, I also lost many during the 27 years I delivered the mail there. But I tell you, some of those senior citizens were the biggest teases, the best storytellers, and were the most excited to meet my children when I brought them around after hours. Many thanks to Emma, Wendy, Betty, Irma, and so many others.

After we cross over a main street and park the car we hit my business section. I used the services on this section for all sorts of transactions. Food. Fresh produce. Haircuts. A family jewelry store, which was and still is the only place I have purchased any kind of jewelry for the past 30 years, even though the location has now changed. Good people and friends there. When they moved, a strip mall was built on the spot and in that mall was an optometrist who was a delightful person to chat with on the occasions I might see her. She honored me with her attendance at my retirement party.

Across the street was one of my fave fast food establishments. I ate there somewhat regularly and they always took good care of me. The day manager became a friend and when he moved to a different store location I made it a point to drop by and say 'hello.'

Also on this section you could find tote bags. Second-hand stores. (I had three of these over the years and became good friends in particular with one proprietor, a man of the highest integrity named Cory). Lawyers.

Ah, let me tell you about one of the attorneys on my route. He was one of the partners in a small firm that had three lawyers. For a couple of reasons that are not germane to the story I got to know this gentleman the best. And I do mean gentleman. Mr. Mains was a most impressive man of high integrity and kindness. I was a lowly blue-collar mailman and he was a well-dressed, highly intelligent attorney. And not once in the 27 years that I was his mailman was I ever made to feel that way. He always treated me as an equal and as if my job was just as important as his. He'd ask about my family and how I was doing. We would readily tease each other about our respective crafts. (He always enjoyed my lawyer jokes.) Just before I retired I was able to tell him how highly I thought of him and how much I appreciated the respect he showed me. He seemed a bit flustered but also pleased. The attorneys' office also had many other terrific folks in and out through the years, including three lovely secretaries who all became very dear friends and who I still am in contact with. One of those secretaries, Jena, worked in that office for 25 of my years on the route.

There were many others who were fabulous people to do business with but not necessarily in products of my interest. A travel agency (where I became very good friends with a lovely woman who I continued to visit for several years after she left this company for another across town). Furniture stores. A dental office. Two bars. At one volunteer organization I met many wonderful receptionists.

———

But no one affected me as deeply as Marie. She was about 15 years my junior and drop-dead gorgeous. We chatted most every day and became good friends.

After a while we discovered that we had gone to the same high school, which further cemented our friendship. We got to know each other very well. She knew all about my family. After working at this establishment for a few years she sadly announced to me that she was leaving and moving across country. On her last day I was quite emotional at the prospect of "losing" her.

She was very busy at her desk so I was only able to give her a little wave before I headed out the door. As I got to my postal vehicle she came running out the door saying, "Wait, wait!" She told me she had to absolutely say goodbye to me. We embraced tightly and thanked each other for our friendship. It was the first time I cried over a customer leaving my route.

We kept in touch for a bit while she was across the country but then lost contact as cell phones came along. I tried a few times to locate her but with no luck. A few years passed. One day I was carrying a section on another route to collect some overtime. At a large older home that had been converted into a small set of apartments I was putting mail in a mailbox and came across her name. Not a common name but neither was it rare. So it could have been her but could very well be someone else.

I knocked on the door but no answer. I debated with myself for a couple of days whether or not I wanted to pursue this. Finally one day after work I decided to stop by again. I was in my postal uniform so as to keep the creep factor out of the equation. I knocked on the door. A young woman answered the door. She kept the screen closed so I could not see her very well.

I said, "Excuse me, I'm sorry to bother you but I'm looking for a Marie _____." Before I could finish the sentence, she exclaimed, "It's YOU!" She burst through the door and wrapped her arms around me. It was just such a sweet reunion. We ended up having coffee together a couple of times, catching up on the years that had passed. Shortly thereafter my son died and I called Marie so that we could have coffee again. She was tender and a fabulous listener. We don't see each other regularly, but I know she is there with an ear and a wonderful history between us. She is dear to my heart.

———— ✿ ————

Up the street we come to another business. Jim was the proprietor of this business when I got on my route and stayed there until his untimely death about 15 years later. Jim is the single best owner/manager/boss of any establishment I have ever known. Friendly. Honest. Giving. Gracious. Funny. Caring. I miss this man terribly. Many years after he passed I wrote about him.

September 15, 2008

One of the businesses on my route was for many years run by Jim. Jim was not only the best CEO I have ever met, he was one of the finest gentlemen I have ever met. He owned and ran a small company in southeast Portland. He employed a handful of ladies (occasionally there was a man working there, but not often) who were taught the wisdom of exemplary customer service. Jim was always beyond gracious to me. I was allowed to use the restroom, grab a bag of fresh popcorn, and use the telephone when needed (before cells).

There was always a cat that lived in the store that Jim cared for. The store was always closed Christmas Eve. One of my fondest memories will be those quiet Christmas Eves when I would bring in the mail and Jim and I would quietly chat about life for just a few minutes as he fed the cat before going home to his family.

We never talked about deep stuff; it was just two gentlemen chatting quietly and maybe having a laugh— because he could have a wickedly funny sense of humor. And every Christmas he would give me a large frozen turkey as a gift of thanks for my service. I considered him a friend. He passed suddenly about ten years ago and I still miss him and think of him. A good man. If you open your dictionary to the page that lists the word "kind," and it doesn't have a picture of Jim, you need a new dictionary.

I still think about those Christmas Eves with Jim. I can still sense the quietness of his abandoned store as he fed the cat and we had a quiet conversation. He was also exceptionally generous to his employees. At Christmas he hosted a huge celebration of some sort (limo and helicopter rides to expensive restaurants and lots of thoughtful, generous gifts) and after the holiday his workers would regale me with the stories of their delightful evening of celebration with Jim, his wife, and their spouses. Truly, a quality human being. Many of those ladies became dear friends over the years and I am still in contact with some of them.

———— ∞∞∞ ————

A few yards down the street were Tony and Glenda, a man and wife who owned a store that was quite famous in the Portland area, known for low prices and iconic TV commercials. As the years passed their children took over the store and I didn't get to see them often. Everyone in Portland knows their TV persona, but I was fortunate to know them as people. Very nice folks. About five years after he had sold the store to his son-in-law I happened to see them as he was getting his famous haircut at one of the barbershops on my route.

July 8, 2011

For many years I was [name of store] mailman. Very nice folks. I had not seen them for the five years since they sold the business. I got to visit with both of them today as Tony was getting a haircut (still has that terrific flattop). It was a very nice time and Glenda especially seemed tickled to see me. They are really genuinely pleasant people. I miss seeing them. And they are of course a Portland institution.

Speaking of haircuts, I had three shops on my route. At one of them I got my hair cut for 24 years until the dear woman retired. She knew she had tough shoes to fill because my dad had been a barber. She did a great job and more importantly became a good friend. Next door to her was Matt, who made custom T-shirts. We got to know each other better when I joined a bowling league that he organized. He died much too young. He could be a rascal, but I miss him.

Before we leave the business section I have one more quick memory to share with you. The first two years I was on my route, from 1988 to 1990, I delivered to a dry-cleaning service. It was run by a married couple in their late 50s to early 60s. I can vividly remember more than one blistering hot day when I would be feeling quite sorry for myself having to work in such miserable conditions, and I would walk into their shop. The heat coming from the huge irons and dry-cleaning equipment would be beyond oppressive. And every day the two of them would look up and smile or wave cheerfully to me and then return to their backbreaking work. It always made an impression on me.

There were two residential streets that were assigned to my route for only ten years. After I'd had the route for nine years our postal station went through a significant change in some of the route boundaries brought about by a huge technological change in how the mail stream throughout the nation was processed. So I was shoved two blocks south. I lost some customers (Mr. Wolf and his four shelties, for one), but gained some new ones.

These next four stories deal with those new patrons I had for just those ten years. Then ten years after that because of other changes I was slid back north. Anyway, during those ten years I was able to develop some good relationships with the folks living on those two streets, including the father and son who received the very late postcard from Alaska.

—— ∞∞∞ ——

Two single guys shared a split-level home in the area. I got to know both of them, one ("Dan") much more than the other. They received parcels frequently, many of them fairly large. They always asked me to not just leave them lying around at the bottom of the stairs but to bring them to the upper porch which was out of sight of the street.

That is not normal procedure for the USPS, but they were exceptionally nice guys, and it was not every day, so I performed this service for them. After I got to know them better I asked what they were receiving in the mail so regularly. Turns out they were heavily involved in purchasing/collecting/reselling buried remains from shipwrecks. Dishware, small furniture, pictures, etc. I was immediately fascinated.

I came around during a lunch break soon after to see some of their treasures. Fabulous stuff. What really caught my eye were several items they had just recently purchased (and I had delivered) from the wreck of the ANDREA DORIA ocean liner that sank after being rammed by a freighter in 1956. It is one of my favorite historical accounts and I've read a terrific book about the event three times.

Over the years as they obtained more items, from time to time they would show me the wares. It was always engaging and they seemed genuinely pleased at the interest I showed in the items they received. When the boundaries of my route shifted again they were no longer my customers.

The postscript to this story? A few weeks later Dan found me out on the route and gave me a small package to say thanks for my years of service and for placing their parcels in a safe place. Imagine my shock when I opened it and found myself holding a plate from the ANDREA DORIA. I was speechless. Dan insisted they wanted me to have it since I had such a passion for the story. So among my treasured gifts from customers I have a plate that was rescued from the bottom of the ocean more than 60 years ago. How cool is THAT?!!?

A couple blocks away lived Mrs. Gregory. I wrote about her a few months before I retired.

January 17, 2015

I try very hard to have relationships with my customers. It is what can make the job enjoyable. If I am your mailman and I see you even just occasionally, I am determined to make a connection. On a corner lot was a house not particularly cared for but surrounded by a huge yard that was. Privacy must have been paramount to the owner because even the gate was padlocked leading to the house.

A few weeks later I finally saw the owner, Mrs. Gregory, an elderly lady. As I came up to the mailbox (perched on the chain-link fence) I said, "Good morning." She didn't so much as look up. That was the extent of our greetings for a year or so.

Then, finally, one day she looked up and nodded. Caught me completely off guard. After about five years she shocked me even more with a "G'morning," barely audible. But I would still faithfully say hello to her every time I saw her.

At about the eight-year mark of me being her mailman she would occasionally initiate the greeting. And once in awhile, she would give me a little wave from across the street. In 2008 they moved my borders again and I lost her street from my route. But in 2009–10 if she was walking through my route on her way to the store, and even if she was across the street, she would call out with a smile, "Hi, how are you!" and wave.

She is gone now. And I don't think she ever even knew my name. But I smile at the thought that my persistence paid off and she and I were finally at the end able to have a pleasant— and for me—satisfactory mailman/patron relationship. The moral of the story: If I got you, I'll get you.

And then up the street was little four-year-old Stevie. He was fairly shy, and if he was out in the yard with his dad when I arrived, he might give me a little wave and a mumbled "hello." But then nearly every day after I got about two or three houses away, he would bellow out, "Goodbye, Mr. Merrit!" Over the next couple years he became un-shy around me, and if he was outside when I arrived we would have a little chat. If he was inside the house when I delivered his family's mail, by the time I was two houses away he would make it outside to the porch and yell out his daily greeting. I loved it. It became a highlight of my mornings, that greeting from Stevie. I was heartsick when he and his parents—also delightful folks—moved away. One day a couple years later they were driving through my route and stopped to say hello. I never saw them after that. They are one of the scores of families that I lost touch with over time. And that paragraph explicitly shows the best and the worst of the job for me.

Speaking of adorable little ones, let me briefly tell you about Harriet. After the boundary changed on my route for that second time, I had three new streets on my route for the final eight years of my career. I met Harriet and her dad when she was six. I was her mailman till she was 12. The story I want to share does not involve me but was shared by a mutual friend about an outing the three of them were on. Parents, listen up, because this is a good one to tuck away. My friend, Steve (the dad), and Harriet were on a drive one day. Harriet was in the back seat working on a picture she was trying to draw and color. She was about eight at the time. Dad was driving and came upon a road that was rougher than normal.

Harriet was having difficulty trying to keep her picture looking good. "Daddy, I can't finish my picture because you are driving so bumpy."

Dad thought to himself for a moment. They were not in a hurry. They were not in a high-traffic area. The picture was obviously important to his daughter. So he pulled the car over to the side of the road so his daughter could finish what was to her a very important project. And why not? After a couple minutes she said thanks to her dad and said she was done. And they continued on their way. I was very impressed with the heart of this dad to stop his schedule for his child. For, to the child, this was an important issue. And you can bet she will take that memory (or at least the attitude that went with it) with her for the rest of her life. Okay, I threw that story in for free. You may now continue on with your regularly scheduled book.

Mrs. Hewlitt was a wonderful and elderly woman who was always very nice to me. She lived next door to her daughter and son-in-law. In what had been converted from a garage into a lovely little collector's room she kept hundreds of dolls. All sizes, styles, and ages. She asked me a couple times to come by on a day off so she could show me her collection in some detail. I knew my wife and her daughter would love it. But I kept putting it off. She passed at the age of 99. Never coming by to see her show off and speak of her doll collection is one of the regrets I carried into retirement.

Next door live Kevin and his fabulous wife, who I love to address as Ireland, for reasons that are clear 17 seconds after you meet her. You will not find two more kindly folks . . . or two more fierce Portland Timber Football Club fanatics.

Speaking of the British Isles, across the street lived Ronald, who was from Scotland and had a delicious accent but who could also speak with a delightful Irish brogue and did so many times for me. He would say the same sentences to me first in Scottish and then in Irish. I loved it. I still can't tell the difference, but it was cool.

As we head on over to the next neighborhood we meet two ladies who live across the street from each other. They are quite opposite in temperament but both became good friends. Joyce is an exuberant and gregarious woman in her 30s. And she was always nice . . . until . . . she put on a pair of short shorts, fishnet stockings, a considerable amount of blush . . . and . . . a pair of skates . . . and turned into . . . a roller-derby queen!!! What a transformation!! She gave me a pair of tickets so I was able to go to one of their matches with a dear friend. Such fun. These ladies are determined. My customer was actually the commissioner of the league for a time. I was delighted to see someone step out of their "normal" life and become a different entity. She turned into someone totally fierce on the rink, but when I spoke with her after the match, there was that sunny smile and disposition I had come to know. Well done. If it is okay for me to be proud of someone I delivered electric bills to, then let me say I was proud of her.

Karolyn is considerably quieter. Over the years she became one of my favorite customers and totally floored me by saying to me one afternoon in my wife's presence (she had come out to bring me some lunch and walked a section with me) that I was one of the nicest men she knew. Not just a mailman, but one of the kindest men she had EVER known. You don't forget moments or people like that.

Next door to Joyce is Mrs. Green and her daughter and granddaughter. A very quiet and private family. I was very surprised and touched when they came to my retirement party. Granddaughter is a complete delight and was very patient with me when it took several weeks for me to remember her very beautiful but difficult to pronounce name.

As we head up a very busy street we meet Gavin and Barbara who ran an auto repair shop and when they retired left me an open invitation to visit them at their home on the Oregon Coast. Four years after I retired I finally made good on that invite.

Across the street we meet a medical facility that mostly caters to the local Hispanic population. Ridiculously friendly folks who tried desperately to teach me Spanish over the years, especially after my youngest daughter married a wonderful Mexican man. Alas, these lessons did not take.

As we keep heading north we meet someone who was part of one of the most frustrating and helpless moments I experienced in my career. Mr. and Mrs. Yonin were an older couple who occupied the house that began the second half of my route. I spoke with Mr. Yonin many times over the years. After he passed away I began to see Mrs. Yonin more often as she walked through the neighborhood on her way to the store. One day when I was still about a block away from her home

I saw a young man go bounding out of her yard, through her gate, and running full blast down the street. She came out to the sidewalk, yelling for him to stop. He was carrying her purse as he fled. As I said, I was a block away and was in my mid-50s. Pursuing the kid was out of the question. I got to her as quickly as I could to find out what had happened. We called the police but the man was never found. If I could erase events from my time as a mailman, this would be very near the top. Dang! Sally lives across the street. She could be found working in her yard from time to time. To the side of Sally's house was a fantastic shade tree. It is my favorite tree ever (no, seriously, I have thought about this) and I parked my postal vehicle under its fabulous covering virtually every day for 27 years. I mean, we are talking serious shade. Across the street from Sally is Stan. In some ways, Stan is the very definition of one of my "regular" customers. Stan and I have not hung out together and probably never will. I didn't see him on any sort of day-to-day basis. He has never met my kids and if I told them his name they would have no idea who he is. But, when I did see Stan – including since I have retired – there was and is an instant recognition of a familiar relationship based on my service to him and his address. It is an idea I tried to aspire to with all of my customers on some level. Up a house and across the street again were Eleanor and Marty. Good people who are part of a good neighborhood. And boy howdy, Eleanor can play a mean fiddle.

At the farthest point east on this street is a five-plex. At the first of this quintet of apartments lived Mr. Baggers. He was always exceptionally nice to me and frequently came out to say hello. After about a dozen years he moved to another part of southeast Portland. For several years I was on the list to work as much overtime as I could. One of the unexpected benefits to this was from time to time I ran into friends of mine from other areas of my past or present life.

And sometimes that rare moment might occur where I would find a former customer. This happened one day with Mr. Baggers. I was on another route and came across his name. I knocked on the door and we had a lovely little reunion.

At the bottom of the street in houses directly across from each other were some of my very fave customers. Kelly and Trent were a couple about my age. Well, that is not entirely true. Kelly was a few years younger and actually went to school with my kids' mother (and our kids went to school with their kids). And Trent made it a point to always remind me that he was exactly ONE DAY younger than me. They have a beautiful home and our relationship became very close over the 27 years I was their mailman.

Their across-the-street neighbor was the beautiful and sweet Jan. She and I did not really become acquainted till after her husband died. Over the next several years she and I became extremely close friends. When she moved across town and off my route, I wept. I simply could not imagine my route without Jan living on it. We have stayed in touch since. I ran into her mom and sister at a social function many years later and was deeply touched when they told me that Jan still spoke of me often and lovingly. Here is my post about that:

December 2011

I had an encounter today with one of my fave customers. I was invited to a fundraiser for her as she is dealing with a serious disease. She no longer lives in the neighborhood of my route. I was astounded to hear from her mother and sister that she still talks about me FIVE YEARS AFTER SHE MOVED OFF MY ROUTE. Also, I was very honored to be invited to the event. She is still quite dear to my heart.

At the top of the street lives Kit, one of the most courageous women I ever knew as a mailman. She is a single mom of a lovely little girl and struggles mightily and with an enormous positive outlook against a major disease. She is an inspirational delight.

Farther down the street lives Paul and Miriam. Before I tell you about Paul, a little background info. In my early days in the Post Office the most annoying package to regularly deliver was a vinyl record. They were oddly shaped and did not fit in your mailbag and also frequently did not fit in many mailboxes and never in any mail slots (unless of course you folded them, but customers didn't seem to like that option). These were the days of mail order record companies and virtually every day you had a handful to deliver. They were a complete pain. Fortunately in the latter part of the 20th century vinyl seemingly went the way of eight-track tapes and disappeared from mailman domain. But with the rise in vinyl popularity there is now a rise in these mailings again. Well, Paul is an avid collector. All styles and from all over the world. Delivering Paul's records was never a pain for me because he was the only one on my route who received them and I knew he had an eclectic and interesting collection. And also a mailbox that would properly house them when I dropped them off. It's true. I never folded any of Paul's records.

If you follow the news you may know of these next folks. Some young people live here and they are terrific musicians. I started getting to know them shortly after they moved in and had begun their career. I got two of their CDs as they began to make a "name" for themselves. I put that word in quotation marks because this is where their story really takes off. Some folks took offense to the name they had chosen for the band. This began a legal battle that went on for years. I didn't see them too often because they were on the road touring much of the time. But when I did see them I'd always ask how the battle was going. Well, that battle actually went all the way to the United States Supreme Court. It is just incredible to me that people I delivered mail to for several years actually appeared before the highest judicial court in the land. And I can say I knew them "when." By the way, they won their case.

Close by lives Maria and her family. This is one of those exceptions where I am using a real name. For a reason. Maria came with her family from the Ukraine. Very sweet. Very broken English. Which was infinitely better than my pathetic attempts at Russian. Oh, she tried very hard and patiently to teach me some basic words and phrases. Futilely.

A few years after she moved in, her mother came over from "the old country" to live with her. Mama spoke no English whatsoever. And was also very sweet. And also named Maria. One day at a local grocery store I was there shopping with MY daughter Maria. Maria and Maria were there in line and I came up behind them to pay for my food. I told route Maria and motioned as best as I could to Mama Maria that this girl was "my" Maria.

They were absolutely tickled and then Mama Maria got this big smile on her face, embraced my daughter, and gave her a big kiss on the cheek. It was a very special moment. Mama Maria could not get comfortable in America and eventually moved back home. I was very sad one day when Maria came out to get the mail with tears in her eyes to tell me that Mama had died. I had one other lovely and funny moment with this lady. I wrote about it.

July 5, 2014.

I have a Ukrainian woman on my route named Maria. She is about my age, has several sons, and has lived at her home for about 12 years. She speaks fairly good English, and over the years has tried to teach me some of her native language, but to no avail. Yesterday I handed her the mail, which consisted of a single bill.

She said, "Oh, a bill."

I said: "Yes Maria, you get your bills, I get mine. Maria, what is your word for "bill"? She hesitated, thought, and said humbly, "I don't remember."

Me: "Maria, what is your word for when you owe money to someone?"

She thought again for a moment, looked at me with a sly twinkle in her eye, and said: "za-billa!"

I gently punched her arm and said, "Maria, I don't think I believe you!"

She walked away giggling.

Down the street lived Dorothy and Dave. A quiet and dignified couple with a gorgeous home, inside and out. After my son died, Dorothy was a source of comfort and knowledge as she had gone through the same loss herself over 30 years previously.

During the final eight years of my career I picked up three streets farther to the west than I'd had before as the Post Office made a final adjustment to my route. Directly across from a park I became friends with a couple who were very nice to me despite a huge opposition we had in a very important aspect of life. Football.

August 3, 2014

    Friendly rivalries. I have had a couple on my route the past six years who are avid Chicago Bears fans. And they know I am a huge Green Bay Packers fan. (For you non-footballers out there, this is the ultimate rivalry in pro football.) As you can imagine there is a lot of needling back and forth. They have occasionally put pictures above their mail slot of famous Bear players. Yesterday they presented me with a really cool gift of a Packers cap (which I had ironically delivered to them in the mail just two days previously) as a way of saying thanks and how much they have enjoyed our football chats over the years.

    Around the corner live Doug and Sharon. Dear Christian folks. I got to know them fairly well over the years. They were thrilled when they heard about my impending marriage in the summer of 2011. They had never met my fiancée . . . to my knowledge. Some weeks after Jill and I got married I stopped for a few minutes to show them my wedding photos. About two pics into my presentation, Sharon suddenly exclaimed, "Isn't that Jill?" Whoa, that caught me totally off guard. "And isn't that [Jill's brother]'s backyard?" Turns out they had known Jill's family for many years and had a regular Bible study held in Jill's brother's backyard, which is where we got married. But this small world moment would blow my mind entirely four years later. You'll read about it in the chapter on connections.

<hr/>

    As we head down the street two of my favorite families live next door to each other. Paul and Rhonda live in a charming house that finds Paul always working on it—or in his yard—regularly. Paul also worked for the Post Office, albeit at the downtown plant as a mail sorter.

    My relationship with them started slow but built into a very close friendship over the years. They are a delightful couple. I am always fond of reminding Paul that he is older than I am, which is alright because he got to retire long before I did and that became an ongoing part of our friendship.

As I mentioned, he was frequently outside working on his yard or in the garage. On this particular section of the route I walked down the street on the opposite side from his house first. And every time I saw him I'd call out with the same greeting: "Are you off again toDAY?" And he would respond with some type of affirmative comment. It became our "thing," which we "performed" countless times over the last several years of my career. Sillily enough, it is actually one of the daily moments that I miss the most.

Next door to Paul and Rhonda is Bonny and her family. Bonny is a lovely woman with a bubbly personality and a large and infectious laugh. I have mentioned this family before. The annual homemade Christmas fudge. The deeply touching note left for me one year that I still have framed. But there is more to this family. Two amazing kids. Well, they used to be kids.

Jackson was only a year old when they moved onto my route. I watched him grow into a terrific young man. Nancy was born a few years later. She grew into a stunningly beautiful young woman who is still one of my favorites.

As I watched Nancy grow into a toddler, little girl, tween, and then into her high school years, one of our routines together was that I would often bop her on the head with the mail I had for them. It got to where she would come outside and stand there waiting for me to tap her on her noggin with an impish grin on her face.

When I retired, she was my second oldest Route Kid, that is, a child born during the time I was the mailman at her house. She was 18 and believe me when I tell you I carry more than a little pride that I was her only mailman for nearly the first two decades of her life. She is a peach. And sometimes she still giggles like that little girl who used to get bopped on the head with a handful of letters.

Bonny and I became close friends over the 26 years I was her mailman. Many talks on her front porch as I took my afternoon break. Our families became acquainted and her house was one of my kids' favorites to go to on Halloween night because they really decorated up for the holiday.

This family became a hugely significant color on the canvas of my postal career. In particular, two highly charged emotional moments stand out. Bonny had gotten to know my kids well, as I said. When my son died she was devastated for me. As I headed out to my route on my first day back to work after his death I made a beeline for Bonny's house. As I pulled around the corner she was outside working in her yard. She saw me as I pulled the car to the curb. I jumped out of the car and ran to her. We embraced and shed tears together for a little bit. Nothing needed to be said.

On the opposite end of the emotional spectrum, when I married Jill a few years later I stopped by to see Bonny one day on the way home from work to show her our wedding pictures. As she was perusing her way through them I looked over and was surprised to see tears rolling down her face. She looked up at me and said, "I'm just so happy for you!" This dear and precious family will be part of my life always. Remember the subtitle of this book? "Why I Liked Being a Mailman." Yeah, these two families . . . that is exactly why.

Even now, when Bonny and I communicate, it is that marvelous porch and the memories it holds that bring smiles to our souls. When I visit, we tend to meander out to it. A good porch.

〰️

Before this turns into a cry-fest, let's continue up the street. I had a superb moment one day at another house where I had watched kids grow up, although not in as tight of a relationship. I know the exact day of this one because I posted about it.

August 1, 2014

Longevity, families, and remembrance. A family moved onto one of my streets 26 years ago, just weeks after I became the mailman on the route. I watched their two daughters grow up off and on (as the girls didn't always live there). Today one of the daughters was there with HER two kids, and as I was walking away after delivering the mail she told her little boy, "That man was the mailman here for Grandma when I was YOUR age."

I stopped and said to her, "And I was probably YOUR age at the time." The boy asked me, "Were you really the mailman here when my mom was six?" So the mom and I got to talking and comparing. Sure enough, we were literally correct. She was six when they moved in and is 32 now. When I started the route I was a few weeks short of 33. Wow, the circle of life.

There are points along the way as I write this book that still astonish me when I recollect them. That is one of those moments.

〰️

Time to head to the next street over. Time to share with you a story that still pains me but that I must share. I am glad for it now. This incident and this gentleman taught me the biggest lesson I learned in my 30 years of delivering the mail.

There is a duplex on this street. Several years ago Mr. Johnson moved into one of the two units. The first time I saw him he was walking up his street about four blocks from his home. He was about 30-ish at the time. He was swaying and stumbling and struggling to walk up the street. The man was obviously sloshed to the gills.

I ignored him and just thought how disgusting it was that he was that drunk in public in the middle of the afternoon. I saw him the next week and about once a week for the next month or so. Same drunken state as he tried to maneuver to his home.

Once or twice I said hello, but he was so intoxicated he was completely unaware of my being there. It would take him several minutes to cover those four blocks. Totally revolting.

One day I was talking to the gentleman who lived next door to him in the other half of the duplex. The conversation got around to Mr. Johnson. He said, "He sure has had a tough time of it." I asked sarcastically, "Oh, really? How so?"

"Well, a few months back he was in a horrendous motorcycle crash. He got both legs broken in multiple places plus a head injury. He has had to re-learn to walk again and has to totally concentrate on landing each of his steps while he walks. It takes everything he has just to walk a few blocks." Oh-h-h-h. Sigh. I don't know if there was ever a time in my career where I felt so abysmally small, stupid, arrogant, self-righteous, and judgmental. Mr. Johnson moved about two years later, but before he did I got to know him to be a very pleasant and sweet man. And, unbeknownst to him, he was also the tool God used to teach me a VERY IMPORTANT lesson. Or rather, lessons plural.

One day many years later I posted this story on social media. As I was typing it I was suddenly smacked across my conscience with lesson number two from Mr. Johnson. So, what if he HAD been intoxicated all those times I saw him struggling to walk? What if he WAS struggling with alcoholism? Did I still have any right to sit on the high throne of judgment on him? Not knowing his story? Never having established any relationship with him? No, no, and no. At the very worst, I should have had pity for him. Not look down my nose at him.

———— ✺ ————

Down the street lived a sweet little old couple. Mr. and Mrs. Kittle became good friends over the 25 years I was the mailman at their residence. Here is my favorite story about them. They moved into the house on Saturday, December 6, 1941. It turned out to be quite a weekend for all Americans. Their mortgage was $10 a month. At the end of their first year of living there, their taxes for the home went up $2.00 per month. Their new payment would now be $12 a month. And they gave serious consideration to selling their home because they did not know how they could possibly come up with that extra two dollars. Can you imagine? Fortunately, they stuck it out and lived there for the next 70 years. Now, this was after Mrs. Kittle had been raised in this house. So she lived in that same house for about 85 of her first 90 years. Incredible.

As we continue on we find a lovely family who lived on my route for several years. They had two little girls who were adorable. When they moved I was heartbroken. Then this happened.

July 17, 2014

Today as I was delivering, a lady was walking down the street toward me with two little girls. I had no idea who they were. Turns out it was one of my very fave customers ever. Her family had moved out of state three years ago and that had been a tough loss for me. When they had moved I had asked the parents to always remind the older girl that I had been her first mailman. The last time I had seen them, the girls were three years old and just a baby. Now they are six and three. The older one remembered me. I was touched that the lady talks about me to her neighbors where she now lives. It was not only the highlight of my day, but of my week. Now THAT is why I like being a mailman.

Update. Recently the mom posted on social media a video of these two little ones who are now selling Girl Scout cookies. I teased her in my comments that it almost hurt to see them so big now.

Across the street lives a woman that I didn't see too often but who did one of the coolest things for me that any customer ever did. It certainly was the most unique thing that any customer ever did.

June 1, 2011

There's a lady who has lived on my route about ten years. Between the previous house I deliver to and hers I have to walk through tall grass and shrubbery. Last week I found a homemade brick walkway between the houses. I asked her about it. She told me she made it FOR ME so my journey between the homes would be easier. She had extra bricks from another project and decided to make it for me. She called it "Merrit's Walkway." Neat-oh!

When I retired I wondered to myself if there was any way I could take this brick pathway with me as a keepsake. Alas, I could not figure out a way. What a fabulous thing for her to do!

Merrit's Walkway.

Emma lived up the street. She was only there for a short time but we formed a casual friendship that continues because we have attended the same church for the past decade. At the corner was Mary Anne. She and hubby Tom were the most amazing gardeners I ever delivered mail to. Their front lawn was filled with a plethora of different plants, flowers, small trees, and shrubs of every variety. They were frequently outside playing in the dirt. Moving on, let me introduce you to another pair of friends who I still have contact with. This social media post actually comes from 16 months after I retired but accurately shows what dear folks these two are.

August 25, 2016

Randall and his wife Janet were customers the entire 27 years I was on my route. It did not take long to realize that he was an avid New York Yankees fan like myself. Over the past 2 1/2 decades we have had countless delightful conversations about baseball and our Yanks. Reliving past victories and moments, commiserating over heartaching losses, kibitzing about trades that were made or suggesting to each other trades that should be. In a phrase, because of baseball and me walking onto their property nearly 6,000 times, we became not just friends, but good friends.

We have lent each other books over the years, have watched some games together at his house (not during work hours, postal bosses! . . though maybe occasionally an inning or two), and he gave me a Mickey Mantle watch, which even now hangs on the wall of my study four feet to my right as I type this.

It was not uncommon for him to pop his head out the door as I was walking across the street delivering mail to a neighbor to give me an updated score. When the Yankees won their last championship in 2009, Randall was the first person I called as we screamed and cheered over the phone. A dear man.

Well, for his birthday this past March, his wife gave him three tickets to see the Yanks play against Seattle up at Safeco Field this season. He was allowed to take any two people he chose (she had to work and was unable to attend). He picked his son, and . . . and . . . ME! When he called to invite me last spring I was astonished, flabbergasted, overwhelmed—and teary.

Yesterday was that game. The Yankees won 5–0 and it was a fun game to watch. But even if that other team had won 19–4, it would have been a day I will never forget. Many stories and laughs and baseball chats throughout the day.

Oh, and these were not nosebleed seats, either. (Which would have been fabulous, by the way!) No, we were in the 17th row just to the right and behind home plate! What a gift! As we parted ways last night I thanked him again—and again got teary-eyed. What a fabulous day! What an off-the-charts gracious gift! What a dear friend! Because of an ongoing, forged, day-by-day relationship. Why did I like being a mailman? Because of the undefinable and glorious blessing of relationships with dear folks like this. I am/was blessed.

Randall and Janet came to my retirement party and two years later when they retired a month apart, I was honored to be invited and to attend their party.

———&&&———

Susan always had a welcoming bathroom if I needed it and over the years we found a myriad of ways to tease each other. But there was also some deep sharing during difficult times.

Around the corner were Pete and Laurie, incredibly friendly and always, ALWAYS asking how my family was doing. They became some of my dearest customers but sadly they moved away several years before I retired. I would have loved having them for my entire career.

Well, we must continue on our way. We are well over halfway done, but there is still a lot of route to cover so let's get on with it. We will keep heading north. A local watering hole became a very welcome stop over the years. Two things. It was a good bathroom break. One I used virtually every day for those 27 years. And if I needed a cold glass of ice water while I briefly chatted with the regulars for a couple minutes, that was a good spot as well. Across the parking lot is a building that was the home of several businesses over the years. The first one back in the late 80's and early 90's was a shop that sold lawn mowers and small farm equipment. The owners were a married couple who were extraordinarily nice. Sadly, I can no longer remember their names. What I do remember however is that her son became a Major League baseball player for the San Francisco Giants. Now that was cool.

———— ❦ ————

Another interesting family and another lesson. An older woman lived with her two middle-aged sons. They were not unfriendly to me at all, but they were very quiet and morose. Shades always pulled. They never seemed happy about anything. I am embarrassed about it now, but I dubbed them "The Miserable Family" in my head. I had been their mailman for several years when my union, the National Association of Letter Carriers, had their first annual food drive. It was a terrific idea that has rightfully blossomed into a huge tradition for the benefit of food banks around the country. If you don't participate, you should. It is a fabulous cause. Anyway, when it was announced that we as mailmen would be picking up bags of food around our route to collect for this food drive, I began to make mental notes of who might give food and how it would affect my delivery times and effort. As I mentally went through my route I came to "The Miserable Family" in my head and laughed at the absurd idea that they of all people would leave some food for me to pick up. You can guess. Not only did they leave some food out for me, but they left an entire paper grocery bag of canned goods. I really must learn to not label people, especially when I don't know them well. Sigh.

———— ❦ ————

Directly to the north as we head down the street were two families who had lived next door to each other for many years before I came along. Mr. and Mrs. Scott were an older couple who lived but one house from the corner of an intersection. They were quiet and mostly kept to themselves, but when they saw me they always greeted me with delightfully friendly smiles. They passed away within a couple weeks of one another.

Their neighbors were the Hamiltons, who were even older. I did not see Mrs. Hamilton often, but Mr. Hamilton was frequently outside sitting on his porch or lightly working on his flowers. If he was inside the house and spotted me as I approached, he would often motion me to come inside to say hello, waving his left arm in a large arch to capture my attention as he sat in his big easy chair. He was in his early 90s when his wife passed.

He lived for a few more years and though his smile grew weaker, his friendliness never did. I was quite saddened by his passing a couple of years later. The four of them—the Scotts and the Hamiltons—were good neighbors and some of the first folks I got to know on my route. Even now, as I think of them, I find myself with a poignant smile on my face. After both the Hamiltons had passed away I got a very sweet note from their daughter, which coincided with the halfway point of my career.

"Again thank you for being so thoughtful to my dad. I know he looked forward to seeing you every day & was disappointed when you were on vacation. I surely appreciate your kindness. Thanks again. Congratulations on 15 years of service."

Long after the Hamiltons were gone, a nice young couple moved into the home and they became good friends. Every year without fail they left me a nice little bag of homemade cookies for Christmas. Really sweet people.

Across the street lived Mr. Brown. Boy, howdy, did he have a story to tell.

September 13, 2011

People have amazing stories sometimes. Historical. I delivered to Mr. Brown and his wife for many years. He was quite the artist. In his home were many paintings he had created. One day I noticed a gorgeous painting of a yellow biplane with a man standing in front of it. I asked him about it. Well, when Mr. Brown was about ten years old it was a year or so after Charles Lindbergh had made his solo crossing of the Atlantic Ocean in his plane, "The Spirit of St. Louis." He was touring the country. Mr. Brown's father took him to see the flying hero . . . AND HE GOT TO MEET CHARLES LINDBERGH!!! He even had a short chat with him! Mr. Brown was obviously admiring the plane so Mr. Lindbergh asked him if he was interested in flying. When Mr. Brown said, "yes," Lindbergh looked down at the ten-year-old boy and told him there was no more rewarding and satisfying career.

So Mr. Brown learned to fly and ended up being a flight instructor during World War II and after. And the painting? It was Lindbergh standing in front of his plane which Mr. Brown painted years later from memory. Mr. Brown passed on many years ago, but before he did I went to see him in a nursing home. Right before I left he asked if I would like to have a painting of his. I was floored with gratitude. He gave me a painting of a head shot of Mr. Charles Lindbergh. It is in storage as I write this. Now, I ask you: how cool is THAT?!!?

Mr. Brown and his wife were good friends with their neighbors, Mr. and Mrs. Danville. Where they live there is a T-intersection. On both sides of the street of the T, plus across from the entering street, and the next address east, are four houses that at one time were owned and occupied by the same family, Mr. Danville's parents. They were purchased/built sometime in the early twentieth century, I think.

When I became the mailman in May of 1988 two of the homes were still within the family. The original owner's son (Mr. Danville) and daughter (Helen) lived in those two houses. The son (30 years older than me) became one of my first acquaintances and was also the first customer to give me a Christmas tip. His sister, who lived across the street, was single (widow?) and also very friendly. I loved my interactions with them. She passed in the mid-1990s.

Then Mr. Danville moved into his sister's old house. Over the years Mr. Danville and his wife were always so graciously kind to me and he and I had dozens of chats over the years. Then around 2000 (?) Mr. Danville's son (same first name) moved into the other house. Mr. Danville and his wife passed away several years ago. I miss them. Two nicer folks you could not meet.

Who is in his house now? His grandson, a wife, and Mr. Danville's great-granddaughter, who would be the original owner's great-great-granddaughter. The last ten years or so Mr. Danville's son from across the street and I became friends and talked frequently. Every person I met in this extended family was terrific and friendly and the definition of why I liked being a mailman.

Directly across the street from the Danville clan was Kanna. She was very sweet and brought me into more than one family gathering as I watched her kids grow up. One of my fave families. Also one of my dumb, klutzy moves happened at one of these gatherings. It was a birthday party. My first time actually inside the home. I made a brisk walk heading to the kitchen and suddenly found myself reeling from a blow to the head. They had a low, angular part of the wall that jutted out a bit. And I had not seen it. Ka-blam. Full on. That's why they invented aspirin, right?

Before we leave this particular neighborhood let me tell you about three more delivery stops. I first met Ethan when he was 14 years old. He lived with his brother and mom. When I retired, Ethan was 41. Those numbers by themselves, 14 and 41, truly show the span of time I trudged through route 0655. Anyway, Ethan is a sports card collector. When I was a kid I collected baseball cards passionately, not selling them until I was in my late 30s.

Over the years Ethan would show me cards that he had purchased, partly because of my still casual interest, but mostly because I was the one who was delivering them to him. I got a real kick out of what he purchased and posted about it on social media a few times.

July 29, 2011

I love baseball cards. I had over 5,000 as a kid. Sold them and paid off debts and purchased new furniture for the living room. But I miss the hobby. A young man on my route is a collector. I deliver most of his cards. So I get to see all this old stuff I never had plus some I did. His oldest cards date to the 1880s. He loves showing them to me. It's a real kick.

December 6, 2011

To anybody out there who is a baseball or baseball card fan: A few months ago I posted about a young man on my route who has some really cool cards. Well, yesterday I delivered to him the 1954 rookie baseball cards of Hall of Famers Ernie Banks, Al Kaline, AND Hank Aaron, all of which were . . . wait for it . . . AUTOGRAPHED!

October 16, 2012

I have mentioned before about the gentleman on my mail route who collects and buys and trades baseball cards. He frequently shows me his old-time cards from a century ago, and it is a real treat. Well, today he comes out and says he has a gift for me. In a plastic case he hands me a Topps 1962 rookie card of Merritt Ranew, the only Major League Baseball player EVER to have my first name (although he has one more "T"). Cool beans!!!

A 1962 Merritt Ranew baseball card,
a special gift from Ethan.

September 29, 2014

First of all, I received the customer's permission to post this if I didn't show their face or reveal their name. Over the years I have delivered just about everything imaginable (dolls, glassware, electronics) and some things unimaginable (fish, human remains), but this may be my most enjoyable delivery as per my tastes. It is a 1952 Topps Mickey Mantle baseball card. I have read about this card for 30 years, but this was the first one I have ever actually seen close up.

I always appreciated Ethan coming out to show me his latest purchases. There were scads more plus football and basketball cards and a few autographed photos of famous actors and musicians. Fun stuff. Ethan also joined me on my trek around the neighborhood, often walking with me for a few minutes to chat as I shoveled out the mail to my patrons.

Across the street was a home that had a room converted into a beauty salon. Victoria and Maggie ran the place there for several years and the three of us had a hoot of a time nearly every day I walked in with the mail. It seemed to be a contest about who could needle the others the quickest and the deepest, always with friendliness and charm. I loved my stops in there to chat with the ladies and was sad when they moved out. I still see Victoria from time to time and we always have a good smiling time between us.

The next house we approach has had many different residents over the years. Allow me to tell you about two in particular. Norma was the first woman I knew who lived in the house. I didn't get to know her very well. But what I do remember is the color of her house. It was a bright lime-green. The outside. No, really. I met her daughter once or twice when she visited her mom. She hated the color of her mom's house.

One day they were chatting about it as I came up to the house with the mail. It simply came down to the fact that the mom really liked the color of her house and saw no reason to change it. Okay. It was pretty weird and wild but we all have our own tastes. There came a time when the two of them went on vacation together. One day shortly after they returned I came by in the afternoon about my usual delivery time and was surprised to see painters working on the house to change the color to a mild beige. Norma was outside watching the work be done. I sidled up to her, dying of curiosity.

"Norma, why are you changing the color of your house? I thought you loved this color."

"I still do but decided I needed to change it to something more mild."

"Why?"

"Do you remember when my daughter and I went on that vacation last month?

"Yes?"

"We flew to [the destination]."

"Right?"

"Well . . . I could see my house from the plane!"

The look on her face was priceless. I doubled over howling with laughter. One of the funniest moments I ever had on my route.

Some years later, an older gentleman moved in. Mr. LaRue was a neighborhood favorite. He would wave and engage with the kids and was just generally a good and friendly neighbor. He was a bit of a character and had a wonderfully bellowing laugh. One day he came out to meet me to receive the mail. He had a very small handmade wooden box in his hand. It was a just a bit bigger than a small matchbox.

"Merrit, do have any idea what I have in this box?" His eyes were mischievous.

"No, Mr. LaRue; what do you have there?"

"Why, it's a three-piece chicken dinner!"

I took another look at this very small box. I had to ask. "No, kidding. Can you show me?"

He opened the box to reveal three small kernels of corn. Then he roared with laughter. Mr. LaRue. What a character. All of the neighborhood was sad when he passed a year or so later.

As we begin to head to the end of the route, let me tell you about my friend Susan. Susan was one of the secretaries at an elementary school on my route. Despite numerous personnel changes within the office at this school, Susan was a constant. She was there when I started on my route in May of 1988. She was there when the boundaries of my route changed and I was no longer the mailman at the school. And she was there for many years after. Beyond simply just delivering the mail to her every day, we became very well-acquainted and eventually dear friends. I would often bring my kids in on my days off or vacations to see her. And the last day before the school's Christmas, spring, and summer breaks, she would come around the desk and embrace me. And when those breaks ended and school resumed, she would greet me the same way. A dear lady. I was very sorry to hear of her passing a few years back.

Around the corner is the sweet Prater family. A very nice Christian family that I had as patrons for my entire 27 years. Nearly every year I was presented a large and varied plateful of Christmas cookies. It was an extra treat watching their three daughters grow up because each of them was within a year or two of the ages of my three daughters. This is the kind of family that if I stopped by and knocked on their door today I know I would be very welcomed. Good people.

Across the street from the Praters in a five-plex. Paul lived in his apartment toward the back for over 25 years. I saw him nearly every day. And on a regular basis he made me my favorite homemade cookies, ginger-bends. That's my name for a gingersnap that is soft. He also made fabulous applesauce that he would ply me with from time to time.

Toward the end of my route was Corina. She is an amazing lady. On her own, she raised a son along with twin girls who were very disabled. When I first met the girls they were just tots and were always very sweet to me. And as the years passed I'd see them out in their wheelchairs with their mom as they went to the store. I saw these three numerous times during my years delivering in southeast Portland. A strong and courageous mom and two lovely daughters. I felt privileged to know them.

On my last section is a gorgeous house where at different times lived two of my best customers. Ethel was a dear lady of advanced years who was as friendly as anyone I ever met in my years as a postman. We had many chats while sitting on her spacious front porch. After she moved away we continued to stay in touch. She is in her 90s now and we still chat by phone from time to time. Following her, another nice family moved in that I didn't get to know super well because of their work hours and also because they moved in toward the tail end of my career. But a nice moment came along during my final weeks on the job.

April 2, 2015

Several weeks ago The Oregonian newspaper ran a fantastic feature story in the Living section about two women who had been very close and dear friends with music as their main bond. They were both musicians of some renown here in the Portland area mostly back in the 1940s. They had stayed close friends through the decades. One of them had died several years ago and the article included an interview with the surviving lady. The last name of the woman who passed away was unusual . . . and the same last name as a family on my route for the past few years. A few days later I saw the woman who lives on my route and told her about the article and asked if by chance they were related. She said no, she had never heard of the lady in the story. About two weeks later she came out of her house as I was delivering the mail, thanking me for telling her about the article. As it turned out the woman in the story was her husband's great-aunt and they had not known about the article. She was really delighted that I had asked about it.

This is but a sampling of the delightful folks I got to encounter and got to know during my 27 years delivering the mail on route 0655. To say it was a privilege and honor would be a gross understatement. But it wasn't just me. Many of my fellow letter carriers have similar relationships with their customers. And that truth carries over to thousands of mailmen and mailwomen across the United States and the world. But it also isn't limited to this era.

Fanny Crosby is perhaps the most famous composer of hymns in history. If not the most famous, then possibly the most prolific. In her autobiography[*] she shares briefly about her mailman when she was a little girl back in the 1820's in New York State. He used to bring the mail on horseback every Thursday and it was her responsibility within her family to collect it from him. She talks about the great affection she had for him and how she got to know him on a personal level. After several years of service his son took over the route from him. Miss Crosby said the son was an adequate mailman, but she never developed the friendship with him that she had with the father. So you see, the potential for this unique connection in society has been around for a very long time.

Finally, let me tell you about the Derringers. Well, I can't tell you much about them. They were only customers of mine for three or four years, and right at the beginning of my time on the route. A nice young couple with two adorable blond-haired little girls. I would have short chats with the girls almost every day they were home. Sweet girls with whom I had lovely encounters for a few short years.

[*] *Fanny J. Crosby: An Autobiography* is gently edited and updated from the original edition published under the title, *Memories of Eighty Years* by James H. Earle and Company, in 1906.

I don't remember any of their names. I would not recognize any of them if they knocked on my door right now. They moved away to who knows where. But what I do remember is one hot, sunny day many years later. I was on the business section of my route so it was mid-morning. I had just walked out of an office building and was starting down the sidewalk to my next delivery.

A man and woman were waiting at the bus stop as I passed by. Suddenly the woman said, "Aren't you Merrit?"

"Yes."

"We're the Derringers. You used to be our mailman several years ago."

My mind searched. An address came to mind. (How, I don't know. Not only had they not lived at that house for many years, it was also on one of the streets I had lost due to a boundary change, so I had not even delivered mail to that house for years).

When I asked if that was where they lived they laughed and said that indeed it was. At that point I remembered them and their two little cuties. We had a delightful visit. They informed me the girls were now in high school. I was so tickled that they had remembered me and stopped me to talk. Then they completely floored me by telling me how much they had loved me being their mailman and how much the girls had enjoyed getting to know me and that the family had never forgotten about me nor had they ever had another mailman they were fond of or that seemed to care about getting to know their family.

It was a short but fabulous visit and gave me a real boost not only on that hot day, but just the idea that people would remember me even though I was only their mailman. What a nice moment. What a nice family. And those two little girls were just so sweet. Great kids.

Please allow me to introduce you to some more great kids. Or at least some great kid moments.

Chapter 18

KIDS *ARE* THE DARNDEST THINGS

"Totally logical reasoning"

Kids. Amazing little creatures, aren't they? I was in my late 20s before I began to understand how amazing they can be. When I was a kid I couldn't stand kids. I mean, as a kid myself I obviously had friends who were kids. But multiple kids meant noise and destruction and messing with my orderly little world.

I was a fairly well-behaved child who didn't make lots of noise and could not understand why other kids did. My two siblings were much older, so in many ways I was raised like an only child. I kept my stuff organized and orderly. Very.

Embarrassingly enough, I found out years later from two of my cousins that when their families would come to visit us (with five kids in each family), just before they reached our house from out of town, their respective parents would pull the car over and remind the kids: stay out of Merrit's room; don't touch Merrit's baseball cards; don't touch Merrit's Matchbox cars; Merrit doesn't like to get dirty or play wild so be nice. Yikes. Must have been a real hoot for them to come visit their cousin Merrit.

As I got older, my dislike of all things children became worse. That all changed when I began to help my wife teach a Sunday school class for four- and five-year-olds at the church we attended. I became good buddies with an adorable little kindergartner and decided these little creatures could be fascinating if handled correctly.

The process was not quite as clinical as it sounds, but soon we jumped into the adventure of parenting and I loved it beyond anything I had ever experienced. I have told people over the years that they should be quite thankful that there was not social media when I had little ones at home because I was an obnoxiously proud parent. I would have posted every picture we took and told about every little accomplishment our children did.

Having my own children opened up my heart to the delight of talking with and engaging with these wee folk. So let me share with you a bunch of delightful and charming stories of my encounters with these little ones as I came to their homes on a regular basis and had the supreme privilege of listening to their viewpoints, brutal honesty, and getting caught off guard with their wisdom and unadorned affection toward me as I watched them grow.

My only regret is that virtually all of these kiddos are from the middle to the end of my career. In the early days I simply was to tuned into my own four at home that I did not notice as much the pleasure of dealing with these little people as I could have, and if I did, I did not record the encounters. Most of these stories come straight from social media posts and I have laid them out in chronological order. After them I have a few more without the dates listed. Enjoy. I certainly did.

May 19, 2010

So today on my route I had a certified letter for a regular customer who homeschools their children. As she was signing the form her son (age 6–8) came up to me and had an empty bag of candy that he had stuffed his hand into and was talking to me with it. I succinctly asked him "Is that a puppet?" His response with a look of disdain: "No, it's a candy bag." I was still chuckling 30 minutes later.

March 9, 2011

So I was about to deliver to a residence today and a little kid there said to her mother, "Mom, the mailbox is here." It's not the first time a child has called me a mailbox. So I'm wondering: do I really walk THAT slow?

June 24, 2011

A lady from my route was taking her two- and four-year-olds to the park. They saw a postal vehicle. The four-year-old says, "Look, it's Mr. Merrit." But a female letter carrier got out of the car. The four-year-old says: "No, it's MerriLEE." Apparently that's my name in the feminine. Cute.

June 27, 2011

Three kids were set to walk to the park to swim. I asked this to the little girl, about five or six years old: "How about if YOU deliver the mail and I go swimming." She wrinkled her nose, looked up at me, and replied: "Nooo, I really can't read small letters very well yet." I walked away chuckling and wondering if that was the only reason she said "no."

July 7, 2011

The youngest of three kids at a house is about five years old. I had not seen her in about two years or more. I saw her today. ME: "Why Elinor, I haven't seen you in such a long time. You look like you have really grown." HER: "Well, I've been drinking a lot of milk." I love the literalness of children.

July 22, 2011

I have been the mailman for a very nice family for 13 years. When I started with them they had two small kids. The girl was four, the boy 18 months. I would see the kids occasionally, then a year or two might pass by without seeing them. But over the years I saw them regularly enough to keep up with their growth and schooling. But it had been quite some time since I last saw either of them. Recently as I was bringing their mail up to the house I noticed a stunningly beautiful young woman sitting on the steps, apparently waiting for someone. I nodded politely to her since she was a stranger to me and I don't make it a habit to start up conversations with gorgeous young women I don't know. She looked up at me and said, "Hi, I haven't seen you in a long time." I stopped dead in my tracks. I sputtered out, "Peggy!?" She giggled and said, "Yes." She is almost 18 and will be a senior this coming school year. Sigh. The years fly.

September 2, 2011

A little four-year-old gal on my route with enormous brown eyes usually opens the door as I am putting mail in their mail slot. She hears me because I have a small pocket radio (we called them transistors back in the day, kids) that is tuned to the classical music station. We chat briefly and I move on. BUT, on Monday, she opened the door and exclaimed, "Hey, I thought you were the ice cream man!" Cracked me up.

September 7, 2011

Yesterday I had to deliver a section on another route. Toward the end a little girl of four or five approached me at what was the house before hers. We had never met before.

SHE: "Do you have bubblegum?"

ME: "Nooo, do YOU have bubblegum?"

SHE (smiling shyly): "No..."

ME: "Then why would you think I have bubblegum?"

SHE: "Because ALL mailmans should have bubblegum!"

I started to walk away smiling.

SHE: "And mailgirls, too!"

I loved the totally logical reasoning of this little girl . . . from her point of view.

September 16, 2011

Once in the checkout line at Safeway on my way home from work and while I was still in my uniform, a small boy kept looking at me. Finally he turned to his dad and asked, "Daddy, why is the mailman buying food?" Apparently at the end of the day I was expected to climb back into my mailman box up on the shelf until the next morning when I was let out to deliver mail again.

August 19, 2012

This happened yesterday. I was doing a section on another route. A man was working on his car with his two small children nearby. He went quickly to go get a letter to hand me. I looked at the little boy. "Are you three?" He nodded. I looked at the older girl. "Are you four?" She said no, she was five. I, of course, apologized profusely for my mistake. Her response: "Oh, that's okay. I was four just a little bit ago." I had to quickly turn away so she wouldn't see me laughing. I felt so fortunate to be given a proper excuse for my stupidity. It made me smile many times the rest of the day.

July 27, 2013

A few months back a young couple and their 18-month-old daughter moved onto my route. They were friendly right from the get-go. The daughter, Allison, was naturally shy. Over the months I would frequently see her playing in the dirt with her mommy while mom planted things. Occasionally she would smile at me or maybe even wave. Then jabbering came along. Then, last Thursday, I hear a little voice quite clearly shouting across the street, "Hi, Mewwit!" Made my day. Same little girl three days later: "Mewwit, (gibberish) yard (gibberish) tent?" Translation from mom: "In my backyard is my tent." I walked over to her and said "Allison, you have a tent?!?" She looked up and said, "mm-hmm . . . wanna see?" Yeah, I'm gonna refuse that request from a two-year-old. I went back and looked. We talked for a minute and then I turned to go as she was still in her tent. Then I heard this dear little voice from the tent: "I love you." . . . Uh, if you are in the neighborhood of my route and notice a big drippy puddle on the sidewalk, that would be my heart.

On my last day of work, this little one – who was 3 ½ at the time – gave me a "map" (a sheet of paper with dozens of colored squiggly lines all over it) so I wouldn't get lost during my retirement. It hangs on the wall of my study even now.

Allison's map she drew for me at my retirement.
I haven't gotten lost yet.

August 27, 2013

We delivered advos today, those lovely pieces of pfft with all the loose coupons. Today a father sitting on the porch told his eight(?)-year-old son to come get the mail from me. I folded the advo over to try to have it not spill and told the youngster to be careful and not lose the pizza coupons. He looked at the mail and went running inside the house yelling, "Mommy, we're rich!" Dad and I cracked up. Now that's the kind of response I want about junk mail, folks!

September 30, 2013

I had two fun kid moments today. I was delivering on SE Woodstock Blvd. A couple of little girls (age four-ish?) were having lunch in the living room. The door was open and I had not seen them in several months. I said, "Hi girls, how are you today?" One of them looked up and said, "Do you know that you are on Woodstock?" I assured her I did. At the end of the day I came up on a Latino family that I chat with frequently, a dad and six-year-old daughter. I handed the dad a letter that was addressed in Spanish. As I was walking away I heard the girl say to her dad, "I can't read that, it's in Mexican!" Cracked me up.

October 10, 2013

I love how little ones will add length or syllables or take away from them with their unique pronunciation. Yesterday a chat with three-year-old Larry, as it was pronounced.

Larry: "Merrrrit, there wuss a bg on ower dooruh."

Me: "Did you eat it?"

Larry: "Nooah!"

Me: "Why not?"

Larry: "Cuz thayerr poyyyzun."

Me: "Oh, well that's a good thing you didn't eat it then."

I'm not sure who was chuckling more, Merrit or Larry's mom.

December 20, 2013

A family moved onto my route about nine months ago. The 18-month-old daughter, Virginia, was not thrilled with my presence at the door/window/mailbox. I told her parents (mom was about eight months pregnant at the time) I would win her over eventually. I always do. So every day I would wave. She would just stare without a smile. Sister was born.

About two months ago Virginia finally started waving gently. Now she bolts to the window and smiles big and waves. Today I had a parcel, so I knocked on the door. Virginia was in a high chair in the kitchen. I was walking away when the mom says, "Oh, wait, Virginia wants to see the mailman!" I popped my head in and got a big wave and smile and a big voice telling me she was having "beckfast and that's baby Su," pointing to sister Susan on the floor. I always get them, eventually. Love them kids.

April 16, 2014

There is a lovely family on my route with two fabulous kids. The girl is eight or nine, the boy a couple years older. They are homeschooled, very respectful, and sharp as can be. The following conversation took place today between me and the boy, Tom. You must understand this happened in rapid-fire communication, not in the speed I am going to render it to you, since I will add commentary. He came running up to me with a large envelope to be sent out about two houses after I had left their premises. He started the conversation:

Tom: I keep forgetting to put this envelope out for you to take.

Me: Oh, oh. You should be fired.

At this point I figure the conversation is over because he probably doesn't get my humor at his age, or the full concept of being fired.

Tom: "Oh, I've been fired already."

This caught me off guard for the above reasons, and he seemed a bit serious.

Me: "Huh?"(I know, clever rejoinder, don't you think?)

Tom: "Yeah, they already fired me, but they had to hire me back because no one else would take the job."

At this point he smiles at me and says, "See ya." I just shook my head and chuckled, then stopped in mild wonder at his quick wit at such a tender age. I walked off still laughing. Made my day.

May 1, 2014

Today I was coming up on a townhouse. There were several young adults and a toddler. Mom was telling the little one to stay out of the mailman's way. As I walked by him I looked down and said, "Hey, bud." As I walk past him he looks up at me and says in this ridiculous old-man voice, "Hey, bud." All of us cracked up. Mom looks at me and says, "Yeah, he is kind of a parrot." So I stand in front of him, look down and ask, "Are you a parrot?" I swear his two-letter answer had three syllables. It sounded something like this: "iiinnnnnnnnnooooooouuuhhh!"

June 20, 2014

Early on in my route I was coming up on two of my route kids, both about age four, playing and running on a huge mound of bark chips (and BAREFOOT! . . . yikes!). Anyway, as I got close one of them took a stance like one of the models on "The Price Is Right" pointing at a new car and said, "Look, Merrit. A big truck brought this big pile. Run up and down it with us." I thought about it for about half a second. Then had visions of my ankles, hips, knees, etc. over the past three to four years. I saw about nine different outcomes if I chose to run up the pile, and none of them were good. So I said, "No thanks." But the boys were adorable and the moment was sweet.

August 5, 2014

I put the mail in a customer's mail receptacle today. A little boy (probably almost three years old) saw me walking away. As I moved to my next delivery his dad, who was at the side of the house, said hello to me. Then he realized his boy had run back around to the front of the house. Just as he was reaching the front and could see his son again he asked, "Oliver, what are you doing?" "I'm getting the mail." The dad saw him and started laughing. Then I saw him and started laughing. Their mail receptacle is a slot in the side of the house and there was Oliver with his arm shoved all the way up to the shoulder trying to retrieve the mail. His dad told him he had to go inside the house to get it. Funny sight.

October 6, 2014

I have written often of my delight with my "route kids." They really make my day, and it is thrilling to watch them grow up. However, you know what REALLY makes a mailman feel old? When one of his route kids who he has known all or nearly all of their lives starts receiving lots of mail from colleges seeking their enrollment. Another one today. I have known her since she was about three. Sigh.

Let me tell you about Mr. and Mrs. Wallace. Terrific folks. Married 60 years. He had been a veteran and hero of World War II. They were exceptionally nice to me and had a beautiful home and one of my five favorite trees ever. (I know, but that's just how my mind works, folks.) But what I want you to know about are their grandkids.

One day as I came by the lady brought out her six-year-old grandson to meet me. He stepped out on the porch from the door, stuck out his little hand, and said, "It is very nice to meet you." He was an extraordinarily polite and respectful youngster and quite the conversationalist. He was always a delight to speak with.

Soon after, I met his two-years-younger brother. It was a treat to watch these two fabulous boys grow up over the succeeding years. They were frequently at their grandparents' house as they lived just two blocks away.

As the years passed and they got old enough I would encounter them walking in the neighborhood, first with their mom and baby sister, then later with just each other, and finally as they became even older, by themselves. Every time—and I mean EVERY time—they greeted me with a handshake and proper greeting, speaking to me with respect, intelligence, and ease.

As teens they were wonderful young men and I always got a kick out of them stopping to chat and catch up on our lives. They are both in college now and I last saw them about the time of my retirement. They will be one of those great memories I will treasure always.

Now I am telling you, I have met some nice kids/little boys/teenagers in my life, but I have never come across two boys/young men like these two. Every visit was courteous, respectful, engaging, and a delight. Great boys. This past summer I had the treat of having coffee with the older young man. He has gone to college and is now an apprentice electrician. What made our time so precious to me were his recollections of me as his grandparents' mailman and how much he appreciated our relationship.

<hr>

One day I had three kid encounters within a span of about seven minutes. I am delivering on a street and this young boy and his mom are riding bikes down the sidewalk next to the yard I am in. He stops his bike and approaches me.

"Have you delivered to our house today?"

ME: "Well, where do you live?"

"On Knight Street."

"Well, I deliver on Knight Street and have already been there."

He gets this goofy grin on his face and says: Yes! mail at my house!"

I said, "What is your address?"

He said, "5 0 3...."

His mom said, "That's your phone number." She told me the address.

I replied, "Oh, I'm sorry, that is not on my route, so I don't know if you got mail or not." Ah, the look of the crestfallen.

She told him they would have to wait till they got home.

Then I walked across the street and a small girl (probably eight to ten) asked for the mail. It was obviously her grandparents' house, who I know very well. Grandma was on the porch.

"Can I have the mail, please?" the youngster asked.

"Well, I don't know; are you trustworthy?"

(giggle, giggle) "Yes." (giggle, giggle)

"Are you sure it is okay to give you the mail?"

(giggle, giggle) "Yes." (giggle, giggle)

"Have you ever robbed a bank?"

(giggle, giggle) "NO!" (giggle, giggle) She was a cutie.

A few minutes later as I approached the porch of a home where a Hispanic family lives, a little boy about four was behind the screen door. He said "Hi."

"Well, hello, how are you today?" I asked.

As I hit the steps he got an odd look on his face, turned around while pointing at me, and said in a loud voice "Grandma, [lots and lots and lots of Spanish]!"

I walked away wondering if he'd said, "Grandma, the man who wants to kill our dog and burn our house down is coming!" or "Grandma, that fabulous mailman who is so brave and handsome is here!" Probably somewhere in between.

October 7, 2012

The difference in how little boys think from little girls. Today a few minutes after noon there was a plethora of sirens going off. It continued for some time, so I suspect it was police, ambulance, and firemen. It was quite extensive. About ten minutes later I came upon a boy and girl riding their bicycles, I would guess about eight or nine years old. I asked them if all the sirens going off were the police chasing them because they were riding their bikes too fast.

GIRL: "Noooo. And I am too little for them to give me a ticket."

BOY (while enthusiastically nodding his head up and down): "YEAH!!!"

October 13, 2012

Why I like being a mailman. Adoration. (I know, I know, but hang with me). First, a definition. There are typically two kinds of mail slots we come across in delivery. Smaller ones off from the main door where the mail hits a wall a few inches past the opening and then slides down, causing mailmen to need to guide the mail into the house. Or large slots that are nearly all in the front door and allow simple penetration of the mail into the house with no impediment. I made it a habit many years ago with this type of slot to forcefully shove the mail several feet into the house.

Three reasons: One, it keeps the mail away from the slot and front door where rainy weather could damage the mail. Two, it keeps prying eyes from peeking through the slot to see what the occupants' mail might be. Three, it protects the mail from being damaged by the opening of the door or feet stepping on it when the owners return home. Okay.

There is a lovely family that lived just a few minutes before the halfway mark of my route. They had two kids of their own plus ran a small daycare so there were frequently many little ones at the house. These little ones went nuts when I delivered the mail by propelling it into the house through the slot as far as I could. Squeals, laughter, clapping. It was a hoot.

Occasionally, a tiny set of fingers would reach back at me as I opened the slot to deliver the mail. I would gently grab and pull and play with those little digits, which would illicit more giggling and squeals. Other times I would fake tossing the mail in a time or two, which also brought laughter. Finally one day I spoke with the mother who ran the daycare. She explained that the kids couldn't wait for me to approach the house and would stop playing or eating or whatever they were doing to watch me go through this routine. They LOVED it. "Oh, yeah," she said. "You are a rock star at this house. They love you. It is one of the highlights of the day for them." Eventually the kids drew me pictures and I got a nice treat of candy at Christmas. Fun times. It became one of the highlights of the day for me as well.

This next post was written just a few months before I retired.

February 9, 2015

About five years ago I had a section added to my route. One day I came up on the porch to deliver the mail to one of these new houses for me. In the window was a little two-year-old tot. Now, you know me. I don't mean anything creepy about this. But this little girl was staggeringly beautiful. I thought at first she was literally a doll. Enormous, deep eyes. Her skin was so perfect it seemed to be lit from inside. And an impish little smile that made my knees wobble.

She and I became great buddies. She would wait for me and tap her fingers on the window at me. Eventually she would come outside and give me a hug. Her name was Mary Jo but I called her my pixie. Off-the-charts adorable. I watched her grow till she reached age four, then they moved.

Her aunt recently moved back onto my route. And yesterday, for the first time in three years I saw my pixie again. Age seven, now. She completely remembered me. We chatted a bit and she gave me a hug. She is still a cutie but looks much like most cute little seven-year-old girls do. It made my day to see her again. There is a part of me that is sad that most of these little ones will have no memory of me a few years (or sooner) after I retire. Dang, I am gonna miss my route kids.

A few years before I retired a nice young couple moved onto my route at the very end of my next to last section. They soon had a sweet little girl who became one of my favorite Route Kids. I so wish I could tell you this little one's name because it was such a charmingly delightful old-fashioned name. I saw her often because the couple ran a small business out of their home and got frequent deliveries (and pick-ups). And also, the mom was in the front yard a lot on nice days. The tot was shy and I didn't get a lot of interaction with her other than maybe a wave or quiet "hello." I went to visit a year after I retired and was thrilled that not only did the child remember me, she was happy to see me and climbed up on my lap and told me all about her life and new little sister. Little sister had actually come along at a very inopportune time . . . for me. This nice family had every intention of attending my retirement party but baby decided to come the day after I retired (thereby missing the great honor of being my youngest and last Route Kid) and the day before my party. The nerve of the kid!

But they weren't always perfect little angels. Right at the end of my route was a lovely young family with two adorable little girls. I wish I could tell you the girls' names because they were fabulous. Both old-fashioned from my grandparents' time. And they were both very sweet although mildly shy. They were two years apart. When they moved in the oldest was but 18 months old. Little sister came along a few months later. Over the years I had many delightful chats with these two and also with their parents. The school they attended was close and frequently I was in their neighborhood about the time school was letting out. Many of our chats centered around what they had done that day during school hours. One day the older girl was walking home with her daddy and I stopped to have my usual encounter with her.

ME: "Hey, Lydia, what did you learn in school today?" I had asked this question of her many times before.

LYDIA (with nose defiantly in the air): "I don't think I want to tell you."

I looked at dad. He rolled his eyes and held out his hands in the universal sign of "I have no idea." I watched Lydia march into the house and then burst out laughing. Kids. But one day I was able to observe a fabulous moment with this marvelous family as I was sitting in my postal car eating lunch.

June 5, 2014

I love getting to watch the interaction between members of loving families. Today I was having my lunch in my car at the end of my route. Two of my fave route kids (siblings) were coming home from school. Ages 9 and 7 (I think). As they approached the front door (screen closed, main door open), their dad jumped out at them from behind the door with a rousing "BOO!" They jumped and laughed. One of my favorite families. Made me smile. Love it.

I worked very hard to establish these friendships with the little ones. I always hoped those feelings would be reciprocated. Sometimes they were:

April 28, 2014

Today I was delivering by Marysville School toward the end of my route. Two young teens were crossing the street about 40 feet from me. I thought I heard the girl say something about "the mailman." I looked over and waved and continued on. Then she said, "Is your name Merrit?" "Yesss . . . ?"

"I'm Annie."

Me: "Annie? Annie WHAT?

"Annie who used to live at (her address)?"

She was. I had been her mailman in a house in a different neighborhood when she was ages 3 through 6. She is 13 now and I had only seen her once in all those years. That she would recognize me, that she would take the time to acknowledge me, that she REMEMBERED MY NAME after all those years. Totally made my day!! I would never have known who she was if she had not initiated the chat. And the other time she had seen me was also a very sweet moment for me. She was about 8 or 9 and her family had moved off my route about three years previously. One afternoon they were driving through my route several blocks from their former residence. Annie had spotted me and yelled at her dad to stop the car because she had seen me and wanted to say hello. She came bounding out of the car and ran into my arms. Those kind of moments—the two I had with Annie—whew . . . they can make an old, grumpy, broken down mailman cry, believe me.

A postscript. I contacted Annie's mom about putting these stories in the book. Annie is now 17. Her mom said these gracious words: "Annie remembers you fondly to this day and refers to you as her favorite 'Merrit.' You made a big city have a small community feeling; it was special. We are grateful for having you as our mailman." I think I may feel more wetness in my eyes commencing.

———

Andddd, sometimes they were not. A young couple moved onto my route when I had been delivering out of Creston Station for about 15 years. They had a little girl who was definitely on the other side of the line of shy. I talked to her gently and tried to start up a friendship. Finally, when she was about three years old I thought it was time to try my best "moves." That is usually when a kid will gain some social awareness and become less fearful.

A day came when she was in front of her home with her grandfather. I squatted down seven or eight feet from her and asked her if she would come over to say hello. Her eyes were round as saucers. She looked up at grandpa. He told her it would be okay. She looked back at me. She looked up at grandpa. She looked back at me. She looked up at grandpa. Then she looked back at me one last time and shook her head with an emphatic "no." Grandpa and I chuckled and I knew I had met my match.

I didn't see her much, and eventually the family moved across town and the mom's sister moved in. Three years later they came to visit the sister (the little girl's aunt). The youngster had no recollection of me, naturally, but now she was a Chatty Cathy, telling me all about . . . well, all the things that six-year-old girls chat about with strangers. But I had to admit, she was one that got away.

———— ◦◦◦◦ ————

There came a day when near-tragedy struck my route kids. I will never forget it . . . or what could have happened.

January 8, 2013

If you have been following these posts, you know that the children on my route are one of the best things about it. Since they are all for the most part in the same neighborhood, most of them attend the same school.

Three years ago in November I was walking my route in southeast Portland. I noticed a menacing black cloud billowing and growing quickly to the north of me. A few minutes later I received a text from a coworker informing me that the school was engulfed in flames. I nearly vomited. It was a school day, and you can imagine the fears that spewed up within me.

Suffice it to say that when I received word that NOT ONE child was lost or even injured I was beyond relieved. What could have been a horrendously tragic day ended very well.

Later that afternoon I chatted briefly with a couple of shook-up parents.

But when I think of what could have happened—. It was pretty cool today to see the doors re-opened and kids from the neighborhood running to and fro. YAY!!

My next chapter is about two of my route kids in particular. But before we get to them, let me tell you about one of the first kids I got to know and the bond that continued between us for more than two decades.

December 12, 2011

Henry was an over-the-top friendly kid who I got to know in the first years of my route. He was Hispanic with a smile that went on forever. I got to talk to him most days, starting when he was about ten years old. He was a great kid, always respectful. He was also the only one in his family who could speak English. His parents were terrific people and it was obvious where he got his smile from. One day, after I had been the mailman at their home for about two years, Henry came out to get the mail as usual. It was a warm spring day and their door was open. I pulled Henry over to the door and asked if he would translate something for me to his parents. He was delighted to do so. I looked in the door at his mom and dad and told him to tell them what he was about to do. They nodded.

I said, "I just wanted to let you know what a wonderful son you have. Henry is always friendly and respectful to me and is one of my favorite people on my route. You should be very proud. He is a great kid."

I wish I had a picture of those three faces that day. Henry was smiling, but also obviously embarrassed . . . and proud. Mom and Dad? You could have read a book in the dark from the light flashing from their smiles and beaming faces. He was a great kid. Unfortunately, his family moved a few miles north. I hated to see them—and especially Henry—move away. It happens.

But about five years later I was delivering one day and suddenly a van pulled up next to me. The side door opened up and out spilled 15-year-old Henry. Same smile. Same friendliness. It happened again three years later. Then I didn't see him for several years.

One day this car stops and there was a man and woman in the front with two kids in the back. The woman rolled the passenger window down and I walked over to see if they needed help. The man said, "Don't you recognize me?"

"Henry?!" I asked. He started laughing and said he realized he looked a bit different. Well, yeah, that and the kids. We had a nice visit.

Well, today I was at my vehicle when I heard a voice say from a car window, "Hey buddy, how ya' doin'?"

I recognized him immediately. "HENRY!" He is in his 30s now with three kids. He still remembers me and we had a nice chat. How cool is that?

The postscript to this post is that three and a half years later—just a few weeks before I retired—Henry was driving through my route again and stopped to chat for a few minutes. Again I did not recognize him, until he smiled and said, "Don't you know who I am?"

"Henry, is that really you?"

"It's me, dude!" This was a bit more poignant because although it was not said, we both were anticipating that this would be our last visit. I watched this youngster grow up. As I watched many youngsters grow up. Can you think of a higher privilege for a mailman to witness? Yeah, me neither.

Now let me introduce you to a couple of extra-special cutie-pies.

Chapter 19

FRIDA AND WANDA

"A mixture of disbelief"

Everyone needs a Frida and a Wanda in their life. Don't get me wrong. These two were not better than the other kiddos on my route. Not smarter. Not cuter. Not even inevitably my two favorites. (Although the mom of one of them says her daughter can be jealous and isn't necessarily thrilled about sharing me with other kids). But because of ages and locations and family dynamics, I simply had more opportunity to spend time with them, which led to them providing more fodder for my musings. And these two little ladies always kept me on my toes with their candid opinions (and then some), penetrating questions, and unbounded enthusiasm for all things mailman. Catch a glimpse.

It was actually a moment with Frida that got this whole idea rummaging around in my noggin to record my encounters with my route kids. Again, I wish I had started earlier. Frida was 18 months old at the time and her family had moved onto my route about two years previously. Here is what I posted on social media:

November 12, 2012

I believe I have shared this before, but I was just recently able to tell the story to the grandmother. I have a cute little gal on my route that I have known since she came home from the stork. As I deliver mail I have a little pocket radio tuned to the classical music station. I would see Frida quite frequently.

One day when she was about 18 months old, I was approaching her mom as she held her little one. I had delivered the mail to their house a few minutes earlier and was now coming up on the opposite side of the street, so I walked over to say hello. The little girl was waving her arms around similar to a musical conductor as she was looking at mommy.

"What's that all about?" I inquired.

Mom told me it was what Frida did when she saw me coming and heard my radio. "It's sign language for music."

Bewildered I asked, "Frida knows sign language!?" Yes, she was learning it. As I walked away I muttered loud enough for mommy to hear, "Great, just what I need. An 18-month-old smarter than me."

An occasional added bonus to developing these relationships with the little ones was getting to know the grandparents. More than once I'd see a grandparent visiting one of the families on my route. I'd start to introduce myself and grandma or grandpa would interrupt with, "Oh, I know who you are. (Grandchild) has told me all about Mr. Merrit and how you come by every day to bring the mail and visit." I would beam every time this happened. Hey, you can't get a truer endorsement than from a grandchild.

∞∞∞

Wanda is a very independent-minded young lady you will quite happily instruct you on proper behavioral etiquette . . . from her point of view. As I found out one day. She and I had been pals for a couple of years. But the winter months had hit and we had not seen each other for several weeks. That led to this exchange, still one of my favorite encounters:

January 15, 2015

I have spoken of this adorable tot before. She is nearly three years old, quite verbal, and has enormous brown eyes. Yesterday she and her daddy stopped in their car by my van as I was preparing my next delivery section. She was in her car seat in the back. I walked over to talk for a minute. As we were chatting, I reached in and gently tapped her adorable little nose with my finger. She immediately—and I mean RIGHT NOW—covered her nose with her hand, gave me a ridiculously stern look, and reprimanded me with this: "We don't touch people's noses without asking!!"

I looked at her dad so I wouldn't burst out laughing. He was also looking away with a wry smile on his face. I was for a moment concerned that I had committed some type of "stranger danger" infraction. He said not to worry but also that she was totally serious and that when anyone asked her if they could touch her nose, she always said "no." Even her parents were not allowed to touch her nose.

I looked back at her, profusely and sincerely saying that I was sorry. Then we were buddies again. A three-year-old's honesty . . . you can't beat it.

But our friendship took some time to develop. She enjoyed my arrivals, but that was only expressed at the beginning to others, not to me.

From summer of 2014:

There is a really adorable three-year-old on my route. She apparently talks about me up until I arrive at her house to deliver the mail, then turns shy and mumbles. Today as I approached I could hear her talking to a woman in a car across the street. She heard my music and saw me and turned to the woman: "Oh, ders Mewwit. I haftogoget da mail now." Cracked me up. She talked TO me just a little, but certainly with many fewer words than she used to talk ABOUT me.

Wanda definitely had boundary standards. This next moment happened a few months later.

September 10, 2014

Yesterday as Wanda came out to get the mail she was dressed all in blue, looking quite cute. I asked her, "What color are you wearing today?"

She said, "I am wearing blue pants—and at this point she pulls a sucker from her mouth and puts it directly in front of my face—"...and a light blue lollipop." I would dearly love to have a recording of her pronouncing that last word.

Today she and her dad were just about to pull out of the driveway when I approached. I gave the mail to dad and asked if I could walk around to the other side of the car and say hello real quick. "Of course!"

I walked around and saw she was eating a small bowl of Cheese Nip crackers and some type of popcorn snack. "Hi, Wanda, how are you today?"

"I am having a snack. I have popcorn and crackers."

Now, since she and I are good buddies, I saw no problem with my next question. "Well, can I have one?" I tell ya, you never saw a tiny little hand with splayed fingers cover a bowl so quickly. "No, these are mine. I hafta eat 'em."

Then she absolutely floored me with her next comment: "Maybe tonight." I said okay, and quickly walked away so I could burst out laughing out of earshot. What a dolly.

I mentioned grandmas earlier. Here was a cool moment with Frida and her grandmother:

May 31, 2011

A family on my route has a three-year-old girl who is

an absolute doll. And she loves when I come by. She tells me about her day, etc. We have lovely chats. Her parents order things through the mail. Her grandma came over to babysit. She saw a pile of books on the floor next to her granddaughter. She looked at Frida and asked, "Frida, where did you get all these books?"

Frida: "Merrit brought them." How cool is that!

As someone responded on my post: "Who needs Santa when they have a Merrit?"

As Wanda got older, her world got larger. She entered preschool. One day, as I was walking away from her house after tossing the mail in their mailbox, her mom opened the door and told me this masterpiece: "So, I arrived to pick up Wanda from preschool today. Her teacher said to me – and I kid you not - 'She's going to be running this place soon!' " I just stared at mom and immediately roared with laughter. That kid.

But despite all her independence and determination to take care of herself, there were still the delightful reminders that Wanda was indeed just a little girl. One day she came up to me to get the mail. I was delivering those infernal advos— the coupon-filled mailer we deliver on Tuesdays. I was trying to fold it so she could take it in her little hands as she was trying to grab it. Finally, she apparently realized the problem, looked up at me with those huge eyes, and said, "You hafta start it." I laughed and finally gave her the mail.

As I walked away I said, "Wanda, you are adorable."

Her: "Yeah, thanks." Again I say, that kid!

———✺———

A few months before I retired I was greeted by Wanda in a special outfit. She was attired in a very fancy dress. The conversation went like this:

ME: "Are you a princess today?"

HER: "Yes, I am a princess. I am Anna from Frozen."

About this time mom shows up in the doorway.

ME: "Oh, I have heard about that movie. Do you like the movie Frozen?"

HER: "Yes, I like it. Do you like that movie?"

ME: "Well, I haven't seen it yet."

I wish you could have seen her face. It was a mixture of disbelief/disgust/disdain and several other "dis" words.

HER: (with what I would describe as an incredulous lilt in her voice) "You haven't seen it?!!?"

ME: "No, do you think I should watch it sometime?"

HER: "Well," (wait for it . . . wait for it . . .), "maybe when you are a bit older, you can come over to our house and watch it."

I am not sure who was struggling more not to laugh, mom or me. I just could not figure out if Wanda thought I was not mature enough to handle the subject matter, or what.

ME: "Well maybe I can do that sometime . . . when I am a bit older."

As I turned to go, mom looked at me and said, "I'll bet I'm going to read about this on (social media), aren't I?"

(Yup).

The postscript to this story is that several months after I retired—when I was apparently old enough—I was invited over to Wanda's house to watch the movie with her and her mom. Mom made popcorn and Wanda and I watched the movie together. Or rather, I watched it while Wanda acted out the scenes in her living room, including using the stairs in their house as a prop at the appropriate time in the movie.

I was interviewed by a local radio station for my last day (details later). The man who did the interview had walked around with me for about an hour with my radio in my pocket playing classical music as per usual. So in the background as I am talking about my career you could hear the music. Wanda and her mom were listening to the radio as my interview aired. Her mom contacted me with this little tidbit: "I just listened to your interview with Wanda next to me. She said, 'Mom, did he say Merrit? He's our friend and that's his music."

―――― ∞ ――――

As I said, Frida was involved with the first story that caused me to start chronicling these precious moments with my route kids. Appropriately enough, she was also the center of one of the last fabulous encounters I had with these amazing little ones.

This happened just a few weeks before I retired and is a memory I will clutch to my heart for the rest of my days.

Frida was older now, about six, with two younger brothers. All three kids were terrific and the family had become very dear to me. One day toward the end of my route I could hear a child wailing in the distance. Someone was really upset about something. I had no idea who it was.

A couple minutes later I could see an adult walking about three blocks away with a stroller and another child walking a considerable distance behind. The wailing was louder. I did not wear my glasses while I walked my route, so I couldn't tell who it was or even if I knew them.

I drove to my next section and was preparing the mail at the back of my car. At about that time Frida's mom came walking through my route with one kid in tow and Frida walking 15 or 20 yards behind, crying very loudly. She was obviously the child I had heard bawling a few minutes earlier. I was stunned. Frida was always pleasant and a total delight to be around. There had to be a story behind this. I looked at her mom, trudging along with a resigned expression on her face.

ME: "What is she so upset about?"

MOM: "I have no idea. But she has been like this for several minutes."

At this point Frida had come up to where I was at the back of my car. Her sweet face was tear-stained and she was quietly sobbing. I felt like I wanted to try to do something. Having been a parent of little ones about 150 years ago, I knew maybe she just needed something to get her mind out of that "crazy cycle."

ME: "Frida, did you get a new haircut?" (She had, and it was ridiculously cute and adorable.)

FRIDA: (sniffling), "Y-y-yes."

ME: "Wow; that is really cute."

FRIDA: "Th-th-thank you." (slightest whisper of a smile).

ME: "May I come over closer to you and see it better, especially the back?"

FRIDA: "Y-y-yes."

I walked over and checked out her cute haircut.

ME: "Wow. That is completely beautiful."

FRIDA: "Thank y-you." (somewhat more genuine smile now).

ME: "So do you have a whole bunch of new boyfriends now?"

FRIDA: "Nooooo!" (bigger smile).

ME: "Well, you better watch out because they are going to want to hang around you with that beautiful haircut."

In that way that only little girls can, she sighed indignantly. They then continued on their way and I went back to my car and continued to prepare my mail for the section I was about to deliver. When I looked back at the family, Frida was walking hand-in-hand with her momma, chattering away about something. Mom caught my eye and mouthed "thank you." This will always be one of my favorite moments, with one of my favorite families, and one of my favorite sweet little route kids.

Frida and brother Lance.

Wanda

I want to also mention that after I retired Wanda's mom hand-crafted a sweet pendant for me. In the pendant are a group of little charms regarding my son. It was and is a very treasured gift.

The pendant Wanda's mom made for me.

I hate to walk away from these two chapters because my route kids were the best part of what I did for 30 years. Just typing these pages has flooded me with sweet memories and an occasional teary eye in thankfulness. So let me publicly say in print: Thank you so much all you parents who entrusted me to chat with, get to know, and become friends with so many of your precious little ones. Believe me, it was a trust received that I never took for granted.

We have talked about encounters with weather, dogs, my coworkers, some regular customers, and the kiddos. But sometimes those encounters . . . they . . . er . . . didn't really fit neatly into any category. They just . . . well, read for yourself.

Chapter 20

AND THEN THERE WAS THE TIME . . .

"A crunchy, muted sound"

We all have those moments. Random. Without warning. Unplanned. They happen and we look around and think, "What the heck was that? What just happened? Say what?" Hopefully most of them are pleasant or even funny. I had my share—that's for certain. Like the other chapters, some of these I recorded on social media. Take a look.

September 23, 2011

Two days ago I was delivering to an apartment complex on my route. A young man and woman were having a discussion just out of earshot. As I made my way past them the man asked me, "Sir, do you know who these two guys are?" He was pointing to two nine-inch figurines standing on the hood of his car.

I looked and answered because it was quite obvious who they were. "Yeah, it's Laurel and Hardy."

He looked at the girl and said, "See, I told you."

I glanced at her and asked, "Who did YOU think they were?"

Her response: "I thought they were . . . (WAIT FOR IT) "the Jonas Brothers." Unbelievable. I was still laughing ten minutes later.

I have a five-plex on my route. The apartments are lined up on my right as I walk in, one after the other. There is a small sidewalk running parallel to the left of them that I traverse and then deliver to each one. After I reach the last apartment in the back, I re-trace my steps back out to the main sidewalk.

A few years back I had just delivered to the third apartment when two men walked past me headed back out to the street. We nodded and said "hey." I continued to walk, fingering through the letter mail in my right hand, getting ready for the next apartment. I suddenly became aware that something didn't feel right. The ground was much too soft.

I looked down and was stunned to discover myself standing in about four inches of wet cement. I had left four shoe imprints behind me. Okay, SERIOUSLY!??! About this time the two guys came back. Oh, they were re-doing the apartment sidewalk. With a graciousness I didn't really feel, I apologized for messing up their work. They said no problem; it would be easy to fix.

I wondered then, and still do, why there was no warning sign, no blockades on the path—but mostly, why the heck they had said NOTHING to me as they walked past me, knowing the direction I was traveling and noting my attire. Did it really not occur to them that I was going to keep walking in the direction where the wet cement was and that they had posted no warning of such a hazard. Good grief. It's funny now, but I was not pleased that day.

⁓

One pleasant day someone else was most definitely not pleased. I was casually walking my route one early afternoon when suddenly I heard a siren in the near distance. No. Sirens, plural. As in many. Coming from behind me. I stopped and looked back and probably had a quizzical look on my face at what I was witnessing.

Here came a rundown little pickup screaming down the middle of the street with a homemade camper-like apparatus attached on top. The young man driving was disheveled-looking to the extreme, bent over the steering wheel with both hands glued to said wheel, frantically trying to escape trouble. He and it looked like something out of a Saturday morning cartoon show.

Flying around the corner in hot pursuit came one, two, three, four . . . FIVE police cars, lights flashing and sirens blaring. It was almost comical. Here was this beat-up compact pickup, weighed down by his makeshift camper—top speed probably in the proximity of 55 mph, trying to outrun five police cars through a crowded and narrow street and neighborhood. I saw little chance of future success for this Bonnie & Clyde character. Reports came back to me later that he pummeled into a nearby park and was finally apprehended. It's 20 years later and I can still see that kid and the crazy look on his face as he wheeled down that street.

———∞———

As the years passed it became clearer and clearer to me that Mailman Mike was fervently correct with his words that we were walking through people's lives and that we needed to respect and appreciate it. This was made clear to me again one day during the final year of my career.

September 10, 2014

This is not to pat myself on the back, but to encourage all of us to develop relationships with those who are put in our path of life. A young couple on my route informed me today that they are moving next week. I have only been their mailman for about 18–22 months, I reckon. I don't see them regularly, but maybe once or twice a month. After they told me they were moving, they profusely thanked me for my service and friendliness. "We have never had a mailman ever who showed the slightest interest in us or our lives, and we have really appreciated getting to know you." Then they teased me and said they "knew people" and were going to have me transferred out of state to where they were moving.

Sometimes those lives walked through me when I was not close to where those people usually were. One day late on a July afternoon I happened upon a young woman on my route, a good friend. Unbeknownst to me as we approached, she had just been struck by a hit-and-run driver as she crossed the street. She came up bruised and crying, but incredibly was not seriously hurt. But she was very angry. We chatted a bit as I tried to comfort her. I contacted her later that day on social media.

July 10, 2012

So I'm minding my own business today delivering the mail when this incredibly beautiful young woman walks up to me and hugs me and cries on my shoulder. Ah, the life of a mailman. Seriously, how are you doing? I drove by the park a few minutes after I saw you to make sure you got there okay, but didn't see you.

Fortunately, this customer was not very seriously hurt. But I did have a customer who met with a horrible tragedy. I barely knew the man. But one afternoon he was murdered in his apartment. This occurred within an hour of when I had put his mail into his receptacle in the mail room of the complex where he resided.

Oh, before I forget, I want to ask you a question. Was this you?

April 17, 2011

So yesterday I'm crossing Foster Road on 82nd Avenue on my route. As I'm walking by the Arby's restaurant, someone calls out, "MERRIT!" I did not have my glasses on. I shouted out, "Who is it?" All I could make out was the sound "ay." It was a male driving a small white car headed south. Was this you? Just curious.

If you're reading this book and this sounds like the person who called out could be you, please contact me and let me know. I'm still curious.

———— ∞ ————

Looking back now after being retired for some years, it has become apparent that I simply cannot remember everyone I delivered mail to. I wish I did, but it is simply not feasible. But there are two people that I will never forget . . . although I never actually met them. Of course, that would have been impossible. Well, technically, I never delivered mail TO them. I delivered mail FOR them to their house, although they never received it. Confused yet?

As I stated earlier I felt that it took about two years to become "one with the route," where I knew everybody and what mail they received. After I had been on route 55 for two years I realized that I had met everyone on the entire route at one point or other except for one couple. I never saw them outside. I never saw them through the windows. I never saw them in the morning if I had a parcel. I never saw them in the late afternoon during the normal time I delivered the mail to their house. I never saw them during the week. I never saw them on Saturdays, when I met several of my customers who worked weekdays. I. Never. Saw. Them. I mean, it was just strange.

The house was well-kept and the yard was maintained. What the heck? Finally, I just had to know what was going on. One day I knocked on the door of the home that I delivered to just before theirs. I knew this family well so I hoped they might be able to shed light on this unusual situation. The lady of the house answered the door with her two little ones at her side. After exchanging pleasantries about the day the conversation went like this:

"Betty," I asked, while motioning in the direction of the house next door with my thumb, "I was wondering if you'd be able to answer a question about your neighbor next door. I have been the mailman here for two years and I have never seen them. What's the deal with them?"

Betty looked down at her children and said, "Kids, go inside the house and play. Mommy will come back inside and read to you in a couple minutes." Then she stepped out onto the porch and shut the door.

Now I was really curious. This was very cryptic. The story she unfolded was ultra-strange and a bit sad. Apparently the couple who had lived next door had died suddenly about three years before. Although they were somewhat elderly, their deaths had been unexpected. Not violent, just sudden. Their daughter had been unable to cope with her grief.

Although she was a fully functioning adult with a job and a life, she was convinced in her mind that somehow and sometime her folks were going to come back and live in the house again. In addition to still having all the utilities in their name, which is why they were still receiving regular mail delivery, she came over to the house EVERY DAY to put out a place setting at the table for them, and once a week she changed the sheets on their bed. But, there was no one actually living at the house! This went on for another year or so before the house was finally sold. I never did meet the daughter or hear what happened to her.

———— ✸ ————

Have you ever had those moments when things just seem like they don't belong?

July 17, 2014

Today while delivering the mail I saw an old wringer washer. A young man was working on it to resell. It was in remarkably good condition. I haven't seen one of those in 50 years.

One day around this same time I was coming up on a small section of my route. Although there are two or three nice homes on this street, it could be described as probably the most economically challenged area of my route. On this particular day I rounded the corner to enter this street and was dumbfounded to see a beautiful Rolls Royce parked out in front of one of the houses. Bizarre. It stayed there for six days and then just as quickly as it appeared, it was gone. No idea why it was there, and I never saw it again.

———— ✸ ————

And speaking of something being where it doesn't belong. Here was a truly idiotic maneuver. For the last 18 years of my career, I drove the same van on my route. It had a sliding door on the passenger side. For several years I loaded the van so as to retrieve the mail out of this side door rather than the hatch in the back. As I got older my shoulder began to cause me problems and closing that heavy hatch 20-plus times a day started to take its toll, so I started using the side door instead.

I'd load up my mailbag, reach my left hand inside the door to grab the handle, then give it a good sliding pull to shut it. One day after I finished dropping off a parcel I shut the door as usual. When it latched I immediately noticed two things. First, the sound of the door closing was odd, not what it usually sounded like. Sort of a crunchy, muted sound. Second (yes, I actually noticed this AFTER the sound), I noticed that my hand felt unpleasant and could not move.

Now, you must understand that I shut this door this way two dozen times a day, five days a week. And since as a mailman you're trying to be somewhat quick, as I slid the door shut I was already starting to walk away, so I would not actually watch the door shut.

Problem number one: this time I had neglected to pull my hand away from the door in time. The sliding door to my van was completely shut and latched—with my left hand still completely inside the door.

Now if this had been a regular car door I most likely would have broken my hand. But these side doors, although a bit heavy, actually had some space in the latch area. Oh, it hurt plenty. But I wasn't dying. But I also knew if I didn't get my hand free fairly quickly I was going to be in a heap of trouble.

Here was problem number two: these van doors were designed rather stupidly. In order to open the sliding door, you had to have two hands free: one to turn the key and one to move the latch. First you had to turn the key. And while the key was still turned in the lock, you could then move the latch. I had but one hand available.

But I had learned with experience that you could do this with one hand by turning the key with your left hand and then working your arm to a point where you had enough leverage to move the latch. It wasn't easy, but it could be done and I had done it before.

Problem number three: I had done this difficult manipulation with my left hand—which was now firmly entrenched inside the door.

Problem number four: I kept my key in the back pocket of my pants. On the left side. Where I would normally get to it by pulling it out of said pocket with my left hand—which was still firmly immobile. By this time my hand was becoming increasingly painful. The adrenaline was flowing (along with my panic).

In the years since, I have replayed the next moments in my head and I am still not sure how I achieved success. But somehow I reached across my backside with my right hand, twisted my arm enough to retrieve the keys, and then proceeded to turn the key in the lock, hold it in place and slid the latch-handle with my left shoulder in order to open the door. I was free! Incredibly, I had done no damage to my hand. It was very tender for a day or so, but no broken bones. Dumb. I mean, just plain dumb. It never happened again, and from then on I was especially careful every time I closed that door.

—— ⚭ ——

Late in the morning one lazy Saturday I had a parcel to deliver to an apartment—a parcel that required a signature from the customer. The apartment was one of a group of three duplexes over a span of four properties. In other words, there was a duplex, a house, a duplex, and then another duplex. I walked up to the door of the apartment and pounded on the door. I was immediately "welcomed" with the wailing of a small baby. The door opened to reveal the dad with red-blazoned eyes, looking like he had not slept all night. Which he hadn't.

He was not angry but quite bewildered and at the end of his rope. He had been awake virtually all night with a crying baby and had just now gotten the little one to sleep a few minutes previously. I apologized for the disruption, but he was gracious, understanding that I was only doing my job.

As I looked at the parcel to show him where to sign, I was horrified. I had gone to the wrong apartment. I was off by one building. I stammered out that I had made a terrible mistake and I was so very sorry for waking him and the baby up for no reason. I felt ghastly. He was frustrated, but incredibly he not only didn't punch me in the mouth, he didn't even yell at me. He mumbled okay and shut—but not slammed—the door.

That moment was one of the worst in my career. Several days later I quietly knocked on the door when I could tell everyone was up and around. I again apologized profusely. He was very sweet and said everyone makes mistakes and that getting the buildings mixed up was an easy thing to do. It was really quite nice of him to say, although not entirely true. Although the three buildings look virtually identical, each of the six apartments have individual addresses. If I had been paying more attention, the error would not have occurred.

———

But sometimes those moments had nothing to do with the job or the route, but just to yours truly. And because of the significance of a special moment, I will always associate a particular address with that moment. I was in the last few months of my career. The date was December 2, 2014. Jill and I had been looking for a house to buy for several months and had finally found one that fit into our budget and our desires. But the financial details were dragging a bit.

We got down to the final day of eligibility for our

offer. There were still a couple of hitches to the contract. We thought it would work out but obviously there are no guarantees in situations like this. Then we were down to 90 minutes. Was it my imagination or was the collar of my uniform getting tight?

In the early afternoon I knocked on a door to get a customer's signature for a certified letter. I had never met this woman before. She opened the door and I gave her the form to sign. I was standing only two or three feet from her. At that moment the text came through on my phone that we had been officially approved to get our house. I let out quite a loud whoop of joy. The startled woman took two steps back and said, "Excuse me?"

I quickly apologized for the outburst and explained my actions. It was all fine from then on. At this house over the years I had been bit by a dog and on another occasion had heard a piece of music over my radio that changed my life (see my book *Lessons from a Son's Life . . . and Death*). But when I see or think about this house from now on, it will always be where I knew Jill and I were going to get our home.

———

Sometimes you deliver mail that just doesn't quite make any sense.

July 31, 2014

I don't know whether you would call this ironic or just a poor choice of wording. Yesterday I delivered several calendars from the American Lung Association. The print headline on the envelope read: "breathtaking photos!"

And sometimes when the folks receive the mail they don't always make sense.

February 3, 2015

Because sometimes you just get to laugh. There is an exotically beautiful young woman on my route who has become a dear friend over the past eight years. Today as I was putting the mail in her mailbox, she opened the door with these words: "He is such an idiot!" She saw me and immediately began stammering that she didn't mean me, as the others in the house started laughing. I said, "Well that is the rudest welcome I have gotten in quite some time." She kept insisting she was talking about someone else. Uh huh. Her payment for this infraction: she had to give me a terrific hug. So, you see, I still came out way ahead—and got a good laugh to boot.

And sometimes the thoughts that run through the mind of your humble letter carrier don't make sense.

June 30, 2012

Today as I was delivering I came up to a yard where a mother was playing the game "Red-Light, Green-Light" with her two small children. I knew I needed to get away quick or I would never finish my route at that rate.

And sometimes the surrounding neighborhoods don't make sense (although this is totally not funny).

January 21, 2014

New experience for me today. I had just started the residential part of my mail route when suddenly I heard: POP . . . POP . . . POP . . . POP. Having little experience with firearms I wasn't sure, but it definitely sounded like gunfire. Sure enough, nine blocks east of me there was a shooting at a gas station. Across the street from where I had been just 30 minutes earlier.

And sometimes, well, sometimes the buildings didn't make any sense.

April 9, 2014

Sometimes you have no idea what you might see—or might not. About five years ago a house was being constructed on my route. It was on a flag lot, so the front of the home was small and the side wall to the back was very long. As it was being put up, something just didn't seem right. I just wasn't sure what. Then it was getting close to completion.

Something was just not the way it was supposed to be. But I still couldn't put my finger on it. But then I ain't no builder (I am not allowed to use those poundy thingies to push in those pointy things), and the builders did not speak any English. (This is not a racist comment, but is important to the story.) About that time I took my two-week vacation (yes, another one).

When I returned, the house had been torn back down so that now it was only about half up. I asked one of the neighbors what had happened. Well, apparently the blueprints and contractor were in one language and the builders were in another, and in the confusion, they had neglected to add something vital to the construction of the house. There were, uh, no . . . windows included. Oops.

Oh, but wait. As odd as that may sound, I have saved two of the most bizarre moments for the end of this chapter. Because sometimes, well, the customers don't make any sense.

February 3, 2015

More than 15 years ago I had a young adult woman as a customer. I constantly had issues with her as she would leave her dog out in the yard, which means I could not deliver her mail. It was a fenced property, but the mail slot was up on the porch. Several times I was unable to make delivery because of this and she was frequently irritated with me because of it. Finally, one day she'd had enough. The conversation went something like this:

WOMAN: Will you please just deliver my mail and not worry about the dog?

ME: I can't do that. We are not allowed to enter a yard with a loose dog.

W: He won't bother you; just deliver my mail!!

M: Ma'am, I cannot do that because I could get in a lot of trouble.

W: I know my rights! You must deliver my mail and my mailbox is on the porch and I am leaving my dog out in the yard!!

M: Well, you could move your mailbox to the outside of the fence or put one on the side of the house.

W: I am not putting my mailbox on the outside of the fence where just anyone could steal my mail. And I don't want to put a box up on the wall of my house!!

(I pointed to the side of her house)

M: Then just put up a big slot.

(At this point there was a pause as she glared at me)

W: WHAT DID YOU CALL ME?!!?

M: Excuse me?

W (screaming now): I HEARD WHAT YOU CALLED ME!! I'M CALLING YOUR BOSS AND REPORTING YOU!!!

M: What are you talking about? What did I call you?

W: YOU KNOW EXACTLY WHAT YOU CALLED ME!!!!

She went stomping into the house while I stood there completely flummoxed as to what had provoked this outburst and what she could possibly have thought I'd said to her.

When I got back to the station my boss pulled me aside and said he had received a strange phone call from my customer. Strange because he knew me fairly well and what type of things I was apt to say and what I would NOT say, especially to a customer. He told me this woman had called up yelling about her rude mailman who had the audacity to call her a "BIG ----."

As the story circulated around our postal station everyone was cracking up at the idea that I would have said this to a customer.

The postscript to the story: the woman moved away a few months later. Then three or four years after that she moved back into the same house. When I first saw her after she returned she apparently had no recollection of our encounters (I didn't say anything and she made no mention of it and acted as though I were a new acquaintance). For the remaining years that she lived there, she was very pleasant and friendly to me. Ya' just gotta shake your head.

———— ∞∞∞ ————

And then there was this incredible incident. Please know that I stand a whopping 5 feet 8 inches tall and weigh about 175 pounds.

October 16, 2013

I know most of you probably see me just as a baseball-loving/list-making/karaoke-singing old guy. But I have very special talents, also. Several years ago I had a couple on my route that was . . . uh . . . .trouble. It finally bubbled over when the man at the residence called my boss to complain that I was stealing his Social Security checks and spending the day at the bar.

He claimed that he saw me at all kinds of work hours at the bar pouring down his money into my mouth. My boss realized the absurdity of this because: A) I was somehow still getting my route done, and B) it was not exactly my style. I don't drink and had never had an accusation like this ever made about me.

The man insisted that he KNEW I was stealing his checks. When my boss asked him how I was cashing them, he then claimed I had also stolen his photo ID and was using that to collect his cash. So you see folks, I am incredibly gifted. For apparently, at will, I am able to turn myself into a 6 foot- 5 inch, 240-pound . . . AFRICAN-AMERICAN man.

Like anyone else in their job, there are just those things that do not connect to anything else. But there also people and events that do connect . . . that you would never have seen coming.

Chapter 21

CONNECTIONS

"Imagine my shock and disbelief"

This is not so much an "it's a small world" chapter as it is a "we are all connected at some level with each other" chapter. These eight vignettes are entwined into my life on different levels and different intensities and occasional coincidences. One of them touches back a century in time. One reaches across the Atlantic Ocean. One touches my mother, another my father, and others touch my son. My wife is tangential to one of them. Even my former wife enters a tale. Two of the stories touch each other. There are only eight stories here, so let's jump in.

Mrs. Kimmer was one of the first folks I met when I began on my route back in May, 1988. She was 75 years old at the time. She was a feisty but very sweet lady. She lived by herself and took care of most of her own yard work and walked all over the neighborhood, including to the store— even into her 90s. I got to know her fairly well, but I'd only consider her an acquaintance as opposed to a friend. She didn't know much of my history, nor I hers. She was always very nice to me and we had many chats over the years.

The older she got the more active it seemed she got. I was her mailman for the last 17 years of her life. Right up to the end—when she was 92—she was physically active. In fact, she was tragically killed during one of her walks when she was hit by a passing car on a nearby street. The next week her obituary appeared in the local newspaper. Imagine my complete surprise when I discovered she had grown up in the same little town in Nebraska that my mother had. And I do mean little. Valley, Nebraska in the 1920s had a population of less than 1,000. The kind of town where I would imagine everybody knew everybody else.

Mrs. Kimmer was eight years older than my mom, but I can't help wonder if they didn't at least know of each other's families. My mom had herself been gone for over a dozen years by this time so there is probably no way I will ever know. Man, if I had only asked Mrs. Kimmer three or four more questions!

But a time came after I retired when I was way beyond surprised to discover a connection between a customer's grandparent and my father. I posted about it.

September 28, 2015

This is a very long post, but if you are a fan of "it's a small world" stories, you should enjoy this one. Here is the story: Saturday evening I was at a birthday party for my brother-in-law. One of his good friends who attended was a favorite customer of mine on my mail route. (This is the same woman who recognized Jill in our wedding pictures.) We got to talking about her past. She is a few years younger than me.

First, you must know that my dad grew up in the area of Baker City, Oregon, which is not a large city. Population under 10,000. He has been gone 43 years and would be almost 104 years old. As my former customer was talking she mentioned that her mother and grandparents grew up in eastern Oregon. I asked her where and she said near Baker City in a place called

Haines. Okay, Haines is a suburb of Baker City with a population of just a few more than 400. Nobody is from there. Nobody. But my dad was, which was amazing in itself.

As we talked I told her that my father had attended Muddy Creek High School—which I was sure she had never heard of—and had graduated around 1930. Now, Muddy Creek WAS a suburb of Haines, lol. It was dirt-tiny even back a century ago and has not existed for several decades. She looked at me and asked when he had attended there. Muddy Creek was a one-room school when it existed. Tiny, tinier, tiniest.

So imagine my shock and disbelief when she told me that her grandmother had been the teacher at Muddy Creek School from after the turn of the century even up to and including . . . RIGHT WHEN MY FATHER WOULD HAVE BEEN ATTENDING!!!!! Yes, my former customer's (whom I had known for only about seven years) grandmother would have been my dad's teacher in little Muddy Creek School—now nonexistent—a small part of Haines, which was and is a very small part of Baker City, Oregon, just about 85 to 95 years ago. Now that is just plain incredible.

As a walking mailman you have the privilege of seeing the span of life. I have been there when new babies are brought home. And I have been there when families must say a final farewell to a loved one. One sunny autumn afternoon the reality of those two life-changing events hit me within a span of just a few minutes. The end . . . and the beginning.

September 20, 2013

When I first started on my route 25 years ago, my mail-casing neighbor (who was a walking mailman for 41 years before he retired, 30 on the same route) wisely told me, "You are walking through your customers' lives. Respect and appreciate it." Well, today I was acutely reminded of that in a different way. I approached a house and walked through a gathering of folks and family remembering the life of the family patriarch who died last month, someone I delivered mail to for 25 years.

I was invited to share in the food, but instead, I offered a warm embrace and continued on. Not ten minutes later I was invited into a home to celebrate the arrival of the newest customer on my route, a little guy just four days old. As I was ruminating on these events later, I was struck again with the sage wisdom of my old mailman friend. I have been there at the first and the last for many customers. And for many huge moments in between. Mr. Green and baby Overton didn't know each other, but I was privileged to have both of them interwoven into the fabric of my life . . . and I in theirs. THAT is major cool.

Obviously my deepest stories and connections usually came from those customers who lived on my route the longest. But that was not always the case.

December 28, 2013

The long and the short of it. As I mentioned before, when I share these stories I always use different names to protect the privacy of my customers. This time I will share an actual first name. You will know why. I love how the people on my route flow into and sometimes out of my life, over different amounts of time.

The short of it: a young couple moved out today. I rarely saw them in the three years they lived on my route, and I have no doubt they will not think of me again. But while they were here we had some cool commonalities. They were married on August 13, 2011, the same day my wife Jill and I were married. The brides shared the same first name. And there was even a small Warner Pacific College connection; the woman had attended there and it is also where my eldest attended school. Nice family.

The long of it: Victor and Nan were on my route when I first started on it 25 years ago. They were an older couple from Latvia. I got to know them quite well. Nan went back to the "old country" for a visit about 15 years ago. While she was there, she became very ill and eventually passed away, never returning to America. I will always remember bringing the mail up to the door one day and Victor was sobbing on the porch. He shared with me what had happened. We had a few minutes together.

About two or three weeks later I met him on the porch again. He was quietly weeping. He told me that he was unable to bring "his Nan" home because the cost was enormous. He never returned to Latvia. Victor eventually remarried. A very nice and lovely lady. Then this year, Victor passed away. I will remember his joviality, his enormous opera collection of vinyl records, and his light and delightfully tasty Latvian pastries. A dear man. All five of these folks made an impact on my life and career. I am grateful for all of them.

These next two connections deal with the life and death of my son Elliott. I could never have planned these two (well, three) items if I had wanted to.

"Cosmic" connections. Two very nice ladies on my route let me call their sons by numbers instead of by their names. This posting is in no way to elicit any comments of sympathy. That is not the idea. The cover picture on my social media page was the last (and best) picture taken of me with my four kids before my son died two months later. (And it actually became the back cover photo of my book about my son's death). I will always remember when it was taken for that reason, and also because the date was May 6, 2007—5/6/7. A woman moved onto my route who had a son born on that day, May 6, 2007. I always called him "5/6/7," rather than his name. Neither his parents nor he minded that I tagged him with that moniker.

Elliott died on July 3, 2007 and I was curious about children who had entered the world close to that day. (Similar to the idea of the Blood, Sweat, & Tears tune, "And When I Die.")

Another young woman moved onto my route who had a son born just four days previously. Hence, I always called him "6/29." These women were both very gracious to allow me to address their children directly and to speak about them to their moms by these numbers. And I know years from now when I see them, I will inquire about their sons by asking, "Hey, how is 6/29?" or "What grade is 5/6/7 in now?"

Making connections with people is important. I am grateful for these two I shall never forget. The postscript to this little story is that I posted about this once again on social media 11 months after I retired. The mom of 5/6/7 commented, "5/6/7 wanted to let you know he is in third grade now. We loved having a nickname, especially one so special."

⸎

But before I knew of these two dear women, I became good friends with a single mom who lived toward the end of my route. We had no idea the tie that would bind us because of tragedy. Joanie was a cute little thing with a young daughter who is rightfully called a "Warrior." (Another story for someone else's book). I would see Joanie fairly regularly, though not daily by any means. One hot, sticky July 3rd as I was making my rounds she was sitting out on her porch. I was making good time and we chatted for just a couple minutes. We talked about nothing of importance. But it became a huge moment of remembrance in my life because of what would follow that evening. I wrote about it on social media.

October 13, 2010

Connections. One hot and muggy summer day I was about three-quarters of the way through my route when I stopped to have a short chat with one of my favorite customers.

I got to see Joanie from time to time just to say hello but on this particular Tuesday afternoon she happened to be working outside in her yard so I stopped and we chatted for just a few minutes. As I said, it was not rare to see Joanie, but it could also be a few weeks between visits so this was a nice surprise. We finished our conversation and I continued on to the end of my day.

After work I headed to the beach to catch my daughter in a concert in Astoria. Well, if you have not guessed yet, this was the evening that my son drowned at Cannon Beach. Over the succeeding days and weeks I was pressed with many memories and thoughts of the entire experience. Yes, I know that is a stupidly insufficient sentence but that is not the point of this story.

Many weeks later I saw Joanie as I was delivering mail to her house. She heard me approach the mailbox on the porch and came out to say hello and inquire as to how I was doing. She had heard about my son's death but had not seen me since the event.

At one point in our sharing she asked when it had happened. I said, "Do you remember the day you were working in your yard and we chatted?" Joanie's face scrunched up into a terribly pained expression and she began to cry and whimper, "no, no, no, no . . ." We threw our arms around one another and held on for dear life. Joanie and I became much closer because of this and over the next months and years we both knew we had a much deeper connection than before. I was no longer "just" her mailman and she was not just another customer. She moved out of town a few years later, but we are still in touch. Her being there on THAT DAY and our friendship following is another of those experiences I do not consider coincidental, nor a triviality. I am grateful to her.

Joanie wrote this response to my social media post: There are no words to describe how much this memory touches me. You have been such an incredible friend and inspiration to me these last difficult years. I will never forget that muggy summer day. My heart breaks for you still as I know the pain of losing a child never goes away. I love you, Merrit. I am so grateful for our friendship over the years that will continue for a lifetime. Hugs to you from sweet (Warrior Daughter) and "Joanie." God bless you always.

————— ∞∞ —————

Let's finish this chapter on a lighter note. And a far wilder and weirder one. As this story unfolded it started out curious, got bizarre, a bit creepy, and finally just one for the books. They say truth is stranger than fiction. Well, if I wrote this story as a piece of fiction, no one would show any interest. It's just too . . . bonkers? And I did receive permission from the customer to share this story and the street name. Cue "Twilight Zone" music.

March 2, 2016

About nine months before I retired one of my customers, who is also a social media friend, sent me a message about some nutzoid information she had discovered while rummaging through some papers in her home. She was reading through her contract papers regarding their house purchase (a home they had lived in for many years and for which I had been the mailman for several years before they moved in) and was shocked to discover (wait for it) MY NAME in the paperwork!

She had come across three sheets of paper, and one of them had my name and my former wife's name on it with an address they were not familiar with. The address was a house I had lived in from 1986 to 2002 and was about 40 blocks north and west of where my customer lived.

It took us a while but we finally surmised that she and her husband had submitted THEIR paperwork for buying their house on the same day and in the same title office that we had submitted OUR paperwork to re-finance our home and that somehow one page of our papers had become mixed up with their papers—AND that neither they nor we had noticed it in all these years.

Needless to say, my customer was a bit freaked out that her mailman's name was on her paperwork for a home she and her husband had purchased nearly TWO DECADES before. After more thought-processing, I came up with what I believe is the answer since as a mailman I have seen this type of mistake happen. Their street is RAMONA (don't worry, I am not giving numbers) and ours was RAYMOND. Similar enough that some clerk during a harried day could easily have gotten the papers shuffled. But still, really, REALLY bizarre.

In a much later chapter you will read about my brushings with two local media stations. But now I wish to share with you my deep love and affection for another local media station, one that became integral to the last eight years of my career as a walking mailman.

Chapter 22

PLEASE STAY TUNED

"One of my trademarks"

The days can drag. I mean, they c a n   r e a l l y . . . D R A G. Most of the time what kept me going were the encounters with my customers that you have read about. But it still helps a lot if you have something going on around you to occupy your mind. I am fanatical about listening to music. I have a very large music collection at home.

A dear friend once told me he knew of no one who had more passion for listening to music than I did (especially considering that I did not play any instruments). So there were a few years when I would listen to the usual available radio stations in the area. But the classic rock or oldies stations tend to play the same 168 songs over and over and over. So I switched to political talk radio for a couple years. That also got old and annoying. I tried Christian programming, which was great but also after a time it gets ho-hum to listen to the same teachers day after day.

After my son Elliott died I REALLY needed something to listen to during the day to occupy my mind . . . and heart. My eldest daughter Maria suggested I give All Classical Portland, the local classical radio station, a try. It was monumentally healing to me and I ended up listening to the phenomenal sounds of Beethoven, Tchaikovsky, Chopin, Respighi, Wagner, and a host of others for the final eight years of my career. It became one of my trademarks in the minds of my customers. They looked forward to hearing the sound of classical music emanating from my pocket—where I kept my small radio (no earbuds for this guy!)—as I walked down the street bringing them their electric bills and pizza coupons.

This little piece of minor technology helped keep me sane for many years.

I cannot overemphasize the importance of this music to me as I migrated and wove my way to the end of my career. The mid-morning host on the station, Christa Wessel, became a huge part of my job as she "walked" the route with me day by day. She became a dear friend over the radio, and later, an actual dear friend as we met and became good pals. She came to Jill's and my wedding reception and also attended my retirement party.

She was followed in the afternoon by Robert McBride who provided more tremendous music and was a much-appreciated "punny" humorist. (For a much more detailed overview of my relationship with these two and the radio station, please check out my book, *Lessons from a Son's Life . . . and Death*.)

I have already mentioned some lovely encounters I had with the cutie-pie gals Wanda and Frida that came about because of the music that accompanied me on my rounds. Here are some more moments that happened because of this marvelous radio station and the first-class folks who worked there.

May 18, 2011

Today while delivering the mail I was listening to the classical station as per usual. I got to enjoy the stunning First Symphony by Mahler, Saint-Saëns' delightful third piano concerto, and the gorgeous "Les Preludes" by Liszt. Hurrah for 89.9 FM and scrumptious music.

September 30, 2011

I was caught off guard and deeply touched today when a lady called in her financial pledge to 89.9 All Classical Portland in honor of her mailman's recent marriage. I knew who she was and that she meant me. And I was further stunned when on-air host and very dear friend Christa Wessel stated on the air that it was me by name and that I also supported the station. I was floored. Both of these dear ladies were at our wedding reception.

After I had been listening to the station for five years I was contacted by the station to be part of a feature to be printed into their annual report. I was beyond delighted to participate. Here it is:

November 30, 2012

All Classical Portland (the public, classical radio station here in Portland, 89.9 FM) just came out with their annual report. In it they have small features on eight of their listeners, including a mailman of your acquaintance. On page two are head shots of the eight of us, then my feature is on page six. There is a bust shot of me in uniform with my summer hat on, my name and occupation and these words that I penned (slightly edited): "My small pocket radio allows me to listen while walking my daily mail route. Life wouldn't be the same without Christa's sparkling personality and Robert's sense of humor. Besides the amazing music, I also appreciate learning little tidbits about the composers.

My customers know I am approaching when they hear Chopin or Respighi wafting through the air. Christa calls me the station's most rabid fan. She's right.

Used with permission

I was very honored to be used for this. And yes, I really did use the word "wafting." Oh, those people I mentioned are Robert McBride, who was formerly the afternoon host on the station (he retired in March 2018), and All Classical host Christa Wessel, who is the current afternoon host, and has become a truly dear friend.

June 7, 2014

Today some folks in a car were talking to one of my regular customers as I approached with the mail. I didn't know who they were nor did I recognize them. We chatted very briefly. I started to walk away and they called out, "Our grandson calls you the music mailman."

"Do you live on my route?" I asked.

"No, but when we walk through the neighborhood our grandson sees you delivering mail and hears the radio in your pocket." This little nugget made my day.

Here was a testimonial the station asked me to write for their Contributor's Corner on their website. I was honored to do so.

I was a walking mailman of 22 years. To pass the time, I carried a small radio in my shirt pocket and listened to various types of radio stations as I made my rounds. I had very little knowledge of, or regard for, classical music prior to July 3, 2007. It was on that day that my 16-year-old son, Elliott, drowned at Cannon Beach after getting caught in a sneaker riptide.

After taking a few weeks off, I returned to work. I needed something to listen to that would keep my mind occupied as I walked my 12-mile route. To just wallow in silence would cause me to spend way too much time thinking of, and being crushed by, nothing but memories of my son and overwhelming grief.

My eldest daughter, Maria, suggested I give All Classical Portland a chance. Luckily for me, I took that chance. The station had just hired a brand new announcer with a bubbly personality and a sultry voice. It was Christa Wessel. I took to the music and to her commentary immediately.

The fulcrum point for me came a couple weeks later when a stunning piece of music came on that seemed to define my son. As I listened I cried and cried. I could hear my son's personality come forth from my radio. The tune was called "The Lark Ascending" by Ralph Vaughn Williams. I was hooked.

Over the succeeding months, the music—along with the vibrant tones of Christa Wessel, and later Robert

McBride—took me through the roughest times of my deep grieving. Gorgeous music by Chopin would seep into my soul and I could relate to the melancholic mood and think, "Yes, that is how I feel today. Thank you for the empathy."

At other times, exciting tunes by Beethoven or Liszt would lift me up above my sorrow for periods of time and carry me on through the trying hours. And every day, Christa was there in my pocket to cheer and inform and keep me company.

I had the privilege to finally meet her and become friends, which made her presence in my shirt pocket more intimate and precious. I told her that it was just her and me out there listening to the music and delivering the mail.

As the years passed, many of my postal customers came to realize their mail was being delivered when they could hear the music coming. One little tot on my route heard some classical music coming from her family's radio one day and told her mom, "Hey, that's Merrit's music!"

I am retired now and have had former customers tell me they miss hearing the music as their mail is delivered. I cannot even fathom how I would have fared on my job the last eight years if All Classical Portland and Christa had not been there for me. The station became my lifeline during my workday, and I became passionate about what they bring to the community. Christa introduced me to a fellow station employee as All Classical Portland's most rabid fan. It is a title I carry proudly.

I love the fact that a person like myself can contribute even in a small way to the ongoing vitality of All Classical Portland. Everyone I have met at the station *is a first-class (a little postal reference there!) person who deeply cares about what All Classical Portland offers to the world. It is a tremendous symbiotic relationship. The station provides a wide variety of staggeringly incredible music that spans several centuries.*

As Robert likes to say, they play the "real" oldies. The on-air talent gives us vital and interesting information about the history of the music and its composers and players. Their sparkling and genuine personalities, plus the superb creativity and skill of those behind the scenes, make for a gold-medal organization from top to bottom, left to right, and back to front.

Our part in that symbiotic relationship is to financially support this station so they can continue to impart their skill, entertainment, personality, and information to us. We MUST do this. The idea that this treasure could slip away from us is tragic. They are an integral, vital, and NECESSARY link for all of us to hook up to. If all will give even just a little, it will accomplish so much. Maybe even allow someone to heal from tremendous pain. Please support. Thank you.

Used with permission

One week before I retired I posted this:

April 9, 2015

As you probably know if you read these posts, I carry my route with a small radio in my pocket, listening to classical music. About halfway through my route is a house with a large dog who watches me from the front window as I approach with the mail. Very responsible owners. The dog was never a problem for me. He would simply stare at me or pay me little or no attention as I came up on the porch to drop off the mail.

Unless . . . I DIDN'T have the music playing. Then he would get agitated, bark aggressively, jump around, and generally be in an unpleasant frame of mind. I never figured out if it was the music itself that soothed him or whether he just associated the music with me specifically and I had proven to be no threat to his household. Since I retired I've had customers tell me they miss hearing my music as I delivered the mail. Maybe I should ask the dog.

To this day I could still take you to specific addresses on my route where I first heard and was moved by "Romeo & Juliet" by Tchaikovsky, "The Butterfly Lover's Concerto," "The Lark Ascending" by Ralph Vaughn Williams (a tune that encapsulates for me my son). Or a place and time when Grieg's "Piano Concerto" brought me to a state of near sobbing from the supreme joy and beauty of the piece. The last years of my career without 89.9? Dry, lifeless, and heavy. Without a doubt All Classical Portland was one of the biggest tools God used to help me deal with the grief of losing my son.

A short time after I retired one of my fave customers sent me a social media post expressing how much she missed hearing my classical music. I'll share that one later. But I think you can easily catch my love for this fabulous radio station, the terrific folks who work there, and the significance that glorious music played in my handling of my son's death and working through the final years of my postal career. I'm grateful for it and them.

Chapter 23

THE INSIDIOUSNESS OF IT ALL

"Lots of damage"

Over the years no one has ever really questioned the idea that my job was physically demanding. If you walk 10 to14 miles a day (depending on overtime), while carrying a pack over your shoulder, in all sorts of weather, you are going to get tired. And, obviously, as the years progress that fatigue comes on deeper, more often, and lasts longer. But when I started I had already had blue-collar jobs of varying degrees of physicality, so the idea of walking around for several hours a day did not seem particularly over-taxing. I had no idea.

One day in my beginning weeks at the Multnomah Station I was having a conversation with one of the many old-timers who had put in multiple decades distributing the mail to the masses. He looked me in the eye and told me I would be shocked with the insidiousness of what this job would do to my body. Those simple words turned out to be a vast understatement.

As I write this now four years into retirement, I am aware daily of the costs and sacrifices I asked of my anatomy—and it is constantly putting out its "hand" for payment. I have varying degrees of arthritis in my hands, fingers, and knees. My ankles are completely shot, particularly my right one. In fact, I have to consciously be aware to place my right foot squarely on the ground when I am barefoot or I tend to walk on the right edge of said foot because the ankle is so weak.

The last several years of my job it was often necessary to coat my knees with a hot rub before bedtime so my legs would be comfortable enough to allow me to sleep. My left thumb is permanently strained from 30 years of holding a handful of letters as I trudged along. Just below my right shoulder the muscles have bunched up into a bump from the pressure of carrying my mailbag. It looks much like two tectonic plates were pushed together to sprout a large hill. Fortunately, that particular item causing me zero discomfort, it just looks odd. It was caused by carrying that mailbag off my right shoulder for 70,000 miles. Which also caused two bouts with "dead" shoulder. Anyway, you get the idea.

I don't list these issues to elicit sympathy (nor to push you away). On the other hand, in the interest of full disclosure, during the first years of my career I suffered from very intense back pain from time to time. This pain came more often and hurt more deeply as the years passed. It got so bad that at one point I had to re-learn how to walk. Let me explain.

— ∞ —

When I was a kid I was very small for my age. Nearly every year I was the shortest kid in my class. As I hit my teens I started playing sports with the other boys in my neighborhood on a regular basis. Again, except for the much younger kids who would occasionally join us, I was much smaller than all the other guys. As we played throughout the area I learned that if I was going to keep up with these larger specimens I was going to have to change the size of my gait.

Some of these boys were considerably taller than I was and we were always running around everywhere. So I deliberately extended the length of my steps so I could casually keep up with their pace without resorting to jogging alongside of them. Which was fine. Until I started daily carrying a mailbag on my shoulder and walking multiple miles.

That unnatural step I had developed began to take a serious toll on my frame and led to issues with my back and feet. Plus, it was at this time we discovered that my hips did not work properly. Apparently a woman's hips rotate differently while walking than a man's do. And my hips— while attached to a male body—were rotating like a woman's. Which was piling on to the above-mentioned problems with my back and feet. A funny moment.

As the chiropractor was explaining this malady and the reasons for it and moving my hips in slow motion to display the problem, my former wife Cynthia suddenly piped up with an excited voice, "That's it! That's what has been bothering me all these years!" She explained that ever since she knew me the way I walked just seemed off but she couldn't figure out what it was that was wrong. It also explained why two different times in my youth as I was walking down the street when I had shoulder-length hair I had been whistled at by guys driving by in their cars.

The chiropractor did an adjustment, showed me how to properly change my walking (shorter steps and putting my weight on my feet and hips differently), and sent me on my way with all of us hoping it would significantly lower the level of my back pain. It took me months of concentrated effort to re-learn how to walk. I wondered if my customers could see the difference or my difficulties. But I was eventually successful. And while it did indeed give a semblance of relief, my back issues were much more serious than we anticipated.

I vividly remember one particular sunny day when I was about halfway through my route. I had not had any back issues in a few months. I was walking down the sidewalk when, without any warning whatsoever, I was suddenly on my hands and knees, facing that hard concrete with incredible pain. It had come from nowhere like a knife blade. Finally, about a year later, the day after Memorial Day, it struck with enough intensity that I could barely walk.

Over the years I had taken a pharmacy full of anti-inflammatory painkillers, and cortisone shots. I had been to more than one chiropractor and even tried acupuncture. Nothing fixed the problem. But finally it was time for surgery.

I had my surgery by the talented Dr. Z in July of 2001. One of the discs in my back had actually disintegrated to the point that tiny pieces of it were floating around in my spinal column. From time to time one of those slivers would slide into the nerves (I know, not very medically accurate but you get the idea) in my back and cause excruciating pain. It was one of these slivers that had brought me to my knees.

Dr. Z removed two of my discs and inserted two titanium screws. They made me one-eighth of an inch taller and finally did the trick—the answer to my years of terrible discomfort. I made a fabulous recovery, returning to part-time work two months ahead of schedule, and back to full-time duty also two months early. This was such a momentous change in my life that even a year after I retired I was still looking back on it with thankfulness and relief.

July 19, 2016

It was 15 years ago this morning that my health changed dramatically for the better. I had suffered from back pain—sometimes quite intense and debilitating—for several years. Over the course of time I had missed well over six months of work due to this ailment. Then I had back surgery at the capable hands of Dr. Z from Kaiser. Between him and his assistant, Mr. Oliver, they got me healthy for the first time in years. My home therapy: they told me I needed to . . . walk. Yeah, fairly certain I could do that.

Anyway, with the help of my kids, the doctors, and some rare self-determination from myself, I was back to work two months ahead of schedule. I never missed another minute of work from back pain for the rest of my career. There were times in the months following the surgery when I would be walking my route, suddenly remember/realize that I was in no pain whatsoever, and silently weep at the sheer joy of it. It was definitely a game-changer.

There was one odd regret I had about the months I was off work from the back surgery. Like all of us who have a job where we work with the same folks year after year, one of the things you share are the national news events that then entail numerous "water-cooler" conversations. When you are a mailman you also have those types of conversations with your customers. I remember being in the office at Multnomah when we heard about the Challenger Space Shuttle explosion. I can take you to the exact spot on my route when I heard about the Columbia disaster. September 11, 2011 happened while I was recuperating on my couch with a hard-shell brace surrounding my torso. I certainly shared the horrors of that day and the ones following with my family and friends.

But it was "strange" (for lack of a better word) to not share those moments of sorrow and anger and unity that we all felt as Americans during that time with my coworkers and customers. By the time I returned to work, several months had slipped by. Just a weird thought that I have kicked around in my brain a time or two.

I was very thankful about one of my back injuries I had before my corrective surgery, however. In the fall of 1992 I was off work for about three weeks. My mother was dying from cancer at the time. During the final few weeks of her life my brother and his wife graciously moved my mother in with them to care for her and make her as comfortable as they could. Because of my injury I was able to visit with my mom nearly every day the final week or two of her life. I hold those last times with her very dearly to my heart.

The rest of my anatomy? Well, it seems to be common for folks to get this incorrect idea that we as mail carriers skip on down the street, whistling to ourselves at the sheer delight we must have of meandering through our neighborhoods, soaking up the sunshine as we are paid to get all this wonderful free exercise. Uh huh. As the years piled on, I began to express myself on the health issues I was facing. Again, not to complain, but to inform and let folks know (especially my customers) what I was facing as the miles added up on my body's odometer.

There were also the injuries that occurred on the job. Nearly all letter carriers get hurt from time to time. I tend to be . . . umm . . . clumsy. I fell down a lot as I got older. Plus the regular aches and pains of advancing age. Oh, remember when I got charged by the pit bull and fell on my elbows and hurt my quad? Those injuries hung on for quite a while. The attack happened in late November 2009. It was still an issue almost three months later.

February 23, 2010

Well it took 12 1/2 weeks, but I finally carried my entire route again today. I felt good. Very tiring. And begs the question. What in the heck am I doing walking 12 miles a day at the age of 54?

March 19, 2010

It's amazing how long it takes a 54-year-old to heal. Fifteen weeks and I still hurt at the end of the day/week. The doctor says back to physical therapy for me. I'm not discouraged. I'm just sayin'.

The single most punished spot on me was my right ankle. When I was 16, I fell down a flight of stairs and tore it up bad enough to spend several weeks on crutches. So I was starting out with one foot . . . er, ankle . . . already in the grave. Over the years I would estimate I sprained that ankle another 10 or 12 times. But nothing prepared me for the tumble I took in March 2012.

I was carrying a section on an unfamiliar route. I came up to a business on the corner of a very busy intersection. The walkway down from the mailbox was much like a pitcher's mound, except not constructed of dirt, but of asphalt. I placed the mail in the box and as I stepped to my right my ankle hit the downward curve of that mound and gave out. I rolled on and over it completely, tumbling down to the sidewalk. It swelled way more than it had ever swollen before, looking as if someone had shoved a golf ball under the skin. This was bad. Very bad. And was going to cause me to miss many weeks of work. I texted my coworker Arlen and asked if he thought folks would be mad at work for me missing some more time. I sent him a pic of my ankle. "Wow! No one is going to be mad when they see this photo!"

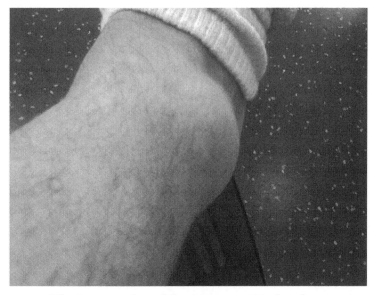

That's not my knee folks, it's my sprained and very swollen ankle.

March 23, 2012

Sometimes being old just sucks. I was delivering a section on an unfamiliar route today and severely sprained my ankle on some steeply sloped asphalt. Ankle completely rolled under me and I fell down. X-Rays were negative but my ankle is very swollen and sore. Off work at least a week. I type this with my teeth clenched in frustration. Grrrh.

April 2, 2012

Arggh! Went to the doctor today. My ankle is very badly sprained. Which means there COULD be pulled ligaments, tendons . . . who knows. I go to see the occupational doctor on Friday, but as it looks know, I will possibly be off a month or two. Dummy me, I don't do this in winter to miss all the snow/ice/freezy stuff, or the summer with the stupid hot weather. Nooooooo, I'm gonna miss one of my fave times of the year . . . SPRING!

April 6, 2012

Egads. Just came from seeing the occupational doctor. My ankle sprain is between a 2 or 3 out of 4 as regards to severity. Three more weeks at home before I can even start light duty at work. Physical therapy starts next week. She was surprised how bruised and swollen I am after 14 days. I showed her the picture from the ER. She called it "gnarly" looking. Gotta love those medical terms.

April 27, 2012

Finally back to work tomorrow. Light duty. Casing mail only. No delivery yet. Gonna get MRI done. Next doctor appointment in two weeks. And no driving yet. And for the first time in five weeks, we have a pair of shoes on.

April 28, 2012

Went back to work today for 2-plus hours. Casing mail at the office only. Came home, went to bed, and didn't move for five hours. I'm too old for this stuff.

May 9, 2012

Got MRI results back today. Good news: no breaks, tears, or stuff pulled off the bone. She (the doctor) was stunned at that and also that there was no fracture or break. She says I have a very strong ankle. Bad news: I have arthritis (not a surprise and not due to injury), tendinitis, AND LOTS (her word) of bone bruising and fluid buildup everywhere around my ankle. It may take considerable time to heal totally. Still can't drive. Still can't deliver mail. Next stop: orthopedics to see about ideas dealing with the damage and maybe more thoughts on how much damage there is and possibly a more specific time frame. To summarize: no breaks or tears, but lots of damage caused by a severe sprain that the doctor figured would have broken my ankle. I knew all that milk I drank would help.

This post got a funny response from J. Lee my substitute: "You'd better hurry up and get back to your route. I'm getting tired of answering questions pertaining to your whereabouts. I'm about ready to start telling people either that you and Jill have run off and joined the circus or that you're dead."

June 6, 2012

Yay. My doctor visit went well about my ankle. Starting Friday I can carry two hours of my route. I miss my customers and am hearing reports they miss me. Next appointment with the doctor is in two weeks and hopefully I will get released for even more then.

June 8, 2012

Finally, after 11—ELEVEN—weeks to the day from when I got injured, I was able to deliver mail today. Just a couple hours' worth, but it was nice. Customers missed me. Remarked I had lost some noticeable weight. (A horrid cold, the flu, a kidney stone, and colitis will do that to ya.) I am sore all over, but it is a good sore.

July 19, 2012

Today, one day short of SEVENTEEN weeks since my injury, I was finally cleared and able to carry my entire route. I got a hug from a seven-year-old and "we missed you" from a couple customers who I thought didn't even know who I was, much less cared about me being gone. It was nice.

July 31, 2012

Eighteen and one-half weeks after my ankle injury, I have been released and cleared completely by my doctor. She said it was a very severe sprain and the ligament that runs across the top of my foot will probably cause me problems for another eight months or so and that my ankle will probably never totally heal to what it was before. But it is all looking good and she says I have done very well considering the severity of the injury.

The severity of this sprain had truly caught me off guard. And a year later I was still having issues.

March 23, 2013

It was a year ago today that I fell while doing a section on another route and severely sprained my ankle. It is incredible to me how much trouble it still gives me lo these 12 months later.

As I said, I did vastly more damage to my right ankle than my left during my career. But ol' lefty was not immune.

July 31, 2013

My body is breaking down on me . . . again. Rolled over on my ankle—the left one this time—at work on Monday. I finished the day but went to the doctor today. Nothing torn but I stretched out two sets of muscles in my foot. So I will be off the rest of this week, and inside duty only next Tuesday and Wednesday till I see the doctor again. I'm too old for this. I told my doc after I retire she would probably never see me again except for yearly check-ups.

The ankle injuries—although there were obviously aging and mileage elements at work—were for the most part specific injuries caused by a specific fall. My knees, however, simply took the pounding year by year and mile by mile. It certainly did not help that I am knock-kneed AND bow-legged (thanks, Mom!), so arduous and accumulated walking was certainly going to take its toll. But a day came within the final two years of my career where there indeed came a fall that did considerable damage.

I was at a house that I had been delivering to for 25 years without incident. As you stepped off of the porch there were two steps leading to a narrow sidewalk that went through the yard leading back to the street. I had taken these two little steps 6,000 times with nary a problem. But this time I mis-stepped and plummeted to the slender concrete path, landing knee-first with a sickening crack-like sound. I had landed directly on my right knee and within 15 minutes I knew I was in trouble. My leg would not take my weight, and the knee was swelling quickly.

October 24, 2013

Annnnd, so, it begins, again. I fell on my route yesterday, landing on my kneecap. Continued to carry mail for about another 30-plus minutes. Then could barely walk, steps near impossible. A trip to the ER. A knee immobilizer, crutches, and home for an indeterminate time. X-rays negative, and ligaments strong. It's wait and see for now. It is not serious, just not sure what I have done or how much. I go see the occupational doctor next week. Rest for now. This is third falling mishap in 18 months. Grrrr.

October 30, 2013

I saw the occupational doctor yesterday. Here is the scoop. The front of my knee is strong and fairly flexible, which leads him to think I don't need an MRI because it seems to indicate no meniscus tear. However, the back of my knee is quite painful to any touch and has a buildup of fluid, which would seem to indicate I may have a tear. So I will get an MRI.

What we do know is I have a bruised/contusion/pulled tendon across the knee. I start PT next week. And I need to realize this will probably take many months to heal totally. My schedule at this point is I am off all this week, next week I work only about two hours a day—just long enough to case and prep my route for someone to carry. The week after that I am actually scheduled for a week's vacation, which comes at a very good time. By then I should have results of the MRI, will have had some PT, and will hopefully have a better grasp on what comes next, how much and how soon.

However, on this day I also had my annual physical. So just to balance things out, let me share about the good health aspect of being a walking mailman.

October 30, 2013

I had my annual check-up today. Other than the whole broken-down body, worthless ankles, damaged knee, weinie quads, and bad sleep thing, I am in excellent health. Really. Cholesterol is good (all four numbers), pulse excellent, breathing/lungs good, and my blood pressure is phenomenal. All of the above I mostly attribute to my job.

As time went by after the fall onto my knee we began to wonder just how severe the injury was. So my doctor scheduled me for an MRI. At night. Somewhat late. So Jill and I decided to make a "date'" of it as we celebrated being married for 27 months.

November 13, 2013

So here is something I have never posted before. Heck, maybe no one has. Today is our 27th monthiversary so we are celebrating with karaoke followed by . . . wait for it . . . an MRI. Yippee?

November 19, 2013

Okay. MRI results. NO TEAR!! NO SURGERY!! YAY!!! I will start carrying about one and a half to two hours of my route starting tomorrow. Will stay that way for about three weeks then increase assuming there are no problems. Continue with PT. Good news is that by carrying some of my route I am, A) helping my employer, and, B) building up knee strength, which is part of what my therapy requires anyway. I have swelling, contusions, blah blah, but nothing that hopefully is permanent. Except for whatever was there before I fell.

December 14, 2013

In health matters, I am now clear to be full-time with all duties starting next Saturday. Which will be just two days short of two months since my fall. However, my PT says because my knees and ankles have gone through so much damage because of my job and injuries, she advises me I should no longer go barefoot or even in just socks around the house. I should always have my inserts in, even while wearing slippers. My right leg/knee/ankle is especially weak and I tend to walk unknowingly on the outside edge of my foot to stay properly balanced. Which is not good. I will need to ponder this for a time.

December 20, 2013

GOOD NEWS: I have been released by my doctor and by PT. Tomorrow for first time in 59 days since I fell I will finally be able to carry my entire route again.

January 10, 2014

I had my scheduled follow-up with the doctor today about my knee. He would have totally released me except that I have had two very bad episodes in the last ten days. He says it means I probably have more damage than we originally thought, although surgery is neither necessary nor could help. He calls my knee "sloppy." It could be this way the rest of my life. For now I just need to take it easy, do my exercises, and wear my brace if it flares up.

May 16, 2014

I've been having some real severe pain and issues with my LEFT knee, especially going up steps, which is also straining my quad and hip injuries from my fall four years ago when I fell on my elbows avoiding the charging pit bull. Well, apparently when I fell in October and hurt my RIGHT knee, the left one picked up the bulk of the extra work in allowing the right one to heal, enough so that it has inflamed my arthritis. To the point that you can see the swelling just by comparing the two knees.

My age and the mileage definitely began to take a heavy toll as I hit my mid-50s (or more accurately, as they hit me).

April 30, 2011

Okay, I am just way too freaking old to be walking this much. I think my elbows don't hurt, that's about it.

As I got older I found it to be essential during my vacation times that I do a lot of walking to keep my legs in shape so that when I returned to work it would not be such a difficulty to get used to walking those 12 daily miles again.

October 29, 2012

Just walked three miles to start getting ready to go back to work next week. First mile was smooth and stride-ful. Last mile was sore and struggling. I am too dang old for this.

May 9, 2014

Well, I walked from Milwaukie to Portland and back to Milwaukie this morning. Don't be too impressed. Time to get my walking in while off this week so I am not crippled when I return to work Monday. Walking north from our home to Johnson Creek Boulevard I cross the city boundary. About two and a half miles round trip. One more time tomorrow or Sunday and I should be ready.

The great health issue about my job was that my "inner stuff"—pulse, blood pressure, cholesterol, lungs— were remarkable for a man my age. My annual physicals were almost always good. Well, mostly.

November 3, 2012

I had my annual physical yesterday. My numbers are excellent for a man my age. The only two real problems at this time are the arthritis in my left knee (which seems to be getting worse) and bursitis in my left shoulder, which may get worse or better. We will re-address these issues in a couple months. But guess who will need to start wearing a knee brace more and more often? This guy!

Off the clock it seemed that at times I was a walking accident waiting to happen. There was the time I stepped onto the cement steps leading into our garage while wearing socks. As my kid's mom said, one minute I was walking and the next I was just no longer there. My socked feet had slipped on the slick concrete and I had fallen as if I was going down a slide. I missed a couple weeks of work. There was the time I was trying to pull off the sock on my right foot while standing on my left foot, lost my balance, and yanked the sock in the wrong direction and sprained my ankle so bad I missed another week of work.

There was the time I was walking on the sidewalk leading to the Post Office as I was headed into work and mis-stepped on the curb and came crashing down onto the side of my face. It was Christmas Eve 2007 and a trip to the Emergency Room for me to celebrate it.

Two bouts of mononucleosis, which caused six weeks off work—each time. You get the idea. It seemed like in my final years I was always wearing some sort of brace or another to hold all my parts together. Ankle braces. Knee braces. Back braces (before the corrective surgery). Bicep braces. Elbow braces. Wrist braces. I was a walking advertisement for velcro. That amazing invention practically kept me from falling to pieces some days. I used to joke if some evil madman had come up with a device that melted velcro, I would have dissolved into a puddle right out there on my route.

It all came to a head about three months before my retirement date. I was recovering from my final postal injury and was at my final appointment with the occupational therapy doctor. I had seen him several times for three different mishaps over the years. He also was getting ready to retire and he kiddingly told me I better not get hurt again because he would no longer be there to treat me.

Right before he left the room he stopped in front of me, shook my hand, then cheered me with these words: "You know, looking back, you probably could not have picked a worse profession for yourself. You have poor feet, very weak ankles, wobbly knees, hips that don't work properly, and a history of back problems. I mean, my hat is off to you for what you have done, but with your body—"

I laughed and said, "Gee, thanks, Doc!" He laughed back at me, shrugged his shoulders, wished me luck and left the room. All I could think was, "Where the heck were you 30 years ago?!" I wasn't upset. I had enjoyed my career. But, MAN!

But as I said, my job may have beat the tar out of my joints and muscles, but on the important internal aspects, my numbers looked—and still look—great. This was all made wonderfully clear 18 months into my retirement. It was time again for my yearly physical. I was having some serious issues with my right shoulder (mailbag, remember?) and was genuinely worried I might need surgery, or at the very least, some lengthy physical therapy. I had my physical first with my regular primary doctor and then she sent me directly to orthopedic therapy to have the damage to my shoulder assessed.

The young man who examined me (when were 16-year-olds allowed to be doctors?) tested my shoulder in a few ways then sat down to talk to me, all the while looking at my numbers from the physical I had just taken. I asked him if he thought I would need shoulder surgery. His reply made me giddy and very thankful for my job.

"Well, I don't think so. We can probably take care of this with some good home therapy." This turned out to be true. Then he said this: "But look at it this way (as he continued to peruse my numbers), if you need to have surgery, it is much better to need orthopedic surgery than heart surgery." Wow, preach that, brother! I have kept that delightful truth pressed to my heart ever since, especially when I feel and hear the creaks and groans emanating from me on those days when my age punches me. Since we are on the topic of numbers, let's look at some others you may or may not find interesting.

Chapter 24

MILESTONES AND SOME OTHER NUMBERS YOU PROBABLY WON'T CARE ABOUT

"Just a hint of OCD"

I may be the only person who will be interested in the contents of this chapter. But I love numbers and lists and more importantly, well, it's my book. The two most important milestones are obviously my 30 years in the postal service and my 27 years on route 0655. I am very proud of those accomplishments. My least favorite number regarding my career is 10. Ten dog bites. Plus that whole rabbit thing. But this will be a combination of miscellaneous knick-knack information and the observations I made as certain numerical milestones came along. So pull out your abacus and let's spin the wheel.

Let's get the main one out of the way. The one most people ask me about first. How many miles did I walk in my postal career? Depending on when you ask me and how tired I am at the time and how sorry for me or impressed with me I want to feel, the answer I usually give is somewhere between 60,000 to 75,000 miles. I usually settle around 70,000. Here is the problem.

First, although I used a pedometer three different times spread out over several years, it is obviously impossible to be truly accurate. Second, my route went through three manifestations over the 27 years.

At the beginning, back in May 1988, it was about (we will henceforth drop the word "about" from this discussion since everything within this topic is "about") nine miles long. When I retired it was bumping up right at 12 miles in length.

Third, although counting the blocks can certainly help with establishing distance, not all blocks are the same length and this takes zero consideration for all the walking from sidewalk to porch and up steps, etc.

Fourth, not every day is the same. Some days you have mail for every (or virtually every) address. Other days, due to a lighter mail volume, you might skip dozens of homes.

Fifth, for many years I was working a lot of overtime including my regularly scheduled days off (my choice . . . ALMOST all of the time). And, as you have read, I missed quite a bit of work due to my injuries and falls, especially in the last few years of my career. Add in (or rather, subtract) sick days and vacations (which increased with seniority). So, to come up with any sort of truly close estimate is simply not practical.

I tend to be more conservative with my guesses so pointing at 60,000 miles is almost certainly much too low. Is it even possible I approached 80,000? Maybe, but I highly doubt it. I missed too much work. If I had to look myself in the mirror and be as accurate as possible I would say between 68,000 and 75,000 miles.

What I like to tell myself is that every year I walked the equivalent of traveling from Portland to Philadelphia. And my hope was that by the time I hung up my mailbag I would have traversed 74,703 miles. Why that number? That would be three full trips walking around the globe. That would be kind of cool. For this book we will use the simple reference of 70,000 miles. Whatever number we use, perhaps you have more insight to why I describe myself as a broken-down, grumpy, old, ex-mailman.

——⚭——

My best estimate (and this is very much a "wibbly-wobbly" estimate) is that I delivered somewhere in the neighborhood of seven or eight million pieces of mail, give or take an electric bill or two. That is a lot of paper (and way too many paper cuts) parading across my fingertips.

I suppose I should have kept track of how much hand lotion I went through, especially in those cold months of winter. There were days when I applied lotion at least every hour just to keep my hands from turning into sandpaper. By the way, have you ever kept track of how much mail you deal with at your home? Whatever it is, be glad you are not the President of the United States. The White House receives 65,000 paper letters per week, not to mention periodicals, plus 7,000 faxes, 21,000 phone calls, and 700,000 emails. I wonder if they have a secretary.

In the previous chapter I mentioned the problems I had with my knees. Seventy thousand miles of walking was certainly the biggest contributor to that. Here was the other part. I posted this three weeks before I retired.

April 7, 2015

People have asked me over the years how many stair-steps I have on my route. I finally took the time to figure out the answer. Somewhere between 850 and 900. Which, actually, is not really a high amount. There are routes at my station that have gobs more stairs than I do. It is one of the reasons I initially stayed on my route in the early years. That many stairs times not quite 6,000 times carrying my route = 5 1/4 million stair-steps.

Also in a previous chapter you read about the wonderful relationships I developed with many, many of my customers. This was written a year before I left the job.

May 7, 2014

Here are some other more personal numbers, also rough approximations: In my 26 years on my route I have known about 300 customers enough to have a "hello, how ya doing?" conversation with them on a regular basis. Another 250 I would say that I know/knew well. Another 135 I would consider friends. Another 90-plus I would consider GOOD friends and will stay in touch with about 50 of them after I retire. That means I have had some type of friendly relationship with nearly 800 customers. I feel tremendously blessed. I have 28 customers left that have been on my route the entire 26 years. I have lost about 130 to death. And I have had about 110 of what I call my "route kids." THAT'S why I like being a mailman.

That was posted on May 7th, the anniversary date of me becoming the regular letter carrier on route 0655 working out of Creston Post Office. I tend to be one who zeros in on key dates. When I came up on the 20-year anniversary of being on my route I received some lovely cards from customers:

"Thank you for 20 years of service as our mail carrier! And your friendship."

"After 20 years, you still show up! Very impressive . . ."

"20 years! It's gone by quickly. Thanks for great service . . . and for not macing me."

"Happy 20th Anniversary. Thanks for being a great mailman & someone we can count on to deliver."

"Congratulations on putting up with us for 20 long years. I hope you have enjoyed it as much as we have. You've actually become a great friend to us. We appreciate your dedication & hard work."

"Congratulations on your 20-year anniversary. It has been a pleasure getting to know you. God bless."

"It is great seeing you often and learning new bits of info on a regular basis. You are more than our mailman; you are a source of knowledge, often a bit of laughter to lighten our day, and a good friend. Congrats on 20 years of great service & friendship. And hopefully many, many more."

"It has been great knowing you all these years. I have always enjoyed our conversations and bouncing movie trivia off you. You've had some tough times and I'm glad we were here for you. "Congratulations on 20 years – that is quite an accomplishment. You are truly part of the [business name] and I'm still looking forward to seeing you coming to the counter!!"

"I enjoy seeing my friend on a regular basis. 20 years at one job is quite an achievement and you should be proud. I appreciate our growing friendship. Stay strong, and when you need it I will always have a hug for you."

May 6, 2011

23 years ago tomorrow I walked into Creston Post Office for the first time. I've been on the same route all these years. I've had mostly fabulous customers and I try to have a Norman Rockwell mailman type relationship with them. I've been blessed. And it was MUCH easier when I was only 32.

May 7, 2013

I have been the mailman on my route 25 years today. I walked into Creston Post Office on May 7, 1988 as green as could be. Since then the friends I have made among my coworkers and on my route are beyond value. I was a mere lad of 32 with two little ones that first day. Maria was not yet 4 and Faitha only 2 years old. I have since delivered my route 5,000-plus times through rain, sleet, blah blah blah. Only two carriers at my station have been on their routes longer than I have. I post this in honor and memory of those I have worked with and delivered mail to that have passed from this life. I miss you. You had an impact on my life.

On my anniversary date in 2014 I added some more thoughts to mark the day.

May 7, 2014

I had spent three years in the Post Office at three different stations. 26 years ago today I walked into Creston Post Office for the first time and walked up to the case of route 0655. I would never have believed I would still be at the same station on the same route over 2 1/2 decades later. What a journey. (Over tens of thousands of miles, actually). I post this as my last noting of my route anniversary date, for (hopefully) this time next year I will be done and reflecting back PERMANENTLY on my career. My blessings to the hundreds of coworkers and customers who have become part of my life story.

My other work anniversary date I never forgot was February 2nd, my hiring day.

February 3, 2010

I wish to offer thanks to my Lord as yesterday I celebrated 25 years in the Post Office. Many prayed way back then that I would land this job and here we are 275,000 advos later. AND my Jill gave me a surprise card and balloons. Hooray!

February 2, 2015

Thirty—30!!—years ago today I walked into the large United States Postal Service building at NW 9th & Hoyt in downtown Portland for my first day of work as a mailman. I had one small baby girl and was still in my 20s. As I ponder these last remaining months of my career, that day is still so crisply fresh in my memory. I had waited three years since the day of my testing for this opportunity and could not wait to get started. Of the original group of 12 employees in my training group, I was the only one still employed with the USPS five years later. I wonder what the rest of them ended up doing. Can you even believe that? THIRTY YEARS!!!!!

In honor of me reaching the plateaus of 25 and then 30 years in the Postal Service, there were small ceremonies at the workplace with middle-management folks coming out from downtown to read a letter of appreciation and give me a pin. I can so clearly remember in my early years of work watching veteran mailmen have these little ceremonies and wondering if I would ever attain those levels of seniority.

When those times did come and I was standing in front of my fellow letter carriers, it was quite surreal and I could not help but wonder if any of the youngsters in the audience were wondering as I had if they would make it that far. And speaking of seniority.

December 11, 2013

I have now been in the Postal Service as a letter carrier for just over 28 years and 10 months. When I started in February of 1985, I was somewhere around #1,080 in seniority in the Portland area. That is, over 1000 mailmen in the metro area had more time in the Post Office than I did. I found out today I am now up to #107. As a wise old mail carrier told me about 25 years ago, this ain't a sprint, bud. It's a marathon. Lord willin', I have about 18 1/2 months to go.

I referenced my seniority listing one last time two days before I retired.

April 28, 2015

Point of fact: when I started at the Post Office in the Portland area 30-plus years ago, there were about 1080 letter carriers here. I was of course at the bottom. As I retire, I am now #78 in years of service in the Portland area. Most—not all—but most of the carriers above me in seniority are driving carriers, not walking ones.

One milestone I did not reach that I REALLY wanted was to be Senior Carrier at Creston. To be the mailman at the station with the most seniority. When you are Senior Carrier it means you get first choice of picking your vacation times. You are the top dog in any item that may come up that is decided by seniority. Number One guy, ahead of all the other carriers. Mostly it is just a matter of pride. Mailman Mike became Senior Carrier at Creston and retained that title for many years. Which he never failed to let us know. I mean that in the sweetest way.

We all got a kick out of his declarations. "Hey, I'm Senior Carrier," he would bellow at the slightest provocation. Well, I wanted it. Bad. When Mike finally retired I slid up to #2, behind Dave, a carrier I mentioned much earlier. And Dave was older than me so it would just be a matter of time. Or rather, SHOULD have been a matter of time. The problem was that Dave wouldn't retire.

I'd mosey over to his case from time to time and "beg" him. "Dave, please retire. I want to be Senior Carrier!" He would just chuckle. And not retire. What was truly funny is that Dave could not have cared less whether he was Senior Carrier or not. So, sigh, I never made it. I had to settle for being second dog. Oh, well. Better than being third dog, I suppose.

The years continued to pile up. As I said, Mailman Mike finally retired. That was sorely difficult for me. I knew it was fast approaching. The guy had put in about 40 years as a walking mailman. But I desperately did not want him to leave. His last day was a very emotional day for me. It just tore me up to see him walk toward his car that last day, knowing I would not see it return in the morning again to bring him back to the Post Office.

Our last few years together were a total hoot. We fought more and more frequently but also with more affection between us. Not that everyone realized that. We found out about more than one new hire who saw us sparring verbally with intensity and volume and approached other workers with a concern that we might come to blows. It was NEVER serious. We were just poking each other more and more for the delight of the sport of it.

Mike is an avid fisherman. Specifically, a sturgeon fisherman. He is a bit of a legend in the area. On his key chain he had a metal attachment shaped like a fish that he had carried for a great many years. When he left the Postal Service, I was deeply touched that I inherited that fish from him. It is a very treasured possession and hangs on the wall of my study.

Mailman Mike's shark key holder which he graciously passed on to me at his retirement.

One day after work I was about to head home and got my personal gear out of my work locker and hung up my mailbag. It suddenly occurred to me that it had probably been quite a long time since I had cleaned out my locker. Um, maybe just a bit.

November 23, 2013

So perhaps I had gone too long since cleaning up my locker at work. Besides the usual crud we all come across with such projects, I discovered two coffee mugs that were shockingly old. One was emblazoned with the name of a furniture store

I have mentioned earlier that had moved off my route many years before. So that cup has been in my locker a good long while. Then I came across another cup buried far in the back. It has a cartoon of a bee on it. The caption reads, "Father To Bee." The two children born into our family since I have been at Creston Post Office were born in 1989 and 1991. So the cup is at least 22 years old and I have no memory if it was from a coworker or a customer. Still works, though.

I was in three parades. Or rather, I was in the same parade three different years. For those of you unfamiliar with the Portland, Oregon area and its traditions and socially important events, we are known for and celebrate the Portland Rose Festival every summer. It is a huge event. More accurately, it is a series of dozens and dozens of events around the area over a span of two to three weeks.

It would take far too long to talk about it on these pages. It is quite magnificent, and if you are ever in the area during the first weeks of June, you should definitely check it out. The kick-off to the festival is the annual Starlight Parade that winds through several of the downtown streets of the city. As you can probably ascertain from the name, it takes place at night. Lots of floats and bands and clowns and princesses. One of those floats is sponsored by the National Association of Letter Carriers. Several mailmen walk in front of the decorated float in uniform, waving at the crowds and having a hoot. I walked in the parade three times, much to the excited delight of my children when they were small. Daddy was in the parade! It was a huge thrill for them, and quite frankly for me as well. I loved it. And a couple of times during the parade I'd hear someone in the crowd call out my name. I'd locate the voice and see one of my customers frantically waving hello at me. Great fun.

Of course, I only walked in the parade in my younger days. When I hit my mid-40s that was just not going to happen anymore. What? Walk on my time off? On purpose? Without getting paid for it? I was too dang old for that stuff. Here are two other examples of that.

During my early days it was not unusual for us to head up to the mall and do some window-shopping (sometimes I was still in my uniform—what was I thinking?!) and spend an hour or so walking back and forth in front of the stores. Later on? Not a chance. But one memory of this type stands out to me the most. I had hit the age of 40 during the summer months and that fall our church had a weekend retreat down at the coast. That Saturday morning a group was heading down to walk on the beach.

"Hey, Merrit, do you want to join us?"

"What are you doing?"

"We are going to walk for a while down at the beach."

"Are you going to pay me?"

"Huh?"

"I said, 'Are you going to pay me?'"

"Well, no."

"Then I ain't going."

That became my mantra from then on whenever anyone wanted me to walk with them anyplace. Were they going to pay me? No? Then I wasn't going.

Here is another number that answers a question I have been asked a few times.

January 28, 2013

I delivered 108 pieces of mail to a business on my route today. I think that is a record for the most pieces of mail I have delivered to one address on one day in the 24 ½-plus years I have been on my route.

I set up one artificial milestone for my own sanity's sake. I had not kept track of how many days I had carried my route. But I wanted to note it.

October 11, 2010

I have no way of pinpointing the EXACT day, but it would be sometime around now so I am designating it for tomorrow, Tuesday, October 12, 2010. I will walk out the door of the Post Office in the morning to go and deliver my mail route (route # 0655) for the 5,000th time. Thanks to so many of my patrons who have become my friends and part of my "walk through life" these past 22 1/2 years.

Here was another number that meant the world to me. I posted this during the final weeks before I retired.

March 17, 2015

I will be tossing some numbers your way in the coming weeks as we head to the finish line. 28. That is how many individual customers I have left who have been with me the entire 27 years. The coincidence is that nine of them live within two blocks of one another.

I must share one more milestone with you, although it is not technically a postal milestone. But it is hugely important to me and it happened while I was in uniform. There is a charming little coffee shop just across and up the street from where the Creston Post Office is located. I am not a coffee drinker (if you cannot tell, I am not a person you want loaded up on caffeine), and I don't really partake of any regular hot beverage, especially in the mornings.

But one day on the way to work I found myself in the mood for a cup of hot chocolate. I had seen this little shop over the years but had never stopped for the aforementioned reasons. I pulled up to the drive-thru window and placed my order. The man who waited on me was the owner and very friendly. He gave me my hot chocolate and I headed off to work.

After I got myself situated at my case I grabbed the cup and sat down to have a few minutes of peace before the workday got under way. On top of the cup was one of those little stickers that covers the hole that you drink from so your beverage doesn't spill. I had recently become a bit more conscious of recycling and waste so instead of tossing this tiny piece of stickiness away, I stuck it to my mail case. I had no way of knowing I had just kicked into gear a behavior that would grab my limited OCD and create a delightful monster.

The hot chocolate was heavenly. I found out years later that the secret ingredient was just the proper amount of vanilla. Anyway, a few days later I tried another cup. And again placed the sticker on my case, right next to the original one. This became part of my morning routine about two or three days a week for the remainder of my career. It lasted through five owners, several baristas, and one name change. Uh, not MY name. The name of the shop.

I cannot remember the original name, but it has been Speedboat Coffee for many years now. So as the years kept piling up, so did the hot chocolates . . . and . . . the little stickers piled onto my case at work.

After several years of being a regular customer I got to wondering one day and wondered just how many cups of hot chocolate I had purchased. It was easy enough to figure out. I merely had to count the stickers. There were . . . hundreds! That first count ended up at 500 and some! (Unfortunately, I had lost track of where the original sticker had been placed). The years, cups, and stickers kept coming. Which led to these two milestones:

August 8, 2013

This is a couple weeks late. There is a lovely neighborhood coffee shop across the street from my Post Office called Speedboat Coffee. I don't drink coffee but have been getting the best cup of hot chocolate in town on a regular basis for many years. I put the stickers that cover the hole to keep the drink from spilling up on my mail case. I just celebrated my 900th cup of hot chocolate from this little shop.

And then ten months later:

June 27, 2014

A MILESTONE today. Over the past 11 years I have frequented a little coffee shop called Speedboat Coffee. Not for coffee, but for the city's best hot chocolate. They put little stickers over the sip holes in the caps. I have collected all those stickers over the years through four owners and many dear baristas. Well, today I had my . . . wait for it . . . 1 0 0 0th cup of hot chocolate from Speedboat. I had been letting them know I was approaching that number. WOW! Was I surprised when I walked in today. They put music on ("Celebrate Good Times, COME ON!"), brought out four Mylar balloons in celebration, and set off 4th of July poppers with a bang and confetti. Left me completely speechless. Thanks to Don, the owner, his wife Carissa, and their two lovely daughters, plus Alyssa, Sam, Wendy, Andy, Dowry, and a host of other fine employees over the years.

It was a very sweet celebration . . . brought on by an old postman with just a hint of OCD. Thanks to all of ya!!!! By the way, you may ask: Do you know what you could have bought with all that money you spent? Yeah, 1000 great cups of hot chocolate and the support of a nice, local, small, neighborhood business.

By the time I retired, that total number of cups of hot chocolate and the accompanying stickers had reached the dizzying number of . . . oh, never mind. You will have to wait till you reach the appropriate chapter about the end of my career. At the onset of this chapter I said my least favorite number about my career was "10," regarding the number of dog bites I received. The first nine were for the most part not traumatic. But during the last few months of my career, I suffered what became the biggest postal tribulation of my career. The stuff of nightmares.

Chapter 25

THE WORST DAY

"Listening to me babble"

Take yourself all the way back to the beginning of my story. My first day as an employee of the United States Postal Service. We sit down in the room and watch "The Dog Movie." As a mailman—especially a walking mailman like myself—the threat of a dog bite or attack is never too far away. As you get your own route and settle into it and learn where the canines reside you can attain a certain level of relaxed detachment.

Over the years I heard the horror stories. Someone at your station or someone who knows someone knows about a letter carrier that got seriously hurt by a dog. It happens. When the pit bull craze started hitting America for the first time in the late 1980s they became the new "boogieman." I remember when Sports Illustrated ran a story about the dangers of the breed with horrifying photos. (Although I have very strong opinions about pit bulls, this chapter is not in any way a political statement on how I think they should be dealt with.)

There was even an episode on the television crime show "Law & Order" about a severe dog attack. But as the years passed I felt like I had escaped. I had my nine dog bites (yes, yes, and the rabbit, I know!) but none of them had even been remotely serious. My worst experience had been the near miss from the unfamiliar pit bull where I fell and hurt myself. But an actual bite/attack from a pit bull? It looked like I was going to escape that dreaded event.

"Hey, all you mailmen who have not been attacked by a pit bull, take one step forward. Uh, not so fast, Hearing." I was within six months of the finish line. A new family had moved onto my route about six months before. I had yet to meet them. There was some sort of monstrous beast living behind the front door because most days when I delivered the mail he came roaring and smashing into it. I was relieved he was always indoors.

It was one of those fabulous crisp fall days where you can deliver your route in complete comfort without a jacket. It was Thursday, October 9, 2014. I could smell retirement, it was so close. This family received frequent parcels, which I always took to the back porch. Although they had a solid wood fence in the front of the yard, they had a back patio that allowed for much more security in keeping their packages from theft, which had become quite a problem in the area.

It was about 10:15 in the morning. I had a large package for them, so I parked my car in front of the house and walked the parcel around to the back. The back door was open but the screen was definitely shut. Someone was obviously home but because of the dog I quickly and quietly set the package down on the patio, walked around to the front of the house, and deposited the rest of their mail in the mail receptacle.

What I did not know at the time—nor did the homeowner realize—was that the glass partition in the screen door had fallen out. It was through this opening that the dog escaped from the house. I was about halfway back to my car when I . . . you know, even now I am just not sure if I heard him coming at me or more sensed it. I am also not clear whether he was barking or growling or just making noise with his running.

I whirled around and he was right THERE. Now I could definitely hear him barking as he barreled down on me like an out-of-control freight train. I had maybe a second to try to avoid him but it did no good. I raised my left arm, which was the nearest to his mouth, to try to get him to miss, but he was very large. And I started screaming at the house for them to come get their dog.

I never did find out, but my suspicion is he was a pit mix with a larger breed, perhaps a shepherd. He sunk six of his large teeth deeply into my left wrist and hand.

At this point it gets weird. I distinctly remember feeling as if time had stopped and clearly thinking to myself, "Oh my goodness, I am actually being bit by a pit bull!" Okay, those may not have been the EXACT words that I was thinking, but you get the idea. But it was all so very slo-motiony. Almost a surreal detachment for a few moments.

At this point I have a blank space of four to seven seconds where I don't know what happened. My next memory is of me laying on the ground on my back. The dog is seven or eight feet away from me, still snarling at me. I have absolutely no memory of him letting go. I have no idea whether I lost my balance from the shock of being bit or if I slipped on the grass or whether he bumped into me. I simply have zero recollection.

But my next move was the same as the time I slipped on the oily driveway five years earlier. I started to turn away from him and cover my neck, presuming that he was about to come in for a second shot at me. And just like five years previously, it was at this time that the owner called the dog into the house and thankfully it obeyed.

My guess is it was about now that I started going into shock, which will explain some of my behavior coming up. I looked up and saw the owner of the dog, a young woman holding an infant. As it turned out she had been in the front room nursing her son (one of the most gorgeous little boys I have ever seen). This explained three things: one, why she was home; two, why it took so long for her to get outside to corral the dog; and three, why the dog had become even more vicious and protective than usual).

I yelled at her, demanding to know if the dog was indeed completely secure. I was starting to feel an enormous level of pain at this point and was bleeding quite a bit. I now heard a female voice say, "What happened?"

The owner responded, "Our dog bit the mailman!" I could not see who was asking because they were on the other side of the fence.

But then I heard these sweet words of concern. "Is it Merrit?"

I knew the owner had no idea of my name so I called out, "Yes, I'm going to need some help!"

It was the woman who lived across the street. I had gotten to know her fairly well over the years. She was very nice. I was sprawled on the ground, unwilling to stand and quite honestly at this point unable to. One of them got me some paper towels to try to stem the bleeding a bit. The owner was hysterical, terrified at what had happened. I was still furious with her, but from somewhere I summoned some respectability and assured her that I would be okay—not completely sure if I actually believed it.

At some point they helped me to sit up. I felt too weak and nauseated to stand up yet. I got on my cell phone and called my boss Marsha to report what had happened and that I would require an ambulance. I then called my wife Jill and then my eldest daughter Maria to tell them what had happened.

I started both of those conversations with these words: "Listen to my words, not my voice!" I knew my voice had to sound strained and pained and overly excited, and I wanted them to get the facts rather than my hyper-emotive reporting of them.

Maria called her sisters and then her mother Cynthia, who in turn called her parents (my former in-laws, in case you have misplaced your program of players). They graciously made their way to the hospital to check on me and arrived 30 minutes or so after I got there.

Now during all this melee something else happened that I have no memory of. Or rather, I did something I have no memory of. Apparently at some point after I got my three phone calls made but before anyone else arrived at the scene, I began to rock back and forth on the ground and kept repeating these words: "I only have six more months till retirement. I only have six more months till retirement. I only have six more months till retirement . . ."

I'm not sure how long I kept saying this because I don't remember it at all. But both of the women who were there told me afterwards that was precisely what I did. My next remembrance is my boss Marsha arriving. I always enjoyed working for Marsha, and she became one of my favorite bosses I ever had. Now that she was there I could relax a bit. And boy did I. I am a showoff and storyteller by nature and am completely at home in front of an audience.

Well, now that I "had an audience," I went into Mr. Entertainment mode. I started joking with Marsha and proceeded to chat up a storm. It is obvious to me now I was still somewhat in shock, especially with what came later. The ambulance arrived with the medical techs. They wheeled me into the ambulance and away we went to the hospital.

Now, keep in mind three things. This was only the second time I had ever been transported in an ambulance. I was starting to feel a much higher level of pain (and still bleeding a lot). And I was as I stated earlier, most likely still in shock. Which all accounts for why I kept up my Mr. Entertainment spiel. I began telling all my best mailman stories (including undoubtedly the rabbit fiasco), cracking jokes and asking a myriad of questions. The guys just played along, listening to me babble while checking my vitals.

We arrived at the hospital. I kept up the chattering as I was initially checked out by a total of six doctors and nurses before they took me into an emergency room to wait for the examining doctor. I was finally and for the first time since the attack quiet and alone. Until Jill walked in. All my pent-up terror and pain and anger and worry and stress came pouring out the instant she walked through the door. Translation: I lost it. Completely.

I started crying and sobbing and shrieking and a maelstrom of words and fear convulsed into a crunch of words . . . some of which actually made sense.

"ItwashorriblethedogwassobigIwassoscaredithurtsobadIdontwanttodelivermailanymore." I am not ashamed to admit I buried my face in her arms shaking and weeping.

The exam went well. Despite the pain and all the bleeding, I was not hurt nearly as much as I could have been. First of all, the dog had only managed to bite me the one time. Second, although I had six very deep bite marks, no tendons or muscles were torn nor any bones broken. Most probably—and most importantly—after he sunk his teeth into my hand and wrist, he had then brought them straight out and then I had (although not consciously so) pulled away from him.

So I had no tears or ripping of skin. Just six deep, but simple bite marks. None of the wounds required any stitches. Which was doubly good because they do not as a practice want to stitch up a dog bite. They cleaned up the holes, wrapped me up and sent me home.

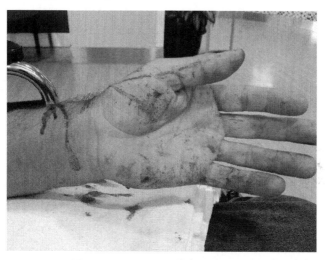

You can see some of the puncture marks in this picture.

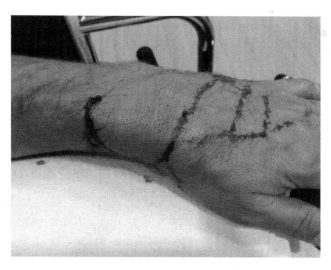

Two more of the bigger wounds.

While on the way home I received a call from my youngest daughter, Valeena, who lives at the Oregon coast. Her voice was shaky and she had been very worried about her daddy. "I just wanted to hear your voice," she quivered. All my kids had known the cloudy fear that was always in the back recesses of my mind about this type of dog attack. Once I assured her I was okay—relatively speaking—she was fine. Jill got me home and I climbed gingerly into my bed . . . where, as far as I was concerned, I intended to stay till my retirement date rolled around.

Although I had had no serious damage done to my arm, it was still very sore and I could do little with it for several days. Fortunately the harm was to my left wrist and I am right-handed. But computer work was out of the question for several days and very limited for some weeks. Five days after the attack I started to share.

October 14, 2014

Had occupational doctor visit this morning. So, here it is. As near as she can tell there is no tendon damage because I am able to move my fingers. There is definitely some soft tissue damage, but my hand is still too swollen to accurately gauge how much, or how severe. She anticipates I will be out at least five more weeks, basing that on one more week before I am able to start PT (due to swelling) and approximating four weeks of PT. She doesn't think I will need to see a hand specialist but will know more next week.

She guesses I should be fully functional no later than Thanksgiving (but no way of knowing how long this will bother, hurt, or affect me), assuming the damage is no more severe than she supposes. I still have to keep taking antibiotics (boo for my stomach) to ward off potential infection, and I need to keep my hand/arm more still than I have been. The really joyous part is starting today Jill has to scrub the wounds to help prevent infection. Which means opening the scabs and rubbing gauze over very, VERY tender skin and sores.

I was dreading the prospect of having the wounds scrubbed and was beyond relieved that Jill was able to do it. It was quite necessary because I had picked up a small infection in one of the wounds. But even with that . . .

October 14, 2014 (7 ½ hours later)

Just got through my first scrubbing of the wounds session. Delighted to have a wife for my nurse. She was great. But I did have "Deep Purple" on my headphones on volume level 8 . . . which is higher than I have ever used headphones before. It definitely helped. I think at level 9 my nose starts to bleed, lol. (psst, sounded FABULOUS!)

I do not honestly remember how many scrubbing sessions I ended up needing, but let's say that my headphones and "Deep Purple" got a solid workout for two weeks. The thought of it just caused a shudder to course through my arms.

October 21, 2014

Had my second occupational doctor appointment today. The swelling is mostly gone, so I can start PT tomorrow morning. I am still very limited with my strength and mobility. He moved my wrist just a bit past a normal place and it really hurt. I would describe my hand as able to grab, but not able to grip.

I will be off work completely at least one more week, but it looks—at this point—as if the damage is not as serious as we were initially thinking. Should know more after PT, and even more after my appointment next week. HOWEVER, I have been ripped off!!! This much pain and terror . . . and zero bruising. That is soooo not fair! Hmmmf. I wanted lots of purples and greens.

Not only was I disappointed with the lack of bruising, I was very surprised. As bad as my hand looked the day of the injury, the depth of pain I had, and the amount of bleeding there was, I assumed there would be wide and colorful bruising. Alas, nothing. And yet when the doctor moved my hand around the discomfort was quite high. That really caught me off guard, especially 12 days after the attack.

October 22, 2014

Had my first PT today. My hand is stronger than I thought, but my mobility is around 50% or less. I asked the therapist if she thought I could be 100% by December. She said she didn't think so, that that would be really pushing it. It took me back how poor my mobility was in my injured hand compared to my normal one, especially in the area at the top of my wrist.

But it wasn't all quite as clear cut as we had hoped.

October 28, 2014

Saw the occupational doctor today. My hand has re-swollen a bit again and is causing me more pain and problems than it was a week ago. Conclusion, although firmly convinced there is no permanent damage because of the mobility of my fingers and the mobility that I DO have in my hand, apparently the muscle damage is more severe and deeper than we were thinking a couple weeks ago. All to say, I am off work for at least two more weeks, while continuing PT. But I am allowed to lift/carry/push/pull no more than . . . ZERO pounds with my left hand. But I must add this: my employer is being totally and wonderfully supportive. I could not be more pleased with that aspect of this situation. But I miss my coworkers and my customers very much.

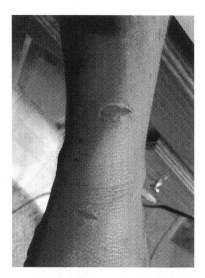

*This is the top of my wrist
three weeks after the attack.*

The road back to full-time work was very slow.

November 13, 2014

Update from dog attack. Starting today I am working two hours/day. In the office only, no delivering. Just preparing mail. Allowed to lift a maximum of two pounds. I will be at this level for the next two weeks. I missed my full work schedule for five weeks exactly.

November 26, 2014

Dog attack update: arm/wrist/hand are healing very well. Still a bit swollen, some definite scar tissue between the two main puncture wounds, but my mobility has improved. Starting on Friday (in two days) I begin delivering for an hour a day, increasing to two hours a day in another week.

December 11, 2014

Today I delivered to a street I have not been on since the dog attack, which is now nine weeks ago. I had my radio on as per usual. I was next door to a house where three kids were jumping on a trampoline. Apparently they heard my radio playing . . .

Kid 1: "Who is that?"

Kid 2: "Is that you Mr. Merrit?"

Me: "Yup."

Kid 3: "It's Mr. Merrit!"

Kid 2: "It's Mr. Merrit!! It's Mr. Merrit!!"

Yeah, that kinda made my day.

December 21, 2014

Ten weeks out from the dog attack. As of two days ago I am released for full-time duty. The doctor says I am about 90% with my mobility and at a 75% strength level. I will NOT let this define my career. I conclude with three gratitudes: that I was not more seriously hurt, that the time off work gave the rest of my body some much needed rest, and for the fabulous outpouring of support I received.

Besides missing five complete weeks of work, I also missed parts of the next five. The next spring, one of my coworkers had open-heart surgery and was back to work full-time in eight weeks. He missed eight weeks for heart surgery; I missed ten weeks for a dog bite. Hmmm. I keep trying to convince myself I am not a wimp. That previous post was in the last days approaching my last Christmas in the Post Office. I will share later about what I was feeling emotionally during this time.

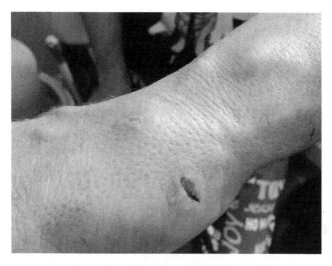

*You can still see some of the wounds
several weeks after the attack.*

April 9, 2015

Incredibly, today marks six months since the dog attack.

Discouraging: I am still uneasy about walking outside in my own neighborhood; my wrist has plateaued at about 90% healing (most days are no problem, but there are days—like yesterday—when there is still considerable discomfort and weakness); obviously, I will always have that terrifying memory implanted within my psyche.

Encouraging: I refused to allow this worst event of my job to define OR end my career. On Tuesday—for the first time—I was able to walk past and stand in front of that house . . . without feeling panicky. I have had terrific support during the healing process from my customers.

Conclusion: as always, it is mind-boggling to again be made aware of how dramatically a life can change in the span of 15 seconds.

I never completely got over my uneasiness after the dog attack. A few weeks after it happened, I started meeting with a professional counselor to learn how to deal with the terror that was gripping me. Many of the dogs from my route who had never caused me any trepidation before now became menacing threats.

There was one house in particular that gave me problems. They had a hugely aggressive dog that had never been a problem for me. It was behind a very tall chain-link fence and would come flying up to the fence snarling and barking like a maniac. He would need to be a professional climber to scale the fence, get across the shed, and somehow get over the top of the fence that had the sharp points at the top. Impossible. But I would freeze in irrational fear.

The counselor gave me some good tools to deal with it, and eventually I was able to get through the entirety of my route without issue. Two years later—long since being retired—it was apparent this event still shook me.

October 9, 2016

Today marks two years since the pit bull attack. Like everything else in life, it is hard to believe that much time has passed. Twice this past week in conversations with folks about me walking, I've had to be honest and share that I am still highly uncomfortable walking around in a public neighborhood, including my own. Which is why I go to the high school track to do my walking.

It still stuns me that this event had such a significant impact on my psyche. I wonder if I will ever fully recover mentally and emotionally or if this is just how I will always be in this one specific area of my life.

Well, even today, over five years later, I am still unable to walk around my own neighborhood with any sense of calmness. I tend to walk overly carefully, furtively looking around at the places where a dog could be lying in wait. It became quite clear that if this incident had happened to me in the first years of my career I would most likely have tried to hitch on with some other profession within the Post Office.

My hand plateaued at about a level of 95% mobility and strength. I never notice it, but if I think about it I can tell there is still a slight limitation.

One very good thing did come about from this time off. I had been feeling more and more run down, both physically and mentally, from the job. The end—although just a few months away (six more months—remember?)—seemed impossibly far away. The time I was able to take off because of the dog attack gave my body and mind a much-needed rest and boost as I made my way to the finish.

The last thing I should add is that I got nothing but the utmost support from my coworkers and also from postal management regarding the attack. I was never made to feel like a slacker or told to hurry back to duty before I was ready. I will always appreciate that. It made the entire process much easier to deal with. But I almost escaped my career without this horrible experience. I was so close. Six more months . . . six more months . . . six more months.

Well, if I am going to ask you to read several pages about my worst day, then at the very least I should spend two pages telling you about my best moment. I am tearing up just thinking about it.

Chapter 26

THE BEST MOMENT

"Defies belief to me"

Over the years I have shared this story multiple times. And every time I do I am unable to finish the story without tears rolling down my face at the sheer magnificence of what happened. A young Christian couple (okay, they were older than me, but looking back they seem very young NOW) lived on my route. They were childless. I got to know them very well over the years. Sweet and friendly folks.

They made a decision to start taking in foster kids with the possibility of maybe adopting at some point in the future. A young twosome came to their home sometime later, a girl and her younger brother. Each was as cute as could be, incredibly adorable, with a big smile and a head topped with bright ginger hair. Their story was the stuff of horror movies. They had been abused almost beyond belief. Intense physical and psychological abuse. Beyond anything I had ever heard before.

And yet—and this still defies belief to me—you could not have met two nicer kids. They were six and four and were always sweet, respectful, and friendly every time I saw them. They slid into this couple's life full blast and were loved back likewise. This became one of my favorite stops because these kids were so delightful. Over the next two years I had many, many encounters with them and they became good buddies of mine. I always looked forward to seeing them, and they me.

After they had been living in this home for two years, a day came when I approached the house to deliver the mail while they were not at home. I began to step toward the house. Precisely at that very moment the car pulled into the driveway loaded with all four members of the household. As they bounded out of the car with their "his" and "hellos," the mom said to the kids, "Tell Mr. Merrit what just happened to us."

Both kids were beaming. The little girl—now eight years old—joyfully responded in one big breath, "We just came from seeing the judge and we have been adopted and this is our mommy and daddy and that is our forever home!"

That was 25 years ago and still now as I type this it brings me to tears. The family eventually moved out of town about five years later. But I tell you, to be there right then, at that exact moment, to hear those words . . . that was about as good a moment as I ever experienced. Not just as a mailman. But as a human soul.

I am certain it has become clear to you by now that dealing with other human souls was what made my job a delight. I have introduced you to many that came across my path over the years. Allow me to tell you about just a few more that I painfully had to say farewell to for one reason or another.

Chapter 27

NO LONGER AT THIS ADDRESS

"I know all about you"

Saying goodbye is tough. Whether you are actually conversing with someone for what you believe will be the final time, or even simply within your heart as someone has died unexpectedly. We have all lost loved ones at varying depths within our lives. As a mailman—at least THIS mailman—saying goodbye could be because of death, or merely that the patron is moving to a different location. I have shared some of those already. I have a few more that were impactful to me and are memories of dear folks I still carry with me.

Before I continue, however, I wish to share with you two social postings that were spurred by cards I received while on my route on the seventh anniversary of my son Elliott's death. July 3rd obviously has always been a tough day for me (and the rest of my family) since my son died in 2007. There were some years when I took vacation that week so as to avoid having to deal with the anguish of grief while trudging through my mail route. But not always. In July of 2014, which ended up being my last July 3rd that I worked, I heard first from my wife Jill via a card she placed (unknown to me) in my lunch, and then from a dear customer you have heard about before.

July 4, 2014

This is the note I found in my lunch yesterday, as I found myself facing the seventh anniversary of my son's death:

"My darling, My love,

Please know that as you walk through this day you are not alone.

You have a myriad of friends who love you and are praying for you today.

You have a multitude of family who love you and are praying for you today.

You have a wife who desperately loves you and is with you today in thought, in spirit, and in love, and praying for you today.

And most importantly, you have a God who loves you deeply and walks with you every step of today."

Love, Jill

Hey, I get that this note and the sender has nothing to do with my route or delivering the mail, but I discovered it while I was on my route and it fits here so I have included it. Plus it shows areas of my life that define who I am: my faith, my family, my friends, and my wife.

July 4, 2014

We will miss you. I might just move after you retire. Just wanted you to know we appreciate you and think you are awesome. Anniversaries of loved ones passing can be difficult, this I know too dearly. Take care.

This was sent by the mom of 6/29, the little guy who was born four days before my son drowned. Which made it even more heartwarming.

*My favorite picture ever. Me with my four kids two
months before my son's death.*

Earlier in this book I mentioned two ladies who had become very close friends and had moved off my route and how those departures had been very emotional for me. Here are four notes I received over the years from folks who were moving off my route.

"Thank you for your attention to detail and for your years of thoughtful service in mail delivery to my household."

"Thanks for dealing with all our packages. We hope you like chocolate . . . if not we really picked bad gifts."

The comment about chocolate made me chuckle. This came from the family of the little girl who just could not get herself to walk away from grandpa and say hello to the mailman.

"Thank you for becoming more than just a mailman, but more importantly a friend. We will miss you."

"Thank you for your excellent service and support for the past eight years. You have been a bright spot for the neighborhood."

I have one final story of this nature, but this caught me off guard because the woman and I had not become what I would describe as truly close friends.

December 21, 2013

If you have been reading these mini-blogs for any amount of time, you know that my people on my route are why I enjoy my job. The hardest part is when they pass on, or, in today's case, move.

Natasha has been on my route for 15 years. She speaks accurate but heavily Russian-accented English. I really first got to know her about ten years ago, and we have become good friends these past five years or so. I only saw her maybe once every month. Her husband died early this year so we had a "grief" connection, also, since she knew about my son. So every time I saw her we would hug and see how each other was doing.

I knew she was planning on moving eventually because she used to talk about it. But I was not aware of when that was going to happen. Well, today the moving van was there. She is going to South Carolina, so I will never see her again. We chatted a bit then embraced. For a while. But I was totally fine, really, until . . . she spoke into my ear these words, "Hava goot life." When we pulled away I was quite relieved to discover I was not the only one with moist eyes.

But death is the ultimate vacater. Over the years I lost hundreds. Three days before I retired I posted a long list of as many of those folks as I could remember with an occasional comment. I do not wish to give the entirety of that list now, but want to give you some idea of a handful of these dear folks who passed on.

April 27, 2015

If you are a regular reader of these blogs, this is one you certainly do not need to go over. This is for my benefit and to acknowledge those who I have lost on my route over the years. It is my list to honor those who have passed and made an impact on my career: Wilma, Alma, Mrs. S, and Delores who all lived at the retirement center; Mike N., maker of fab custom T-shirts; Jim, the finest business owner I have ever known. I miss our Christmas Eve chats while you fed the cat (you have read about him before); Judee (who you will read about later); Mr. Wolf (and his four Shelties), who produced homemade wine; Bernice and both of your husbands you lost; Mr. and Mrs. Newman, thanks for all the times I used your bathroom; Lucille N., the last stop on my route from the very first day. I will be thinking of you when I make my VERY LAST stop on my very last day; Ed. W., who was the mailman on my route back in the 1970s; Mr. McG., who also lost a son; William (he of the $10-a-month mortgage back in the '40s); Mr. Brown (who met Charles Lindbergh); the two young women who lived on Reedway Street and were run over by a car and killed while crossing Foster Avenue; Dee, a great neighbor first and then a great customer; Harold (I delivered to four generations of his family). This is by no means extensive. I know that over the years I have forgotten many. I listed about 100 here, but I have lost about 150 or so. May they be remembered beyond my feeble attempts. Thank you to all of you who were such friendly faces to engage with. Blessings.

As I said in the post, the list was nowhere near extensive, and I have listed only a portion of that post on this page. I just want you to get even a shadow of a taste of what these dear folks meant to me. Here are four more I wrote specifically about. I have listed them in reverse chronological order. This first one came about shortly after I had returned to full-time work after the dog attack.

January 6, 2015

What I DON'T like about being a mailman. Saying goodbye . . . or not getting to. One of the fun things about having your own route are the souls who pass through it on a regular basis . . . who are NOT your actual customers. Over the 27 years on my route I have had dozens. Some of them I never had a conversation with, some of them would be occasional chats, some became friends.

In the latter group belongs John. John lived a few blocks west of my route, but he made frequent walking trips to Fred Meyer and other locales in the area. Over the past ten years we have talked and gotten to know each other fairly well. I had not seen him since my injury, but we came upon each other today. He has since moved several miles away and I probably won't see him again, especially since I will hopefully be retiring this spring. We had a final chat, a hug, and very sincere well-wishes. A friendly, lovely man. I will miss him.

Karen has been one of my 27-year customers. A very beautiful woman, slightly younger than me. We talked many times over the years as she also worked at one of the businesses on my route. Many years ago she was diagnosed with MS. It worked hideously fast on her body. She was in a wheelchair within a couple years. But then the disease plateaued and she had remained about the same for quite some time. When I returned to work just before Christmas, I learned that she had died just three days previously. And worse, her husband had had a massive stroke just a week or so before that and is in a facility for what remains of his life. I will miss them both.

As I approach the end of my postal days, I am sadly ruminating on the fact that over the 27 years I have been on my route, I have lost to death about 120 to 140 customers, many of them friends. It hits harder than usual that I am walking through these folks' lives. I have been so privileged to have been a daily part of their life.

Karen's death hit me hard. To finally return to work and discover she had passed while I was away was difficult for me to process. As I was coming up on my final months, the patrons I had delivered the mail to for the entire 27 years of my route were becoming even more precious to me. To lose one in this manner was distressing.

July 18, 2014

When I started my route 26 years ago I met a Mr. Howard. He lived in a small apartment complex toward the end of my route. He was a very simple man, quite pleasant, a bit shy. He had a horrendous limp due to an artificial leg and was a huge baseball fan. I was his mailman for ten years, which was unusual because folks usually do not stay for long periods of time at these apartments. My boundaries changed and I no longer delivered there for the next ten years.

Six years ago, my boundaries switched again and I got the complex again. Mr. Howard still lived there. He is a big San Francisco Giants fan and so was delighted with their recent championships. About a week ago I noticed he was not picking up his mail from his mailbox. His mail eventually stacked up for ten days or so.

Yesterday I asked a neighbor if anyone had seen him. They had not and were concerned because no one had seen him nor had his newspapers been picked up. The manager had not been reachable so no one had checked on him. I suggested someone call the police. I continued on with my route.

Well, they called the police. Sadly, Mr. Howard had died in his apartment about eight or nine days ago. I have no idea if he has any family. I didn't see him often. But I will miss his smile and our occasional chats about baseball. He lived in the same little apartment for 33 years.

January 17, 2014

I lost two more folks. A 99-year-old lady who was a real sweetheart died about two weeks ago. I did not see her often, but she was very nice. She had an amazing doll collection and lived next door to her daughter and son-in-law. Always very gracious and generous with me.

Then today as I was delivering I approached a home where I have had the customers for 16 years. I noticed an unusual amount of cards in the mail. And it was obvious they weren't birthday cards.

I knocked on the door. Doris and her daughter (late 30s?) answered. "I'm so sorry to bother you, but did you lose your husband?" I found out her husband of 46 years had passed a couple of days ago from cancer. He was a character. Occasionally I would see the two of them walking the neighborhood hand in hand. We chatted a bit; I gave her a hug. The look on her daughter's face was lovely. She remarked, "Wow, in Portland a mailman shows this much concern."

As I left and made my way down the driveway, the daughter came out of the house and said, "Thank you SO much for that! That really meant a lot." We talked a bit more and I told her how much I enjoyed her dad and that the people on my route were what made my job enjoyable. Hey, folks, this is what it is all about.

I had a duplex on my route where a son lived in one apartment and his dad lived in the other one with his wife. I got to know this family very well.

September 18, 2013

The best part of being a mailman: yesterday I was about half done with my route. As I rounded a corner and from two houses away, I suddenly heard three little ones shrieking, "HI, MR. MERRIT!!!!!" I chatted with them as I delivered to their home. About six minutes later as I made my way down the other side of the street, I was greeted the same way by some other little ones.

Later, I was reflecting on how much I'm going to miss this part of the job. The worst part of being a mailman: a lady on my route—one of my 25-year folks—has cancer. Her sister was just arriving at the house as I came by. I had never met her before. I asked her how her sister was doing. Not well. They give her about a week. So sad. Her husband lost his son about a year before I lost mine so we have had that in common.

Anyway, I started to tell her who I was. She told me, "Oh, I know all about you, Merrit. My sister told me you are her favorite." I was touched, then honored, then humbled that this woman, who is about to lose her battle with cancer, had told her sister about me, to the point that her sister knew my name.

These two events were good reminders that although these people are important to me, apparently I have made a difference in their lives, also. I will miss this dear lady. She will be my second death of longtime customers in the past three weeks. I also lost one to a move and will be losing three more to moves in the coming weeks. People—the best part of having the same route for 25 years. Losing them . . . the hardest part. I am not ashamed to tell you I had red-rimmed eyes for the next hour or so.

The next week I posted this:

September 28, 2013

Here in Portland the weather was quite nasty yesterday. No one came out to chat with the mailman. Well, except one. Remember last week the lady who was dying of cancer and her sister talked to me? She passed the night before last. And her daughter took the time to come out in the cruddy weather to tell me about it "because I know Mom just loved you, and I wanted to let you know." Yup, there ain't no price to put on that, folks.

As I think back on my career and the 140 or more customers who passed away during the time I was their letter carrier, the first one still stings the most. Partially because it was the first, partly because this lady had become a very dear friend, but mostly because this was not an aspect of the job that I had considered nor did I have any idea how deeply it would affect me. So if I may, let me dedicate this chapter to Judee. I wrote this a year after I retired.

June 18, 2016

WHY I LIKED (AND DIDN'T LIKE) BEING A MAILMAN

My friend Judee. She lived at the front end of a duplex on Ramona Street. She was one of the very first customers I got to know as a friend 28 years ago. She was a single woman about ten years my senior. Very sweet. She let me use her bathroom when needed, offered me cookies and water on a regular basis, and was almost always there daily with a smile and greeting.

We became good friends and she was one of the first folks I brought my family around to meet. I eventually also got to meet her daughter. She was very sweet to my children and was someone who I always looked forward to seeing. Judee and I were more than mailman-patron. She became a true friend. And this friendship lasted for several years.

But then she slowly started to look less than her normal healthy and vivacious self. Then more quickly. She had cancer. She got to a point where she was going to have to move in with her daughter who lived in Idaho for more personal care.

For Christmas 1995 she gave me (along with her neighbor Irene) a Thomas Kinkade Engagement Diary. She stuck a note inside that read: "Even though I won't be on your route in 1996, there will still be a little left of me in Portland, and if you use this book through the year maybe you'll remember me!"

She remained incredibly upbeat and always assured me that she was going to beat it. It was not to be. From the time of her diagnosis to her death was just a few months. She was the first customer I lost. It is now about 20 years later and I still lament her passing. It still chokes me up to think or talk about her. She was a dear woman, a very kind customer, and a good friend. People like her who entered my life through the delivery of mail (and there were hundreds) enriched my career beyond what I can express. Those that I lost (way too many) I still mourn as we all do with lost friends. Thank you, Judee (and all the rest of you, whether gone or still here), for graciously reaching out to your mailman and being a friend.

Looking back, it is stunning to me how many folks passed into and out of my career lifespan. Well, it is time for us to start getting to the end of the miles. Let's keep going.

Chapter 28

LAST LAPS

"Flailing my arms around"

The rats were starting to win the race and I was wearing down and out. The years and miles continued to pile on and I began to entertain thoughts that possibly the end of the row was in sight. The signals began to fly at me fast and furious. Mailman Mike's retirement put my seniority and age right in front of my face. Looking back from this safe distance, it appears four clues presented themselves, two that were symbolic, and two that smacked me flush on.

Every few months a supervisor is supposed to walk our route with us. It is a practice designed to check that we are being safe and also that we are doing our route in a timely manner. Sometimes the person walking with you is one of your direct supervisors; other times the downtown Portland main Post Office sends someone out that you don't know.

It usually is a fairly harmless day, but occasionally you get stuck with a real . . . um . . . let's use the word "jerk." Someone who just wants to ride your butt all day and tell you how bad you are at your job. Yeah, I know. Fun times. Bosses. What are you going to do?

Anyway, during the last decade or so I had gotten off with these tests (called 99s) pretty easily. But one day I got stuck with a know-it-all from downtown. He was way young and just knew how best I could improve how I did my job. You know. The job I had now done for more than 25 years and walked tens of thousands of miles. He wasn't a jerk, just an upstart. The next day I spoke with my boss at the station—someone I got along with very well—and begged. "Look, if I have to keep getting these tests done up until I retire, could you please try to keep people from following me who have not been alive for as long as I have been doing my job?" Thankfully, they obliged.

—⊶⊷—

I knew the end was approaching, but I was not at all sure how to recognize it. In a span of a few months three things happened that as I look back were flags waving at me that the time to exit was nearing.

One day a new carrier started at Creston Station. She was very young and a bit quiet at first so I did not get to know her very well for a quite a while. She eventually was assigned to a route that was located in the same aisle as mine so we began to chat and formed what became a good friendship. By this point in my career I had been in the Post Office 28 years and on my route for 25. One morning before we started work I sidled up to her. "Dominique, how old are you?"

She replied in her soft voice, "24."

I just glared at her.

"What?" she asked.

I told her, "I have been on my route longer than you have been alive!" I felt so blasted old. What was I doing working with these kids?

That summer I was walking my route one hot, sticky, disgusting day. I was about 70% done with my route. I could take you to the exact spot today. It was mid-afternoon. It was 97 degrees. I was hot. I was tired. And I just stopped. Stopped walking. Stopped delivering the mail. Stopped dead in my tracks and just stood there, miserable. I asked and thought to myself, "What the heck are you doing!? It's 97 degrees! You are 57 years old! You've been doing this for 28 years. Just what the heck are you doing and why are you still doing it!?"

I was quite agitated and totally fed up with my job and these weather conditions at my age. At that moment three things occurred and became abundantly clear to me.

First, I wasn't actually thinking these words to myself. I had been unknowingly speaking out loud, the key word being "loud."

Second, I was not in some secluded isolated spot on my route. I was standing 25 feet from the corner of a busy intersection with traffic rumbling by me. I had probably been seen flailing my arms around and speaking in a voluminous voice.

Third, I also realized that I was doing this because it was my job and I had become used to eating and having electricity. But it was a moment that seared its way onto my conscience and made me understand that I could not and would not do this physically demanding job indefinitely.

Then one day I came through the swinging doors into Creston Station to begin my day and noticed an older boy milling around. It was not rare for employees to bring in their kids for a minute to say hello or something so it was not an earth-shattering moment for him to be there. Or so I thought. He looked somewhere between the ages of 12 to 16, certainly no older than 18.

I asked around and was quite taken aback to be told he was our newest employee. What?! Since when does the Post Office hire 12-year-olds to deliver the mail?! I walked over to my route muttering to myself that I had to get out of this place! It was being overrun with kids! This young man was John and he was actually 22 years old and became a very good mailman for the USPS. But the point had been made to my soul. It was time to seriously start heading toward the proverbial door.

This happened in April of 2014, but I had already started directing my mind about a year and a half earlier toward finishing my career. And as it often did, my brain headed in the direction of dealing with the ugly summer heat.

October 12, 2012

As a walking mailman for the past 25 years, I officially declare the warm days of summer gone for this year. Which means, Lord willing and the creeks don't rise, I only have two more summers of wretched hot weather to get through before retirement. I always say, you can do anything twice.

June 30, 2013

So, IF everything goes to according to plan—and that is the most ginormous IIIFFF in memory—I will wake up two years from today and walk into the Post Office for my last day of work . . . I F.

I actually got out in 22 months, but that was as much as I could foresee at the time. As you have already seen multiple times, I did not like delivering mail in the summer and August was my least favorite month to work. Once I got some seniority behind me I always took my longest vacation (usually two weeks) during August to avoid as many of those miserable 31 days as possible.

August 31, 2013

Well, as another dreaded August is lowered into the ground; I say "good riddance." I hate the month, mostly because of stupid hot weather. And the demonic (business name) catalogs. Good news, if . . . IF all goes to plan, I only got ONE more to deal with.

Two months later on Halloween I spoke to much the same idea.

October 31, 2013

As a walking mailman, I hereby officially declare summer to be over. No more having to wear short pants to stay comfortable. No more sweating like a pig. No more . . . ickiness. I say that to say this: if . . . IF work goes according to plan, I have just one more disgusting summer to work in as a mailman. After that, it's jake. And I always say, you can do anything once more.

Apparently I always say "I always say" about more than one thing. As I said, the "12-year-old" John started in April 2014. I was getting serious about retirement and my memory and emotions began to go into overdrive.

April 28, 2014

My dad was a barber. He died when I was in high school. I have nothing from his work history. No razor straps, no glass bottle comb holders (with those wonderful aromas), etc. My most important work tool is my mailbag. I am currently using the fourth one over the past 29 years and will finish my career with it. It is like an old friend hanging off my right shoulder mile after mile. It takes months for it to fit smoothly and comfortably around my hip. I will use one until it is threadbare. My last one (which I stopped using about six years ago) got so thin on the bottom that it would no longer hold magazines. My plan is to give one of my mailbags to each of my kids when I retire. I will keep the one that would have gone to my son. It seems weird that I will have walked 70,000 miles with a strap across my right shoulder. We all have that kind of stuff in our jobs.

The postscript is that when I cleaned out my locker when I retired it turned out that I had used FIVE, and not four. I gave the one I would have given to my son to my dear friend Jason, who I talked about in an earlier chapter. The last one I used currently hangs in my study.

—❦—

Finally, I got to the point on the calendar where I had but one year to go. And then I had one last summer to plod through. By this time I was also madly posting on social media nearly daily. (Don't worry, that's not going to happen on these pages.) Both at the beginning of summer and as I stepped out of it for the last time, I thought of other summer moments firmly impressed on my memories.

I remembered being on a route out of Multnomah my first summer in the Post Office, back in 1985. I was on a difficult route, on a hot and dusty day, walking up a steep hill. I can distinctly remember stepping up into my postal vehicle and thinking to myself I could never do this job for 30 years.

I remembered a blistering hot day my one summer at Sellwood Station. I don't remember the route I did that particular day but I returned to the office completely depleted and spent. Were these hot days always going to be this difficult or would it get easier with experience?

About this time one of the old vets walked in. No, no. That is not even remotely accurate. He plodded, dripped, and slimed his way into the office. Alan had about 20 years' seniority at the time. He spotted me and broke out in a worn and cracked grin. He began to walk with a heavily exaggerated dragging gait and said, "Merrit, I swear this is how I was walking the last two hours of my route."

I didn't doubt him. It had been a deplorable day. And I still had 27 more summers to wade through at that point. Sigh. But I battled and sweated and Gatoraded my way through the next 26 until I stepped up to the plate for my final beat-down with my dreaded nemesis.

June 20, 2014

Hey! Hey YOU!! Yeah, you . . . Mr. Summer. Tomorrow our last clash starts. There is nothing good about you but baseball and fresh fruit. You have dogged me with your stupid weather while I delivered mail for the past 29 summers. I hate your stickiness, the exhaustion you cause, and the misery of 97 degrees. Well, give me your best shot, pal, cuz in late September or early October the weather will get comfortable again and I am going to shake the dust of you off my shoes for the last time as a postal employee. Let's get this tango started, because I am going to win no matter WHAT you throw at me, and this time next year I'll be sitting on my porch drinking a Snapple and laughing. So bring it on and pffftt!! to you!!!

September 6, 2014

Since I am planning on being retired by next summer, I am truly hoping that today was the last stupid 90-degree day I will have to work in my career.

But I also had other thoughts and feelings about approaching the end of the line.

June 20, 2014

I know this is six weeks late, but it occurred to me the other day, that I will never again enjoy the fragrance of lilacs while I deliver mail. One of the things I will definitely miss.

And a few days later the reality of the other side of retirement really hit me for the first time.

June 28, 2014

It's weird the moments that catch me off guard as I approach my retirement next year. My shoes are my most important equipment. Every year I buy two or three pair, wearing them on alternate days. After a few months I take them to a shoe repair shop to have the heels redone, giving me many more months of comfortable wear. I have been going to the same shop for almost ten years. The owner recognizes me as a regular customer. Today I picked up my repaired shoes, and had to say goodbye and thanks for the great service . . . for the final time. You know, we walk through our lives (no pun intended) and there are people everywhere we touch and are touched by. I will miss our regular meetings with this man of high quality and integrity. I was appreciative that he and his son both asked me to stop in occasionally and say "hello."

A couple months later the reality of doing something for the final time filled me with terrific joy. Remember those despicable catalogs from a certain store that I hated delivering. Well, my final battle with those ghastly things finally arrived.

August 7, 2014

As a mailman, I HATE (blank) catalogs. They are horrible things, straight from the gates of you-know-where. They are heavy, slickery, and a total pain. They come out every August and go to every residential customer. I was hoping to avoid them by having my vacation this month, but I missed missing them by two days. HOWEVER, my route—for some reason—only received four bundles instead of a full coverage of my entire route. (About 80 catalogs instead of the usual 500+). Four bundles is a mere pittance. So, today, at precisely 1:16 pm, God willing, I delivered the last (blank) catalog of my career. They will NOT be missed.

If you remember it was in October that I got attacked by the pit bull. When I realized that I was going to be off work for a few weeks, a wonderful thought invaded my mind. Oh, I LOVED writing this one:

October 14, 2014

So, with me being off work for some weeks, I can officially declare this mailman's summer over. You gave me a good shot this year, Mr. Summer. Hot weather for many days, very warm ones into October. There was great baseball and phenomenal plums. That dog-bite thing at the end was not very nice, but I will consider it your last shot at me. So I will see you again next. . . wait a min, let me think about this . . . seems like there was something . . . oh YEAH!! I won't be back next summer!! So pffft! on you, Mr. Summer. Let's tally up the final score: Grumpy Broken-Down Old Mailman—30; Mr. Summer—0. I WIN! ol' pal. You were a formidable enemy, but I am walking out DA WINNA!!! Go pick on somebody else. I'm ooooooooouuuuutttttttttttttttttta here!

Did I mention I really hated delivering mail in the summer? I tend to be subdued with my opinions so just wanted to make sure I had been clear about this.

And then I began to approach my final Christmas season. This was going to be tough. I lived for delivering those final three or four weeks before Christmas. But something went terribly wrong. I got attacked by the pit bull in early October and recovery time took much longer than anticipated. I was going to miss most of the holiday season. It was a bitter pill to swallow, but there was nothing I could do. I got some good counseling about it and so although I was only going to be fulltime for the last three delivery days before Christmas, I was going to make the very most of it.

December 23, 2014, 6:07 p.m.

Tomorrow is Christmas Eve. My 30th and last as a mailman, my 27th and last on my route. You MAY have picked up that I am a mite looking forward to retirement later this spring. I am NOT looking forward to the end of my last Christmas season. I L O V E working the three to four weeks before Christmas. To finally bring stuff folks want instead of bills and junk. I LOVE handling and delivering Christmas cards. And there is nothing—NOTHING—better or sweeter than walking up to a house with a package in the late afternoon the last few days before the holiday and there are a couple of little excited faces staring at you from the window as you approach. I have had the privilege of working Christmas Eves with little ones at a home on my route . . . and those little ones are now young adults with little ones of their own visiting their parents and remembering me from when they were kids.

Christmas Eve is usually a late day for us, with hugs and "Merry Christmas" being wished by many of my coworkers as we finally stumble out the door for our own homes. Boy howdy, how I will miss that, too. Sometime tomorrow in the late afternoon, I will deliver my last and final Christmas package as a United States Postal Service mailman. Here's hoping for one more little shining face in the window. Dang, I have had the BEST job you could have at Christmas! It has been a delight. Merry Christmas, route 0655! I'm going to savor tomorrow.

God was very gracious. It became a Christmas Eve for the ages.

December 24, 2014

I want to share my last Christmas experience as a mailman. I missed most of my last holiday season because of the pit bull attack. So I immersed myself in those last days I did get to have. This is what happened. It is December 24th. I am delivering the very last of my Christmas parcels. It is about 6 p.m. Very dark. It worked out so that my very last stop delivering my very last package on my very last day of my very last Christmas as a mailman was to a couple who are one of my very favorites and were customers for my entire 27 years.

They invited me inside for a cookie or two and we chatted for a few minutes, reminiscing while enjoying the warmth of their beautiful home. It was very emotional. We hugged, laughed at old memories, and I thanked them for being such dear friends to their old, broken-down, grumpy mailman. And then I went on my way. When I got to my car it took all I had to hold it together and not start crying. For, as I said, I had just delivered my very last Christmas package. EVER. And I loved working the Christmas season.

The New Year arrived. I got through my final winter. Ironically enough, my final summer and winter delivering mail may have been the mildest ones I ever worked in. And I got out at just the right time because the following summer and winter were both brutal. But let's not get ahead of ourselves. As spring approached, the time arose when we could officially hit the home stretch.

Chapter 29

T-MINUS

"Watch what Daddy did"

When you're in the middle stages of any large project it's easy to look around and be overwhelmed with the idea that you will never finish. Whether it be painting the house, unpacking the boxes after a move, getting home after a long drive with the kids crawling all over each other . . . or finishing a career in any sector. The end can frequently seem many tads beyond the horizon. But as the fabulous baseball ambassador Buck O'Neill (okay, if you have no idea who that is, put this book down immediately and do some research; you will not be sorry) used to say to his teammates on excruciatingly long and hot bus rides when it seemed as if they would never arrive at their next destination: "We always get there!"

There finally came a day when I looked at that oh so distant horizon and it was no longer very distant. I was going to make it. Mailman Mike used to tell me that a mailman's career was like picking strawberries. You weren't done until you got to the end of the row. Suddenly my berry basket was nearly full and the end of the row was just a few more steps away.

March 19, 2015

Here is the official announcement that many folks have been wondering about. My last day as a mailman for the Post Office will be April 30th. After 30 years—27 on the same route—it's time to say goodbye.

This social media posting was very emotional for me to write. I remember a huge lump forming in my throat at the idea that the moment was finally arriving—the good, the bad, and the ugly of all it represented. I quickly followed it up with a more staid statement.

March 19, 2015

42/30. Because today the countdown begins. Forty-two days till retirement, thirty workdays till retirement. 350 miles to go.

The comments came in quickly.

We will miss you, Merrit Hearing; you are a great mailman.

Noooooooooooo! (from Wanda's mom).

Wow, Merrit, that's great! Before you leave could you check on a couple birthday packages my mom swears she actually mailed to me?

You have been the best mailman; time went by quickly. Wishing you all the happiness; you will be missed.

Bittersweet for us. I'm so happy for you, but we'll miss your face and expertise. Thank you so much for being a part of our lives all these years, my friend. (from Bonny and the family who sent the wonderful Christmas card and greeted me first after my son's death).

So I only had 42 days to go. Six weeks. SIX. WEEKS!!! Was it possible? Gulp. Now what? My first face-to-face reaction came from one of my 27-year customers the very next day.

March 20, 2015

Today there were the first tears from a customer. I told an 80ish-year-old lady that after 27 years as her mailman I was retiring. She remarked how she and I had been through much in that time (thinking of my son and her late [two years ago, the patriarch I mentioned earlier at the same time as another family welcomed a new baby] husband of 60 years). She got choked up for a quick moment and then we talked about other things.

My favorite flower even came into the conversation a final time.

March 30, 2015

Lilacs!! My fave flower and fragrance. I am so delighted that I get one more season of delivering in the lilacs.

And on the same day I also officially said farewell to Mr. Winter with no regrets. Although he had certainly caused me less trouble than Mr. Summer.

March 30, 2015

I forgot to say goodbye to Mr. Winter. Although I prefer him to evil Mr. Summer, I will not miss torrential downpours, sleet, freezing rain, or snow. In my 30 years of delivering mail, this was easily my most mild winter.

On consecutive days I posted about the enormity of my impending retirement.

March 31, 2015

As I sit here today, I have been IN the postal service 30 years. In 30 days, I will be OUT.

April 1, 2015

Psst! (I retire this month). Hee hee hee.

One of the joys I had reeled in over the years was when my kids would come out and walk a bit of my route with me. During the early days their mom would bring them out and I would walk along with one of my adorable little ones tagging with me to say hello to my customers and to watch what Daddy did all day. All four of them had joined me at different times and at different ages, either together or by themselves. By the time retirement neared, only one was living close enough to come alongside me.

April 4, 2015

Over the years my kids have walked a section or two on my route with me. Today, for the last time, Maria walked a section with me. Thank you, Maria Hearing.

It was a very emotional moment for the both of us. I had not known she was coming. Suddenly she pulled up in her car and stepped out. Yes, it was a long time from the days when Mom had to bring her. I asked her what was up. She swallowed hard and said she wanted to walk with me one last time. I think we both had wet eyes after she walked next to me for about 30 minutes and then embraced me and said goodbye. Daddy and daughter once more together into the fray. A representation of many glorious memories.

As the days dwindled down (to a precious few), I kept a running total on social media of how many calendar days/

workdays I had left. I had started at 42/30 and worked my way down, the two numbers drawing closer together as my days off cut the first number at a faster rate than the second number.

I reached 16 calendar days to go. Two similar but completely distinct ideas hit me the same day. The first idea hit me when I remembered that my favorite baseball player, Derek Jeter, had been in his final year of his career at the same time that I had been in mine. He had retired the previous September. And it had been made clear and evident that no New York Yankee would ever wear his jersey number 2 ever again because of his iconic career. Well, after 27 years on the same route, I saw my career as also being iconic, thank you very much.

April 14, 2015

So I have a fabulous idea. When a professional athlete retires after spending several years with one team, they will sometimes retire his number. I think when a mailman retires AND he has been on the same route for at least 20 years, they should retire his route number. The route I have been on for the past 27 years should no longer be known as route 0655. I should get to keep that. Assign those streets a new number. Just sayin'.

So far I have not convinced the United States Postal Service to capture and implement my idea. But I can always hope, right?

April 14, 2015

I presumed I would wade through many heavy emotions regarding my retirement. Relief. Joy. Melancholy. But I am dealing with one I never figured on. For 27 years I have been THE mailman for route 0655. I have tried to be the very best letter carrier I could be. These are MY people, MY customers, MY neighborhoods. I am not keen on turning over that privilege to someone else. It seriously just hit me a couple days ago: I will no longer be the mailman for these dear folks. That is a tough pill to swallow for me. Not enough to change my mind, but still . . . phew.

The comments I received from this post caught me off guard and were a wonderful massage to my aching heart.

I honestly wondered about that. You have been a very special mailman! They should do a story about you on the news. Honest!

I'm sure they are feeling the same way. A really good mailman is hard to find!

You will always be part of our neighborhood. Always! And you have touched my life and my daughter's so you've made a difference that means a lot.

Hi, Merrit. You were the best mailman I have ever met! You deserve every day of your retirement! I'm sure you will find something you enjoy doing! Love you from your favorite retired secretary, Susan.

You're more than just a mailman, you're Our mailman, but also a dear friend. I can't wait to hear about your next adventures! Bonny.

You will always be our mailman, and the best mailman I've ever had and/or met, xo. (from 6/29's mom).

You know that we have moved and you're STILL The Mailman. You always will be—retired or not!

The days kept slipping by, almost too fast. I hit the point where I was two weeks from retirement, but with less than ten workdays to go.

April 16, 2015

14/ . . . and . . . NINE! We are down to single digits in workdays left. Time to rest the next three days, then on to the finish.

My head, my heart, and my stomach were a whirlwind of emotions. How had this finally come about? How was I going to deal with it and make it part of my life?

April 17, 2015

Another small reality check. For several years I have planned out my life in two week increments on a yellow legal pad. Today was my day to map out the next 14 days. I got to Thursday, April 30th and wrote out LAST DAY. Then for Friday, May 1st.....DON'T GO TO WORK. Weird.

April 19, 2015

I have two weeks left of work. Next week my day off is Monday. So tomorrow is the last Monday of my postal career.

The reality of the end of my mileage also came clearly into focus.

April 20, 2015

Ten calendar days left, eight workdays left. But more significantly for me: in the 30 years and 3 months I have been carrying mail, I have walked approximately 70,000 miles. I now have less than 100 more to go.

April 25, 2015 (a Saturday)

5/3. (Five calendar and three workdays left). Two days off—Sunday and Monday—then three days to the finish—Tuesday, Wednesday, and Thursday. 70,000 miles walked . . . about 35 miles to go.

April 27, 2015

T H R E E. The old, broken-down mailman takes a deep breath and heads for the home stretch.

Also on this day I posted the list of folks I had lost to death that I mentioned two chapters back. It was far from exhaustive and overwhelmed me with deep emotion. And elicited some lovely responses from a handful of my customers.

You are the best mailman a girl could ever ask for! (from 6/29's mom)

You were not just a mailman to us—you were and are part of the family. Miss you.

Thank you so much for this. (Bonny)

That's wild you remember my dad. I don't know if you remember my grandma. (I did.) Thank you; you're like the best mailman in the world.

I was so delighted when I found out that you were our mailman down at the club! Congratulations, my old friend!!

On that Monday of my final week as a postman, a strange truth crept into my mind.

April 27, 2015

I received a card that stated the bad thing about retirement is there are no days off. With that thought in mind: today is my last day off.

April 28, 2015

And then there were TWO (days left). Since my wife Jill will accompany me on my very last day, tomorrow is the last normal day of mail delivery in my career. My last day solo. I am coming to realize that I am being affected in three ways.

Physically, I am soooo ready. Mentally, I am also a bit worn with all the daily grind of prepping for work, etc., like all of us are who work regularly. But emotionally, I am torn up. Not seeing my coworkers, not engaging with my customers. When I contemplate these things, it nearly overwhelms me.

That last sentence is one of the very most gigantic understatements of my entire life. I was a wreck and slipping into basket-case territory. My final days were a cacophonous and chaotic array of swirling emotions, throat-lumping verbiage, and frequently dampening eyes.

On the morning before my last day I went into my boss's office to chat and say goodbye to her since she would not be at work on my final day. She took an iconic photo of me with my feet up on her desk. It is one of my fave pictures ever taken of me.

I got though my next-to-last day and suddenly (or so it seemed) was facing my final and last day of serving my customers with the delivery of mail as a distributor for the United States Postal Service. As I looked forward to my final day I knew that besides saying farewell to so many folks, four unusual things were going to happen.

First, in the morning at work I would be giving my goodbye speech. I had made copious notes, but knew I would be fighting heavy emotion as I spoke.

Second, my tender wife Jill would be walking with me through my entire route (although a terribly unpleasant experience would interrupt part of that).

Third, All Classical Portland, the radio station I had carried with me in my pocket for the past eight years, had graciously agreed to play a request for me on the air at about 1:00 in the afternoon.

And fourth—and this was the nuttiest thing (or so I thought at the time)—a local radio station had interviewed me a few weeks earlier about me retiring after 27 years as a walking mailman on the same route and was going to air the interview a few times the next day. I was blown away by both of these features and had written about it the previous day.

April 28, 2015

There are two cool things going on the radio on my last day of work, which is THIS THURSDAY, April 30th. On KXL-FM radio—101.1—at 5:19 and 7:19 in the morning and an as yet undetermined time in the afternoon, there will be a three minute feature about me. Also, a few minutes before 1 p.m. the classical station—89.9—will play a song for me at the end of Christa Wessel's show. There will be nothing said, but they are playing something for me.

All these items were crashing through my heart and brain as I sat down at my computer to record my final social media post as a city letter carrier. As I began to write I let it all hang out. But, um, sorry. You will have to wait to read it.

It was now time to face the last day of my career. It was time for my swan song.

Chapter 30

THE LAST DAY

"Genuine warmth and tenderness"

It was Thursday, April 30, 2015. My final day as a City Letter Carrier for the United States Postal Service. I was not sure how it had arrived—and the idea that somehow 30 years had passed since I tentatively walked into the Multnomah Station in February of 1985 seemed incomprehensible—but here I was at the end of my career. The end - for me - of the strawberry row as Mailman Mike had said so many times over the years.

I slowly pulled on my blue uniform for one last time and had Jill take a picture. On my way to work I stopped for one last fabulous cup of hot chocolate from Speedboat Coffee. I said goodbye to my two lovely favorite female baristas, Dow-Dow and Moosh and got a lovely photo of the three of us. Funny thing, it was "just" a coffee shop, but I was not the only one with wet eyes. And here is that number I teased you with several chapters ago. The ladies served me with my 1,103rd cup of dazzlingly good hot chocolate. That final sticker—and all the other ones—is still at my postal case even now, along with that number circled in highlighter. It may seem silly to you, but I am proud of that number 1,103 and the significance it played in my career and in a lovely small local business.

I got to work early so I could begin the emotional process of saying goodbye to everyone. I was a wreck. And very shaky. Jill came in and brought my stepdaughter Jael. We heard the first airing of my radio interview.

My eldest daughter Maria came, and to my delightful surprise, Mailman Mike shuffled through the door. (I think he secretly had his doubts I was going to finish. He had questioned the idea since I met him that I was cut out to be a mailman. In a nice way). I went around and hugged pretty much everybody.

Remember Donny, the carrier who I had the fake fights with over the years? I asked him if I could "win" our last battle and proceeded to smash and crash him to the ground in my most annihilating way. It was glorious.

I went from person to person and, depending on the depth of the friendship with each person, there were different levels of emotion and tears. I was delighted to discover that Gordon had made up a button that was attached to his shirt that read: NOTHIN' BUT TILE, BABY!

Then it was time for the ceremony and my speech.
The speech that I had heard others make countless times over
the decades. I had worked on it for a long time. I had things I
wanted and needed to say and this was my last chance. When
a mailman retires it is a big deal. The local postmaster comes
out and says a few words and presents the retiree with a pin
and a letter in a hardbound folder.

But I had erred in sending in my paperwork so no
one came out from downtown to wish me well. It was my
own fault, but it was still annoying. The local vice-president
of our union came out to say some words and introduce me.
As he began to speak I was sitting in the front row, clinging
to Janelle—my utility carrier—hanging onto her hand with a
grip of desperation as I tried to curb my emotions enough to
get through this. My family was in the back. Here is V.P. Jerry's
words followed by my speech, with editing and comments
included for clarity. It was about 7:45 in the morning.

"Here is the example. This is somebody that loves his
job. He's loved his job for his whole career."
(Well . . .)
"You can tell this by the things he writes on [social
media] about 'I love being a mailman.' It's pretty special. I
don't get to do retirements for people like Merrit very often,
because Merrit is kind of a different guy." (Laughter among
the group.) "He likes to let his emotions out on his sleeve. He
likes to tell you how he feels. He likes to tell you what he's
doing. And he likes to sing. So this is pretty special for me as
well.

"You know, the letter carriers are considered the
most trusted federal employees on the planet. And one of the
reasons is because of people like Merrit. So it gives me great
pleasure to be here for his last day.

"One of the things that he is going to find out is that now in the morning when he gets up he has to turn the light on to put some clothes on because he can't get dressed in the dark like we all do on a regular basis. I noticed that myself. And so on behalf of the national president [of our union] and our local president and all the members of Branch 82 [our local union] and all the members of the National Association of Letter Carriers, I want to thank you for your [30] years of dedicated service to the postal service and dedication to the union and dedication to your fellow carriers as well as your customers who are going to miss you a lot. Thanks for all you've done."

At this point I was presented with my first retirement check, an official letter from the union and a pin commemorating my retirement. Jerry then concluded with these words as I stood up to embrace him.

"And I hope you have a long and healthy and happy retirement."

I turned around to face the masses and give my farewell speech as a mailman. I was fighting a surging wave of emotion and tears that were ready to spill out at any moment. I started by explaining why there was no management present and a quick promo for my radio interview that I had heard about 30 minutes earlier on the air.

"It sounds pretty cool except that I am talking way too fast. Can you imagine that?"

There was some mild laughter at this remark because everyone knows I am always talking too fast. I took a deep breath, pulled out my notes, and started my "official" discourse.

"I'm not going to miss commitment times." [When we are required to let our supervisors know how long it will take us to deliver our route each day.] "I'm not going to miss advos. Or 99s. Or 3996s." [The form we fill out whenever we leave notice with a customer that they have a package to pick up at the Post Office or any time we have certified or registered mail, regardless of whether we deliver it or leave notice].

At this point someone asked me if I would miss delivering those special catalogs I have mentioned in these pages.

"I'm not even going to say that word. [pause] I want to introduce some special people who are here."

I then introduced Jill, Maria, and Jael.

"And that old grizzled guy way back in the back is Mailman Mike; that's what my kids know him as. Mike worked for the Post Office for 77 years [laughter], and though he doesn't want to admit it, he worked next to me longer than anybody else he worked next to. And I learned a lot from him.

"I want to thank the union. Many of you know that I have not always seen eye-to-eye with some of the union's viewpoints. But, if you work for the Post Office, you should be in the union. Period. You have the right not to be, and you shouldn't be harassed if you make that decision. I want to thank—and I can't thank all of them—the union people who have taken care of me specifically as stewards here. The late, great, Kelly P. [I choked up as I spoke this dear lady's name; again, I am omitting last names], Mike M., Linda S., Kimmy. [And as I said the next person's name and looked at her, I almost lost it] And the greatest ute carrier in the universe, Janelle L.

"I remember really specifically—trying to remember what it was like at the start—I was out at Multnomah on route 32. Heck of a route. It was a hot summer day. It was dusty. Hills. Dismount. I can picture where it was. Getting out of that car. And going, 'I can't do this for 30 years.' And it's like John B. [a retiree from a few years earlier] says, 'The days drag and the years fly.' And here I am.

"I want to thank Mailman Mike. I learned a lot from you."

It was getting harder and harder to speak through my choked-up throat.

"Probably the most important was that we are not just delivering mail. We are walking through people's lives. You need to respect it. You need to appreciate it."

This should be the last time you have to read this sentiment.

"Mike and Dave W.—many of you don't know this—brought me to work for years and years and years, picked me up and took me home and would take no gas money because they knew we didn't have it at the time."

I looked over at Doug the Slug.

"Where's Dougie? Doug and I have worked together for 29 of my 30 years. We've gone through some stuff."

At this point Doug piped up. "I've got 29 years to go!"

"I've worked between Annie and Victoria for the last several years. It's the best blond/brunette sandwich I could ever ask for."

As I started to speak the next words my voice broke.

"TP in da house!"

She responded with, "Come on, brother!"

"JAY-son bo-NAY!"

And of course I got back, "Merrit Hearing!"

"Arlen."

In his best Eeyore voice, "Take it easy, old man. Take it easy."

"Tyra. Gordon. Happy Pam. Tin-Man. I wish I could name you all but I can't. I want to thank you for your support. For carrying my route all the times that I fell down."

This drew some laughs and a retort from TP: "So about for ten years then." That cracked me up and got a lot more laughter. I walked over and TP and we gave each other a high-five.

"When I came in here I had two kids. You were excited with me for two more births that I had. You supported me when I lost my son in ways I could not imagine. And I've never told you this before out loud. For some silly reason I have a reputation for being a bit of a smart-aleck. I'm not sure where that comes from."

Uh-huh.

"But quite honestly I didn't expect but maybe three or four of you to come to my son's memorial. And when there were two dozen of you there . . . that's something that I'll never forget. You also took up a collection for me so I wouldn't have to worry about finances. I don't know if anyone has ever told you how much it was, but I'm going to tell you now. I was expecting 150 to 200 bucks because we do that for people here. Guys, Kimmy came over to my house and handed me an envelope with ($$) in it. That's you guys.

"I'm going to miss the camaraderie. I'm going to miss getting to say all your names in all the weird ways that I say it . . . CHUCK-AY!! . . . every day.

"People ask me what I'm going to do. I'm going to do a lot of writing. I've already written one book and I've got ideas for two more. I have lots of books to read and unfortunately—though it's now fortunate—I'm the world's slowest reader, so I can actually get my reading done. I'm going to listen to a lot of music. I have 1700 CDs to listen to. I have 60 that I haven't even opened yet. I'm going to watch a looooot of baseball. Visit my kids, my grandkids. Take up some amateur astronomy. And for the next hundred days I'm going to rest."

I folded my notes. I knew there was more to say and emotions were beginning to make it difficult.

"Two last things. Like you, we get so frustrated with downtown" [middle management].

At this point I took a step toward vice-president Jerry and addressed him.

"Can I say this out loud? They can't fire me, can they?"

Everyone chuckled and he said, "That's right, you can say whatever you want to." I rolled my eyes about what I was thinking about middle management. This will be the only time in the book where I will complain about aspects of my employer. But this was my chance to spell out and spill out what virtually all letter carriers feel from time to time.

"I get so disgusted with the idiotic decisions that are made. And there have been times when I've just been so frustrated with the organization I work for."

Here I became very emotional and choked up. And a bit fierce.

"But I'll be darned if I didn't wear this uniform with pride for what WE DO! Because we're the backbone of this organization whether they know it or not. And [as I tapped my postal shirt] it's going to be hard to take this off tonight. Because I've worn it with pride.

"Lastly. Because I kept thinking, how do I get off? I'm a big music fan and one of my favorites is Lyle Lovett. He does a song called "Simple Song" and the last verse I think sums up how I feel about you guys."

I then quoted the verse which ends with the words, "Remember, part of me is you."

I said thanks and sat down. I was quite spent . . . and still had the whole day in front of me.

I cased up and prepared the mail for that day's delivery. For the last time. I loaded up my vehicle. For the last time. And with emotional difficulty. I posted a picture of it (along with dozens more of my last day) for social media and wrote:

April 30, 2015

I know I am a sentimental old fool, but I got choked up saying goodbye to this old friend. She and I have been together for 18 years and 30,000 miles.

I pulled out my needed supplies from my locker. For the last time. It had been my locker for 27 years and still had the torn, tattered, and faded remains of a page from a coloring book that one of my kids had made for me at least two decades previously. It was a picture of a mailman. I still have it. And for the last and very final time just before I walked out of the building I stopped and called out for everyone—and especially Gordon—to hear: "Nothin' but tile, baby!" (To my memory, it was the only time I said this when I knowingly knew it to be a falsehood. With my supervisor's permission I had indeed left some third-class mail to be delivered on the next day. But I HAD to say it!)

On to the route. For the last time. The day was filled with goodbyes, tears, cards, balloons, and surprises. Including one terrible one that I will drop into the story now and be done with. As I said, Jill walked nearly my entire route with me, soaking in the sentiments and taking oodles of pics. Oh, before I get to the terrible moment let me shoehorn in two items from the social media aspect of Jill being with me for the day. I had posted the night before that my wife Jill would be walking my route with me on my last day because it is a tradition in the Post Office. My friend Ed commented: "Why is it a tradition in the Post Office for your wife Jill to walk the route with people who retire?" That cracked me up. But the next day she posted and got some terrific remarks.

April 30, 2015 (from Jill's page)

Walking Merrit's route with him on his last day!

Comments:

Please don't let him fall down on his last day.

I bet the Post Office is saying the same thing (in response to the previous comment).

Jill, what an incredible and I'm sure emotional day. It is so cool that you can go with him.

Keep the dogs away from him today, too.

Jill, just remember if you help place even one piece of mail in a customer's box he better dibby up some of his pay for your last day services. Like a giant ice cream cone on his way back to the office or something just as good.

Anyway, about halfway through my route while she was out walking a section with me someone broke into her car and stole her purse. What an awful thing. So she had to spend about an hour on the phone with her bank and the police and DMV. Unfortunately, the culprit was never found. But fortunately, nothing ever happened because of the items taken. No one was able to use her credit cards or identification or anything else.

As I said, as I made my way through MY route for the final time, I was inundated with hugs and cards and balloons and well wishes. It was an enjoyable but emotional minefield. I was staggered with the love that came pouring out of those homes onto me all day long. At the halfway point of my route the time came for my requested tune to be played on All Classical Portland, 89.9. Jill and I took a brief break and sat at the back of my postal vehicle to listen. I was expecting nothing more than the song to air, much to my enjoyment.

At precisely 1:00 came the announcer shift change from my dear friend Christa Wessel to the dapper and punny Robert McBride. Christa and Robert exchanged their usual daily bantering, mentioning the music that would be played on air over the coming afternoon.

Then I was dumbfounded to hear Robert speak the following words: "But first, we are going to make a mailman cry." Which they most certainly did. He went on to share "my story," telling how I had been a rapt listener to the station for the past eight years while delivering my mail route and that I was retiring after 30 years in the postal service. It was a lovely tribute that caught me completely off guard and touched my heart to the depths.

As he continued to speak of me I wept more and more in unabashed gratitude. Robert then finished with this statement: "Merrit, this one's for you." Then they played the "Flower Duet," a gorgeously chiffon-like song sung by two women from the opera "Lakme" by Leo Delibes.

At that moment my daughter Maria popped her head around the corner of the car and asked me if they had indeed made me cry. My face displayed the answer. Maria had decided to join me for just a little bit, soaking in the day with me.

I collected myself as best I could and prepared to deliver the next street on my route. And was met with another wonderful and unexpected surprise. Many folks from the neighborhood had gathered together and been waiting for me to show up to celebrate my retirement with banners, flags, noise-makers, balloons—and lots and lots of love. But it was even more than that. Because of how the day had been progressing I was running 30 to 45 minutes late and these dear folks had been waiting for over an hour for me to arrive. But it was even more than that.

This group of 10 to15 people—made up of both adults and kids—then walked the entire section with me like a parade, waving the aforementioned devices as they accompanied me up the sidewalk on one side of the street and down the other. It was one of the most glorious moments of my career, let alone the day.

In the middle of this trek one of my 27-year customers came out, and just about the time I was finally getting myself together she started crying, which then brought more tears from me. The parade continued on down the street until it was time for me to move on to the next section. This little corner of the neighborhood was very dear to me, and after I retired I was still invited to street-wide cookouts where I happily returned to share my exploits and hear about their new ones. By the way, this group included the famous Wanda and her parents.

The 'occasional' balloons from my last day.

The day continued and I plodded along, trying to drink in every smell, sight, and sound as I continued to take in greetings, well wishes, and the occasional balloon. About 45 minutes later I came upon Paul and Rhonda's dear home. They were on the porch waiting for me. One last time we did our daily routine: "Are you off again toDAY?!" Followed by more hugs and then they graciously took a photo with Jill, Maria, and myself. I received that photo in a lovely frame from them at my retirement party. It hangs on my wall next to my postman memorabilia even today. On my social media post I remarked about this "last" meeting with these two dear folks a week after I retired.

May 6, 2015

Two of the best folks a mailman could ever know, Paul and Rhonda. He is a retired postal worker. Every day I saw him I would ask him the same thing: "Are you off again today?" Now, he can ask me.

Three houses later I met up with Trena, the dear woman I had bonded with one emotional Christmas season many years previously. I also got a picture taken with her, which I posted. She attached this gracious comment to the photo:

May 6, 2015

The reason for this photo is wonderful. You are such a wonderful human, Merrit. Thank you for being such a positive part of the neighborhood, and for being a friend to so many of us.

The day kept speeding by. I got to my next-to-last section and had my final route kid moment. It was one for the ages. And wrapped up in that poignant moment was the reason why I liked being a mailman and why I miss the people aspect of it so much. About 20 stops from the end of my route was a super nice Hispanic family. I had many chats with the father over the years, frequently about how highly I thought of his kids. The youngest of the two siblings was a darling little gal named Goldy. I first met her when she was two and she had now reached the grand old age of eight.

We had become good buds and I saw her and her brother often, especially during summer days. I had not seen her in a couple of weeks. She was alone on the back patio this day, where I always saw her since that was where the mailbox was located. She was playing with her puppy, a new addition to the family. I greeted her and introduced Jill to her and the dog. We chatted a moment then I said this to Goldy:

"Hey, do you remember how I have been telling you that I was going to be retiring and wouldn't be your mailman anymore?"

"Oh, yeah."

"Well, this is my last day. This is the last time I will be here to deliver your mail."

"Oh. Okay."

We then chatted a minute more, exchanging "so longs" and me telling her to be good and do well in school. Jill took a picture of the three of us (puppy included, of course). I said goodbye and headed out the gate and finished the section, which concluded a few houses down the street. Jill got a fantastic shot of me standing on a slanted concrete handrail.

Jill and I stopped at the back of my postal car to prepare the last section of mail and also for me to gather myself a bit as I faced the last minutes of my career. Two or three minutes later here came Goldy's dad driving his pickup down the street past us. He stopped parallel to us and motioned for us to come over to the truck.

I walked up and was stunned to see Goldy sitting in the front seat next to her dad and sobbing. Her dad looked at me with genuine warmth and tenderness and said that she was so upset that she would not see Mr. Merrit delivering the mail anymore. His words and temperament spoke loudly to me that he had appreciated the years when I had befriended his precious children. He fondly wished me "good luck" and drove off. Those few moments define and encapsulate so much of what my career meant to me.

There was also one last little ceremony I had to do for myself. I have a little bit of OCD that pops up from time to time. It is not so much that I must do certain things, nor do I feel the necessity to repeat actions. But there are routines I do because I want to and have always done so. Again, if I was prevented from doing these things, there would be zero anxiety or consternation on my part. I just enjoy the idea of certain small routines.

There were four places on my route where I set my footstep in or on specific spots every day. Two rocks (one that bore a striking resemblance to the state of Nevada), a place on a sidewalk with a strange foot-like shape irregularly traced in the concrete, and this final spot that had been with me the entire 27 years I had been on my route. It was embedded in the asphalt of the driveway for a five-plex. It mildly resembled a footprint. Sort of.

Anyway, for 27 years I had stepped into this spot virtually every day (unless it was full of water from heavy rains). I would step in with my right foot one day and my left foot the next and so on. Again, it was not an obsession. If I forgot which foot I had last used I didn't worry about it. When I returned to work after a vacation I gave no thought to which foot I had last used, but merely began again with my left foot. So what was I going to do, on this my final day?

Three years after I retired I was sharing this story with a dear friend who knows of my . . . um . . . oddities in this area. She asked me that very question. Which foot did I use on my last day? I simply stared at her and smiled, waiting for her to arrive at the inevitable answer. Finally, she closed her eyes and said, "Oh, brother. You stepped in it with BOTH of them, didn't you?" That would be affirmative. I first stepped in the hole with my left foot, walked around in a very tiny circle, and then very deliberately stepped in the hole—for the very last time—with my right foot. What else could I do?

*The footprint shaped indention I stepped into
for 27 years. Because it was there.*

We continued on to my very last section. Nineteen
more homes to bring mail to. I went down the street on one
side, just like I had done 6,000 times before. Then I crossed
over for the final eight stops of my postal career. After 70,000
miles of walking, I had but one more block to traverse. Jill
took out her phone and took a video of these two and a half
minutes.

I went through the gate of the very last house on this
section, the very last house on my route, the very last house
of my 27 years as a city letter carrier for the Post Office on
route 0655. I trudged up the steps to the porch, flipped open
the mailbox lid, hesitated for just the briefest of moments,

took one of the biggest and deepest breaths of my life . . . and placed the mail into the mailbox. The very last time I would place mail into a mailbox on my route. It was done.

We headed back to the Creston Station. I parked my postal van in its assigned place for the very last time. Then I received a delightful surprise when I entered the building. My middle daughter Faitha had driven up from Cannon Beach with her son William to greet me as I finished the day. It was such a wonderfully sweet gift because she had made that trip knowing she could only stay for a few minutes before heading back.

I had no idea she would come all that way, and I was deeply appreciative of the gesture. I organized my returned and outgoing mail and turned in my keys—for the very last time. I grabbed my personal belongings, threw them into my mailbag which I then tossed over my shoulder, and swiped out my time card—for the very last time. I was truly finished. After 30 years, two months, and 28 days, I now was officially no longer an employee of the United States Postal Service.

The rest of the afternoon and evening is a blur in my memory. Several of my coworkers—including some former coworkers, either retired or now working at other stations—joined my family at a local establishment where we told stories and celebrated the completion of my "appointed rounds."

Two very vivid and poignant moments do stick with me, however. And always will. Mailman Mike came to this party and we naturally shared many a story and laugh, especially as he regaled everyone else with his eternal doubts that I would ever make it as a mailman. I spoke with dozens of folks over the hours I spent there that evening.

As I made my way to the door to head to my car and make my drive home I spotted Mike chatting with a group of people while sitting at a table about ten feet from me. I stopped walking and was suddenly very overcome with emotion. And in a span of about four seconds my entire 30 year career swept before my eyes. I was awash in memories and gratitude for . . . well . . . all of it.

"Hey, Mike!" I called out. He looked over at me. And I choked out these very significant nine words between the two of us: "I made it to the end of the row!" He smiled knowingly, nodded, and gave me a thumbs-up. Because, indeed, I had.

There was one final "ceremony" to accomplish. One more thing to do for the very last time. After arriving home from the party I walked into our bedroom. I took one last look at myself in the mirror wearing that old familiar uniform that had adorned my person for 30 years. Jill took a picture of me. And then—for the last time—I peeled off that old friend, never to wear those blue-striped pants again, those seemingly inseparable pants that so identified my job and who I had been for three decades. Before we conclude this chapter, please allow me to share from a different perspective how the day had hit me. Much of this is a condensed version of what you have just read. But I felt it necessary to include it. This was my social media post the next morning:

May 1, 2015

What a day it was! It is unfathomable to me how I can possibly express in words what all you folks did for me yesterday on my last day of work. First, let me get the one cruddy item out of the way. While walking my route with me, Jill's purse was stolen from her car. So she is having to spend much of today doing DMV, banking, etc., as I stay at home (BECAUSE I DIDN'T HAVE TO GO TO WORK!!!) to allow our contractor to come to the house to re-do all the locks. WE will NOT allow some idiot to spoil this weekend.

Our union VP, Jerry F. came out to the station in the morning and said some very kind words about me and about what my fellow mailmen do. I was able to deliver my speech to my dear coworkers, telling them the affection I have for them and the pride I feel in what they and I do.   Throughout my route I was met with handshakes, good wishes, cards, gifts, and LOTS of balloons. On one street many of the neighbors had gathered and greeted me with drums, balloons, streamers, poppers, and then those dear folks of the hood walked the street with me as a parade while carrying above-mentioned items and flags, including one little one who carried a huge American flag that was bigger than her.

There were many goodbyes, hugs, laughs, and a lake full of tears (mostly mine). Then many of my coworkers and I, plus several other retirees, gathered together over food and beverages for more of the same. The radio interview that was done by Jim Ferretti on KXL radio was incredible, and the classical station not only played a song for me, but host Robert McBride had some truly lovely words for me.

Then to come home and see the myriad of wishes, thoughts, and comments from y'all . . . well, I am still coming down from an emotional high I would not have thought possible. Jill took dozens of photos, plus video of the parade of kids, and finally, video of me coming down the street delivering my last few stops. We will post those soon. It was delightful having Jill walk my route with me. Daughter Maria came along for a while and was at both morning and evening celebrations, as was my lovely stepdaughter Jael.

I got several phone messages of love, including one from daughter Valeena. And the cupcake on top was as I returned to the postal station for the last time, I was bowled over to walk in and find daughter Faitha waiting for me with grandson William. I have maybe never felt so appreciated and cared for so deeply by so many at one time. A truly, TRULY extraordinary day. Thank you.

Comments:

We love you, Daddy! (no, this is not a bad mailman joke, it actually came from one of my daughters)

Wow! What a day!

Congratulations, Merrit! I hope your retirement will be as rich as your career was. Cheers and best wishes.

So happy for you! Now every day is a day off!!

You will be missed, Merrit. Enjoy your retirement!

Congratulations, Merrit! Looking forward to your epistles describing the next leg of your amazing life journey.

Aweeee, such a bittersweet moment! It's not every day a customer makes me cry at work!

You'll be missed! (this was from one of the hot chocolate ladies)

Congrats! I can't wait until I am that old! ;)

Welcome to the Retired People's Club! Congratulations on a job well done!

Sooooo, are you bored yet? Lol.

Sounds like a beautiful send-off! May this next chapter in your life be as fulfilling as the last! I'm looking forward to reading your book!! (Well....)

Merrit, you have obviously ministered in Jesus' name to those on your route and those with whom you worked. May the Lord bless your retirement years.

Loving you so much. Thanks for sharing your thoughts and life. Always your friend.

What a wonderful testimony to your faithfulness over the years, Merrit! Many who are proud of you, many who will miss you, and many, many folks who honestly care about and love you. You must have felt like some sort of dignitary.

The day was done. A day I had anticipated for just over half of my life. And now I was a "civilian" again. But, about the media.

Chapter 31

AS FAMOUS AS I WILL EVER BE

"Delighted to do so"

In my youth I was fascinated with the medium of radio. For several years it was the vocation I passionately pursued. But it was not meant to be. After being involved in radio in varying aspects for nearly a decade, all that remains of my "career" is a three-minute recording of me losing my mind in excitement at the end of a collegiate basketball game. (When my kids were little and brought a new friend to the house it was not unusual for them to request me to play this recording so they could poke fun at Daddy. I loved it!)

It is still a means of communication that I love. My dearest friend Roger has been a radio broadcaster for decades. And I love to visit the local classical music radio station any chance I get. I have earlier expressed my undying devotion to that station, 89.9, All Classical Portland. Their gift to play a tune I requested and their kind words are something I will always treasure. I kicked the idea around for some time before I contacted them.

What I did not expect were two local stations—one radio and one television—to contact me for a story. I first met Jim Ferretti through my oldest daughter Maria and their mutual love of bowling. Over the years I had occasional casual chats with him at the bowling alley or at social gatherings. He got involved in radio and eventually went to work at KXL radio as a reporter. He began to see and read my social media posts and would sometimes comment on them.

About two months before I retired, he contacted me and stunned me with the idea of doing a feature story about me and my career as a mailman. The combination of the stories I had published on social media, along with the idea that I had spent my entire 30-year career as a walking mailman (as opposed to driving or some other area in the postal service) and the further unusualness of being on the same route for 27 years intrigued him enough to convince him it might make for a good radio feature.

I got permission from postal management for him to tag along with me on my route for an hour or so and two weeks later he joined me as I delivered to my business section and my first residential section. I spun my tales, answered his questions, and he chatted with some of my customers. He did a beautiful job of editing and arranged the airing of it to coincide with my final day of work. Here is part of the written transcript, used with his permission.

A SOUTHEAST PORTLAND NEIGHBORHOOD WILL NEVER BE THE SAME
Written by Jim Ferretti on April 30, 2015

PORTLAND, Ore – The Mt. Scott/Arleta neighborhood has had a familiar face delivering letters, magazines and junk mail for the past 27 years. But starting May 1st, Merrit Hearing will be sitting at home drinking tea instead of being a long time postal carrier.

Merrit has been with the U.S. Postal Service for the past 30 years and has delivered to the same neighborhood for the past 27 years. Merrit said when he started working for the Post Office he was young and naive and thought he would only do it for a little while and see what happens.

"I had no idea I would be stepping into, in a way I consider it a ministry. I have talked to people who have lost children. I have made dear friends, people who came to my son's memorial, people who came to my wedding reception, people who mean a lot to me. And I didn't expect that."

Merrit, like many other postal carriers has had his run-ins with mean dogs. He has suffered 10 dog bites including a serious bite last year. But what he is most famous for around the post office is his run-in with an angry bunny.

Jim then told about the rabbit attack. Following that was this statement:

Merrit saw a lot of things during his 30 years of service, but he summed it all up with a very touching story.

He then shared the story of the two little kids who were adopted on my route. Here is the finish of that interview.

Merrit says during his retirement he is going to watch a lot of baseball, drink a lot of iced tea, visit with his kids and grandkids and do some writing.

"And probably for two or three months, I'm not going to walk anywhere!"

Congratulations Merrit on a wonderful three decade career and a well-deserved rest.

In the three-minute audio version that aired on the radio you can hear neighborhood sounds in the background, and in a decision that surprised and pleased me greatly, you can very clearly hear my little radio from my pocket playing classical music. In other words, Jim's radio station played an audio recording with a competing radio station playing in the background. Very cool. It was this interview I referenced earlier that my little friend Wanda heard with her mom and remarked that it was Merrit and that was his music.

The day after I retired was Friday, May 1, 2015. I had just gotten into my car to run some errands and pick up supplies for my retirement party the next evening when I got a phone call. It was from KATU television, our local ABC affiliate. They had received a phone call from one of my customers (one of the dear folks in the neighborhood where I had my "parade"). He had strongly suggested to them that my story might prove of interest to their viewers. So the next morning a woman came out to our home to interview me along with a cameraman. They set up in our driveway and did a quick feature. It lasted about 90 seconds and consisted of me sharing a few thoughts, some commentary from the interviewer, and some photos of me in my postal gear I had collected over the years. It was short but very well done.

I didn't seek out either of these opportunities and both caught me very much off guard. But I was more than delighted to do so. As a famous baseball announcer once said, I don't seek out attention but I don't turn it down when it is offered. Actually, my wife might disagree with part of that statement. And considering the next chapter, she might be right.

Chapter 32

PLEASE PARDON THIS CHAPTER

"A man of letters"

Is it unusual for a letter carrier to spend 30 years as a walking mailman, never moving onto another aspect of the postal service? A bit. Is it also unusual for said mailman to stay on the same route for 27 years? Somewhat more. Are either of these accomplishments newsworthy? In the grand scheme of things, no. During my time at Creston, three other carriers—Mailman Mike, Doug the Slug, and Dave W.—all surpassed both of those numbers. And, like me, I also know that each of these gentlemen was proud of what he completed. But this is my book, so please indulge me with the next part of these writings. If you slide through a career of 30 years in any sort of service industry with the idea of wanting to please the public, it is a fine thing and very encouraging to be recognized and have some of that public go out of their way to say "thank you."

My postal retirement party was, well, jusssst a bit over the top. We invited more than 200 folks to come celebrate with us. It was loud and crowded and warm . . . and oh, so wonderful. One of my customers—Curt, the man who had called the TV station about me—got up and spoke a few words.

Apparently that morning he had received mail that did not belong to him and he concluded with these words: "Well, here we go. I already miss Merrit." It got lots of laughs.

I brought Aaron up in front of everyone ("the worst carrier in the station") and officially presented him with my postal coat. As I placed it on him, I asked him if he knew what size it was. He didn't. I said: "42, extra legend."

My daughter Valeena got up and told how one of her deepest memories from when she was a little girl is that Daddy always wore these long postal socks that went almost to his knees and that she loved to tease me by rolling them down. Then she and her husband Rigo sang a song with personalized lyrics adapted from a tune called "I'm Gonna Be (500 Miles)" by the Proclaimers.

If you know of the song, you will understand where they substituted some of these very personal lyrics:

"who rolls socks to my knees."
"that goes out with good shoes."
"if I fall down . . . it's gonna be right before the holidays."
"if I get bit."
"by a crazy red-eyed rabbit."
"to drop mail at your door."
"the back pain and the knee pain"
"numb toes and cold nose."
"get that mail to your door."
"when it's rainin' or it's snowin' or it's hailin'."
"gets that mail to you."

Valeena sang the verses while Rigo played guitar, then he joined her for the chorus. It was very sweet, very touching, and both my daughter and I seemed to have trouble with our eyes, especially when during the last verse her emotions caught up with her and caused her voice to catch and crack.

I had my wife take a fabulous picture of me with my two oldest "Route Kids." Corrie was 23 and Nancy was 18. I had been their mailman for their entire lives. I already mentioned how I used to bop Nancy on the head with my handful of mail. Somewhere in a box I still have pictures that Corrie drew for me when she was a little girl. Now they were both beautiful grown up young women. One other fascinating aspect about Corrie. Over the years I had been the mailman to her great-grandmother, her grandfather, her mother, her aunt, and her uncle. Talk about walking through a family's life! What a privilege.

Corrie and Nancy, my two oldest Route Kids.
If you are retired you probably love my shirt.
If you are not, then I would politely ask you not to
spit on this page. Unless you actually own the book.
Then feel free.

The most surprising moment for me and others came when off-the-cuff I suddenly had the idea to celebrate my customers who had shown up for the festivities. I said a few words of appreciation for my job and the customers who had helped to make it so rewarding. Then I said, "Just out of curiosity, if you have been or ever were a customer of mine during my career, would you please stand up?"

I was astonished when well over 125 of the attendees rose to their feet. Even now, the thought of that moment overwhelms me. My only regret of the evening is that I had not thought to have someone record it. So I will keep those memories fresh and pressed to my heart with as much detail as I can recall. It was a glorious night.

But I was caught off guard yet again in the following days as I began to read the cards that so many of these dear folks had written to me. So for the remainder of this chapter, please allow me to share some of those sentiments with you. Not so much to say "hey, look at me and how much I was loved." No, more to give testimony to the reward that can be attained through simple caring and doing what could be a monotonous job with a bit of personal-ness and with a sincere people-oriented focus.

Thank you for rescuing our package [mis-addressed]. Sorry our dog is a jerk to you.

Thank you so much for delivering our mail each and every day! We truly appreciate your hard work and we are sorry the dogs are so loud!

Hi Neighbor! Thanks for two decades of love & friendship. I will be forever grateful! With much affection & endless hugs, Annie. (my blond postal neighbor I have mentioned)

What a blessing it has been to be on your mail route and a little part of your story . . . you've been a treasured part of ours.

You've been a constant for so many, many years—always positive, always joyful, always just you. I will miss you.

Thank you for your many superb years of service delivering our mail. I will miss hearing your music as you walked up our porch steps.

We have enjoyed our Chicago Bears–Green Bay Packers rivalry! Will keep those fun memories. And our mutual dislike (to put it mildly) of Seahawks (ugh)!! Fondly.

Although we will miss your grumpy (broken-down) old face we are thrilled for your new life.

We count ourselves very lucky to spend the last 4-plus years with you. We are very excited that you are about to embark on this new journey. We hope to keep in touch. You will be missed!

For four years you have been such a wonderful presence in my life. Always joyful and ready with a smile and hello. When my daughter was born I appreciated you sharing your story and advice.

Thank you for all your years of good service; we could always count on it being done right.

Thanks for the heartfelt conversations at the mailbox.

Dharma [her dog] barked: "I love you and will miss you!" Me too.

With all the dog bites and miles of walking, you have never given up on bringing the mail.

Congratulations. After many thousands, enjoy your next step.

I loved drawing pictures for you and leaving them in the mail.

Sincere congratulations to a man of letters.

Thank you for all the years—snow, freezing rain, summer scorchers, pleasant spring days, too.

Congratulations on a graceful end to a worthy and well-lived career.

When you introduced yourself as I was moving in three years ago, it was another sign to me that I had picked the right place—such great people!

Thank you for all of the years you spent not just delivering mail but getting to know us.

You were my best mailman EVER.

God has truly blessed you.

Merrit, I admire you, I envy you, but most of all congratulate you for LIVING your work. Enjoy your transition to retirement, I know it will be an awesome chapter to your life!

What a legacy. Our lives have all been changed for the better, having known you. Congrats, buddy.

We could really tell how much you put into doing your job well. We could always trust that you would hide packages in the back for us and it means a lot for that rapport to be so incredibly high.

You worked hard, put in your time, and earned this retirement.

Just think, no more dog bites, hot weather or ice to contend with. How great is that?

Now you can take up a new hobby. Long-distance hiking! No? Well, whatever you do, have a great time.

It was great having you as our postman. It will never be the same. You made me feel like I lived in Mayberry right in the middle of Portland.

And finally, from the dear family that wrote that amazing Christmas card to me thanking me for showing the sense of a community aspect in their neighborhood.

Used with permission.

Dear Merrit, Let me start by saying thank you. Thank you so much for being a part of our lives. Thank you. You are so much more to my family than "just" our mailman (which is significant in and of itself!) You have always been "Our" mailman, but you're also an old friend. You would have been my mailman for 25 years in September, the 11th to be precise. Your young family once lived in my apartment. (I love that!) Over those 25 years I've had 3 relationships, 2 marriages, 1 divorce (thank you for the "wait 6 months for every year married" advice—it was accurate), 1 major home purchase and remodel. 3 cats. 1 dog (oh, what I would change if I could!). 1 bunny. [No, not THAT one.] 2 guinea pigs. 2 beautiful children! We've shared, you and I, conversations about all of the above, as well as your life's milestones, the good and the bad. Not everyone shares themselves like us. I'm blessed to have been a part of this incredible journey, so far. I say "so far" because the next phase is just beginning for you and I'm not going anywhere, friend. You know where I live! Ha ha! All my love, Bonnie.

As you can see, this idea of walking through people's lives—it was very true. But now it was time to take those next steps. But I had no idea of the grip the Post Office still had on me.

Chapter 33

POSTMORTEM

"An abundance of friendships"

Soooo, now what? It was time to start getting used to being an EX-mailman. But even now, a few years later, that concept still jars me a bit. When I speak of the Post Office I still tend to use "we" rather than "they" in telling stories and events. This organization does not let go easily. That certainly is not necessarily its fault.

One of the first surprises was a prophecy of Jill's that came to pass in a big way. I presumed I would take it easy for a few days and then feel rested and get on with life. Jill warned me I would most likely be very worn down for a LONG time. Oh, my. It was months before I felt remotely rested. It was not like having an extended vacation. This time my body seemed to be asking, "Are you really done this time? Is this it or are you simply recovering from yet another injury? Okay, if you are actually finished for good then we are shutting down for an extended time." And I really did. I just felt run over and blitzed for weeks and weeks.

I had been entwined within the postal doors for 30 years. I was simply not emotionally or mentally ready to let go of the folks so easily. I was determined to stay in touch somewhat regularly and also keep letting the folks know how and what I was doing and that I was certainly not going to forget about them. I was delighted when the first volley came from a customer.

It was a social media post from Sally to me a mere four days after my retirement. She had mentioned a few times over the years that she enjoyed hearing my radio playing as I approached the house with their mail.

May 4, 2015

I had a very bittersweet moment, returning home from work today around 5:00 p.m. There was no classical music playing as my mail was delivered, so I opted to put on a Stevie Wonder record (guess which song was up first?). [Signed Sealed Delivered I'm Yours]. I got back to my Michigan roots with Stevie, and thought about how much I dug seeing and talking with you. I'm thinking tomorrow's selection will be something in the way of Tchaikovsky.

Oh, thank you, Sally! I was missed already! Yay! But my emotions and reflections were still running on overtime so I looked for any excuse to share them.

June 4, 2015

Today I am five weeks out from my last day delivering mail. Here are some of my meandering thoughts. I do not miss work one iota. I had had enough to know that I had had enough. I miss my customers terribly and worry occasionally about the quality of service they have been receiving since I left. (Hey, just being honest, folks.)

I feel extremely blessed to have relationships with so many of them. I miss many of my coworkers so much. But I was soooo done. I have been caught off guard with how spent I was, both physically and even more so mentally. I am just now starting to relax in a restful fashion and truly realizing that I am done with my career. That I am not coming back.

All of that is bringing me to a point where I actually feel more fatigued now than I did 35 days ago. Jill has been after me to allow myself to just do nothing for several weeks—or even longer, if necessary—and my doctor urged me to rest (not sleep) whenever my body tells me to for the first few months.

I still need to get regular exercise, go to karaoke (well, duh), attend church, spend time with friends, etc. But it is time for me to finally take a heavy sigh and do some major chillin'. It will take some serious discipline to not stare at a "to-do" list all the time. But I am going to stop feeling guilty about not working and soak up this new chapter in my life. I have enjoyed the past month, but much of it has seemed raggedy to me within myself. Time to get smoother.

Five more weeks passed.

July 9, 2015

Ten weeks into retirement. I do not miss work AT ALL!!! I am torn between feeling terrible about this horrid hot weather my (ex) coworkers have been working in, BUT really, really thankful that I have not had to. And remembering that my final dealings with Mr. Summer last year were the mildest I had in 30 years on the job. I had two large reality checks this past week. A few days ago while watching World Cup action on TV with Jill, it hit me out of nowhere like a hammer: "Good grief! I am never going to deliver mail again!" That hit me hard. And I just found out yesterday that my route—MY route (it will always be so in my heart, those are MY people) —has officially been assigned to another person. For the first time since early May 1988, route 0655 in southeast Portland, Oregon does not belong to Merrit Hearing. I miss my coworkers and the daily banter. But I REALLY miss my customers and those interactions. I miss the wisdom from the little ones, my route kids. So grateful for social media and being able to stay in touch with all those friends. P.S. – But my knees have not felt this good in Y E A R S!!!

Some comments about that post. First, the weather. My last summer AND winter had been if not THE mildest, then certainly one of the very mildest seasons respectively I had in my 30 years of delivering mail. My first summer after I retired was a blazing inferno for weeks. At the time it set the record for the most 90-degree days in one year for the Portland area. And that first winter was one Noah's Ark day after another.

And as those days would hit I would be caught between dichotomous emotions. I would gaze out the window and think, "Oh, those poor mailmen!" Which would be almost immediately followed with giggling.

And I did feel some guilt about not being out there in the elements with my comrades. But one day it occurred to me that I had no business feeling guilty. I had put in my time. Much of it while some of those still working mailmen were in grade school (or in Dominique's case, not even born yet). So now it was their turn. I had done my duty and my time.

Regarding the moment that hit during the World Cup. I can still picture it to this day. I was sitting at the far end of our couch as we watched the soccer match. Then the thought pummeled me. Suddenly I leaped up. Jill asked me what was wrong. And it had truly and finally hit me. I was really, REALLY never going to deliver mail again! Not. Ever. Again. I had done one occupation for 30 years. And that time was accomplished. Whew.

August 8, 2015

100 days into retirement.

SURPRISES: As Jill warned me, how utterly spent my body was. I am still so very worn out. Also, I didn't anticipate it taking so long to get used to this schedule.

WHAT I EXPECTED: I am never bored. I read a lot and have watched oodles of baseball games.

WHAT I MISS: My customers. Oh, my customers. My goodness, how I miss those daily moments of life-sharing. I thought I would, but it is waaayyy more than I figured.

WHAT I DON'T MISS: (blank) catalogs, advos, political mail, walking in this ghastly heat, and although my last bosses were ones I liked, I don't miss having to report to one.

FRUSTRATION: I have been ill since Father's Day. Nothing at all serious. Intestinal issues that are starting to slowly improve with new meds. But I have been mostly confined to the house.

JOYS: Two main ones. The time to go about my projects and activities at a leisurely pace, knowing I have "tomorrow." I have found a special place at our home. In a comfy love seat on our back patio, overlooking our yard, numerous trees, and the wetlands behind our property. It is shaded and allows for a nice breeze and the view is fabulous. I love to just stare out through the trees into the high grass and just read, listen to a ballgame (or the simple sounds of nature), or just sit and contemplate, as I enjoy the glorious colors of green, red, or gold that are within my visual grasp. I liked being a mailman. I am loving being an EX.

WARNING: Once I am feeling a bit better, many of you will be receiving visits from me. I can't wait. Blessings.

P.S. THANKFUL that I didn't have to deal with this illness while trying to work, especially in this horrid hot weather. Oh, I have also been walking a couple miles two or three times a week. And one final huge bonus, my knees have not felt this good in over 20 years.

Yes, the thing with the knees was a huge deal for me. As tired as I still felt, my knees were recovering at a much quicker pace than I had anticipated from 70,000 miles of walking.

I heard from dear Sally again.

August 16, 2015
    We miss you!

I was hoping she was not alone in that sentiment. So I expressed it in regard to the new style of walking I was doing.

August 18, 2015
    I do not enjoy walking on our treadmill. My doctor says I need to walk in order to stay in good health. The first few weeks after I retired were totally unpleasant. Then it dawned on me that I needed to be listening to Christa Wessel on the All Classical Portland radio station like I did when delivering my mail route. That helped a little.

    But the other day it suddenly occurred to me that what I am really missing . . . is YOU, my customers. I estimated that during the course of a normal day I MIGHT have as many as 60 to 125 interpersonal chats with you dear folks as I made my rounds. By the way, in case any ex-bosses read this, they were ALWAYS of course substantially short conversations.

    Anyway, my idea is to get a sign-up sheet going and have my customers take turns stopping by my house for a few minutes while I get my walking done. It would be a rotating list so each of you would only need to stop by once every several months. What do you think? In other words, I am missing:

At this point I listed dozens of names from my route. Folks that you have already read about and some you have not. I continued:

I fear I have missed someone. My sincere apologies. Plus, scads more that are not on social media. This was fairly off the top of my head. Warning: I should be feeling better soon and I will come see many of you. Kidding about the sign-up sheet. Although—

October 30, 2015

So, today marks six months since I retired. I've had several folks ask me, "What's it like, being retired?" I can only come up with one word: weird. It's not just that I am done with my 30 years in the USPS. I have—like most folks—been working in some capacity since I was about 10 or 12. Paper routes, picking fruit, college campus jobs, warehouse/shipping work. It is supremely odd to not have that inner clock still yammering.

I love the time I now have to read, listen to music, watch baseball. I do not miss the grind delivering mail had on my body. And when the weather is unpleasant, I must admit I take a real pleasure in knowing I don't have to go out in it and deal with it for miles and hours. I miss my cowor . . . EX-coworkers, and my former customers. But now socialization, although not as regular, is more relaxed.

I do miss the daily chats with folks, but social media helps with that. In other words, I miss the people, not the job. Probably the most poignant thing for myself is the idea that somehow the Postal Service is still functioning without me, lol. People still receive their mail. Not as well . . . but certainly faster now that I am off the job. I am proud of my career and extremely grateful for the dear friends I made, both in the office and on the street. I must say, however, that my body feels better than it has in years, especially my knees. As soon as the World Series is over, I anticipate getting more into some type of routine with the activities I wish to throw myself into. Onward.

I know, I know. Again with the knees. Hey, it is what it was. A funny moment came along about two weeks later. It was Veteran's Day. And another reminder my life was so very different.

November 11, 2015

I think I am officially retired. Today I could not figure out why the mail had not come.

That coming weekend the weather turned truly nasty. I threw out a thought for all.

November 17, 2015

For those living in the Portland area, be extra nice to your mailman today. This is truly miserable weather for them. Don't make them wait or call them back because you didn't have your outgoing mail ready to go. I can remember during last winter thinking I was almost done working in this kind of mess. Today is my first time not having to do so since I retired. Soooooo glad to be indoors. Hang in there my ex-coworkers; you will get through this.

My first Christmas season not being a mailman in 31 years approached. Tough times for my heart. What you are about to read is not new information to you if you have read this far in my book. But it was a brand-new viewpoint of an old experience for me.

December 1, 2015

I have posted in the past a few times how much I miss my customers, but not the job. Well, for the next 3 1/2 weeks I will for the first time be missing my job. I positively LOVED working the Christmas season. The sights, sounds, lights, smells, familial love, joyous greetings, and, if it didn't get too bad, even the crisp chilly weather.

I loved delivering colorful Christmas card envelopes rather than the same old bills/junk. Loved delivering parcels. Yes, it was delightful getting treats and tips from some of my customers (that's a hint if you have a good mailman). But I just loved the atmosphere.

And every once in a while, I might get dosed with a little magic. Two things would thrill me. Delivery to a house where I had watched kids grow up and eventually move away. They come back to visit their folks for Christmas and see me. "Mr. Merrit, are you still the mailman here?"

Hugs all around and maybe meeting THEIR little ones. And, for me, there was nothing—NOTHING—better than approaching a house the last few days before the 25th with a large package to deliver and spotting a little face or two in the window with total wonderment in their eyes watching me come up the walk. And THAT is why I liked being a mailman. To my former customers: thanks for all the joy, treats, hugs, and love. I will REALLY miss you these next weeks. Happy Holidays, everybody!!

However, there was also the realization that not everything during the Christmas season was magical and exciting. That first December after my retirement also brought on some very unpleasant and overly soggy weather.

December 7, 2015

Sooo, remember how last week I said how much I was missing working this month? Well, I be looking outside and thinking not so much!

There was another part of the season that I was desperately missing, and I used it as an opportunity to nudge people a bit in regards to those in the different service industries.

December 19, 2015

I will be blunt. One of the things I am missing about my job is the treats/tipping I received from many of my customers this time every year. It wasn't the cash or the stuff—it was being remembered and appreciated. Homemade cookies, fudge, candy . . . Always . . . ALWAYS touched my heart. One lady for 25-plus Christmases in a row left me some homemade Chex mix. So, PLEASE, if you have any kind of good & friendly mailman, say thanks with something tangible. Even a card.

For that matter, remember your garbageman, fave waitress or barkeep, gas station attendant, your kids' teacher(s), anyone who brings you regular, consistent, friendly service. You have NO idea how much it will mean to them that you took the time, effort, and cost to say "thanks."

The month slid by and I was hit with an unexpected—and truth be told, silly—emotional moment.

December 30, 2015

My wife Jill always tells me I am a sentimental old fool. This post will prove her correct. After 30 years, I am using an item for the last time tomorrow. My faithful six-color postal calendar. Mailmen's days' off rotate weekly. Monday off one week, Tuesday the next, etc. Letter carriers' days off are divided into six colors: green, blue, red, black, yellow, and brown. That way they can plan their activities to correspond to their off days months in advance despite the rotating schedule.

For 30 years I have used these calendars to schedule doctor appointments, ballgames, social events, reminders to call friends, children's sports or school events, church meetings, expectant delivery dates for grandchildren (and way-back-when . . . MY children), etc.

Tomorrow marks the last day on my very last postal calendar. I COULD continue to get and use them, but I have chosen and wish to not do so. These calendars are for working employees of the United States Postal Service. For me, it would not be appropriate to continue to use them. So tomorrow I will do the one last thing written down as a reminder, fold up the calendar, and store it for posterity. It/they have been great tool(s) down through the years. Oh, the very last item on the very last day of the very last month of my very last calendar? Why, to remind myself that it was the last day of my last calendar, of course.

The retirement months continued to fly by. That is how I saw them in my head. I had counted down the months until I retired. They were "work" months. Now I was in my "retirement" months. The year 2016 became a year of much less transition and easing into this new life. Well, easing would not be the most accurate word to use. Perhaps walking jaggedly. But my . . . er, physical problems were not always . . . um . . . terribly serious.

January 13, 2016

OK, as I post this I am completely aware that it is a first-world prob. Like most untalented men my age, I love to play air-drums. Well, since I have had tendonitis in my right elbow for the past year and since I am having some real tightness and pain issues with my right shoulder as my body learns to adapt to NOT carrying a mailbag, I am having to air-drum left-handed. Which is not nearly as smooth or powerful as right-handed. Fortunately, I am semi-ambidextrous, so there is hope.

But I was also beginning to miss my folks, especially the little ones. One lovely winter afternoon while waiting for a small repair on my car in the same neighborhood (Leonard, of course) as my route I stopped by to see a couple families.

January 28, 2016

Got to see one of my route kids on Tuesday. In the four years I was her mailman she was very shy and would usually not engage with me beyond a shy wave. Not so much now. We had a giggle time wrestling around and tickling. She has a baby sister who was born the day after I retired, thus missing by one day of being my last Route Kid. Many thanks to mommy for letting me drop by for a few delightful minutes. One of many families I miss seeing regularly.

The postscript to this family's story is that because of this baby sister's "rudeness" of being born the same weekend as my retirement, the family had to miss my party. We have seen each other occasionally since then and one or the other of us will complain about it. It always brings a smile.

But the steps slowly became smoother as the days passed. Part of what helped were visits. I arranged to stop and visit two of my dear families who had little ones I was missing. The day ended up with a couple of sightings I was not expecting.

May 12, 2016

Do I miss the dear folks from my mail route of 27 years? I saw about a dozen of them tonight in three different locales. I am still beaming. Me be blessed. Then and now.

In June I stopped doing my walking on the treadmill and instead headed over to a nearby high school track to tally up some miles. The idea of walking outside had come from a dear friend and it made all the difference in the world. My track went from being six feet long to a quarter mile. And there were trees to look at and breezes to feel and sounds to listen to. And as I got to know some of the regulars there was also human interaction. Sometimes I would envy the younger folks who would fly around the lanes at speeds I had not attained in 30 years. Then I began to notice some of these folks were not all that much younger than me! I had to resign myself to the fact that I probably had tens of thousands more miles on my deteriorated frame than they did. Hey, pal, I already did my miles, thank you very much.

In August of that year I was treated to the Yankees game in Seattle by one of my customers that I have already told you about. It had become more obvious to me than I had ever realized that keeping in contact with these dear folks was going to be a huge key in my healthy transition.

That summer I also attended the retirement party of my dear little friend, Dwyn, the sweet little lady who had marched into Multnomah Station for her first day in the

Post Office a few months after I had started. For reasons that still escape me, it really smacked me hard with the reality of my extinguished career. Dwyn spent her entire career at Multnomah and her party was in that area. I had not been out there in several years and on the way to the event I kept pointing out misty but familiar memories to Jill of streets I had delivered mail on 30 years previously. At the party were a couple of the old-timers who had worked at Multnomah when I was there. When I saw Dwyn, we embraced tightly. I looked at her and said, "We made it, kid." I kept looking at her and all I could think about was the overwhelming reality of the passage of a LOT of time. That here in front of me was a woman who had seemed like a kid on that first day. That she had started AFTER me. And that she had now also reached retirement. Dwyn and I had turned over the reins to the next generation of mail carriers. We did our bit. We did it well. Time to move on.

September 12, 2016

Yesterday marked 500 days into retirement for me. Unexpectedly, today was the day I celebrated it. I had a scheduled coffee with a former coworker who had retired. We had a lovely visit, of which a chunk of the time was us reminiscing about former bosses we'd had that we despised working for. (No former bosses of mine that I am social media friends with were brought up because I LIKED working for them). We'd mention a name, share an awful story, then (unplanned by the two of us) laugh uproariously because we were no longer in that environment and having to deal with these folks who could be so unpleasant.

On my way home I drove through my route and was able to have a delightful visit with three of my former customers. A mother and daughter and their neighbor. These memories and stories were rich with love and smiles and warmth.

On the drive home I felt blessed and thankful to God that despite the unpleasant times with some of postal management, my memories of work are interlaced with an abundance of friendships like my coworker and these three dear ladies who I delivered mail to for 27 years. The cherry on top was that as one of the women was getting out of her vehicle to come hug and greet me, I heard her exclaim, "What a treat!" That simple comment, said 16-plus months after I last delivered her mail, overwhelmed me. Ah, the treat was mine, believe me.

Along came the first national election since my retirement. As you can see, some memories do not fade.

October 14, 2016

I gotta tell you, I am really, really . . . REALLY enjoying not delivering mail during this national election time frame. Other than [blank] catalogs (yes, again), political mail is the WORST!!

The Christmas season rolled around again and the Portland area was inundated with its heaviest snowfall in eight years. That led to this quip:

December 8, 2016

"Oh, it's beginning to look a lot like . . . I'm-really-glad-I'm-not-a-mailman-anymore . . . everywhere you go."

The third summer since I had retired came along. I couldn't help but ruminate once again on my relationship with that particular season.

June 6, 2017

Mr. Summer approaches. During the 30 years that I was a walking mailman I hated Mr. Summer. Fortunately, my last summer was the mildest I had during my career. And, fortunately (for me), the succeeding two summers were ghastly.

(The two succeeding winters were pretty bad, too). I don't miss delivering mail during Mr. Summer AT ALL.

What I do miss is this: the camaraderie of a group of folks plowing through hot, sticky, endless summer days and accomplishing their "appointed rounds." You arrive at work and know that you and your fellow letter carriers are going to have a tough go of it. You take in enough Gatorade, tea, and water to supply a small African village, and as the hours melt by, most of that fluid ends up under your arms, down your back, and in your shoes. You catch a whiff of breeze and it is nearly paradise to your being.

I always felt sorry for those with fair skin who had to lather with sunscreen 17 times during the day to keep from turning into tomatoes. The other difficulty in these summer days is that all the dogs are out and to make matters even worse, all the kids are out, too, and the dogs are in extra-protective mode over their kiddos—plus they ain't exactly reveling in the beastly weather, either.

And then you hear some guy on the radio blathering on about what a wonderful sunny day it is—you know, the guy who has central air in his house, a freeze-box A.C. system in his car, and works (while sitting on his behind) in an air-conditioned office. Anyway, I say all that to say these two things. One, while I don't miss bringing the bills in the warm weather, I do miss my compatriots who are still out there today and who I slogged through many a day with. Hats off to them, my pals.

Two, don't greet your mailman with a "hot enough for ya?" It is not funny and they don't appreciate it . . . REALLY. Offer a cool drink and don't yell at them when they are three houses past yours to come back and get your outgoing mail that you forgot to leave at the mailbox. It's tough work, and they are doing the best they can. Hang in there, my ol' friends! I survived 30 summers and you will and can, too! Cheers! (Oh, and just from me to Mr. Summer: PFFFT!!! I outlasted and beat you, you miserable old beast. Hah!!!)

As you can see, I enjoy talking about my career and sharing the myriad of stories that accompany said talk. But

I began to realize that in regard to social media at any rate, I could not and should not continue indefinitely. So I made an executive decision. Partly because I knew I wanted to write this book, but mostly so as not to become that old fuddy-duddy with the creaky voice who tells the same stories at every family gathering. I decided to make one final original social media post about being a mailman.

January 24, 2018

This will PROBABLY be my final ORIGINAL post of this type. Why today and why the last? Today marks—wait for it—1,000 days since I retired. One thousand?! How can that be? I've barely gotten used to 30 years of my career having passed by. In the 2 ½-plus years since I walked my route for the final time, I have gone through many moods, reflections, and thoughts about my career—and the end of it.

I now understand that I was a bit lost for the first several months after I left the USPS. When you are part of something for so long it gets into your very identity. I mean, I walked my route about 6,000 times. For three decades the idea of being a letter carrier was a significant chunk of who I was. To have that just be lopped off of my personal psyche was jarring, to say the least.

Initially I saw retirement as just a long succession of days off and vacation. It was not so. It was only after speaking with other retirees that this came to be clearly in focus. Don't get me wrong. I didn't nor don't want to come back. My body had had enough. And I look outside on sloppy wet days or days where the thermometer punches into the 90s and I giggle inside (and sometimes out loud) that I am not out in those elements any longer.

For the past 32 months I have filled my life with baseball, people, writing, music, reading, and much more time with Jill. I have yet to have even a single bored minute. Most of the time I am looking at my list and wondering WHICH thing I want to do, but NEVER wondering IF I have something to do.

And in the past several months, I have come to a better and deeper peace about really being done as a walking mailman. It is what I DID, no longer what I DO. This is just a last rambling of an old, broken-down, grumpy, EX-mailman who is looking back and being very grateful for a career that brought scores of fabulous folks into his life. THEY are the reason that I LIKED being a mailman. So glad to have many of them at my fingertips via social media. To my coworkers and customers: thanks and heartfelt cheers! You know who you are. Oh, and thanks to y'all who so faithfully read these posts for so many years.

How are your shoes and water holding out? Well, we are just about done with this mailmanpalooza. But you can't quite turn in your keys just yet.

Chapter 34

FINAL CORRESPONDENCE (INCLUDING MY BEST)

"Given me the privilege"

How did 30 years go by so fast? A man who retired a few years before me said during his farewell speech, "The days drag but the years fly." Is it that way for all people in all jobs or is this truth more to the heart for those who are blue-collar workers? I am not the one to ask. But that statement was certainly true for me.

As I wrote in my final social media post, I had anticipated retirement to feel like an endless succession of days off. It did not. And it hit me hard. There were times I was reeling internally trying to find my new balance of life. My new (I hate using this overused word) identity. I was never bored. I had lots to do and was enjoying all those things. I reveled in the lack of physical punishment my body was not marinating in. I loved having my time be my own and not having a boss or time clock to report to every day. All the individual parts to retirement were wonderful. But my insides were not.

Jill was fabulously patient and understanding and tried to help me navigate through my uneasiness. I missed the identification of being a mailman. No, that is not quite right. I missed the identification of my friends and acquaintances of me being a mailman. If anyone in my circle of people heard a joke about the Post Office, or saw something on the news, or had a question, they always came to me. I enjoyed that. I did not want to lose that identification. It was who I was.

After I had been unemployed for nearly 21 months, I met with some other postal retirees who gather once a month for dinner, drinks, and rehashing of stories. I had been there about an hour when one of the guys (who I called J.B.) pulled me to the side to chat. We exchanged some basic greetings; then he asked me how I was doing. I gave a superficial answer.

Then he caught me off guard with this statement: "I was depressed for the first year and a half or two after I retired." I was astonished. This gentleman is not anywhere the emotional vehicle that I am. This was a revelation! We talked at length about how much we missed the camaraderie of getting the job done with a batch of folks you encountered day by day. J.B. was the one who had coined the phrase, "The days drag but the years fly." We talked about missing the camaraderie of the Post Office. That feeling of group accomplishment at the end of a difficult day. And the longer we talked the more the murkiness cleared from the eyes of my heart. I was depressed! Yes!

Finally, a name to put on my mental weariness. I drove home that evening after dinner, bounded through the door, grabbed Jill by the shoulders and announced with a sheepish grin plastered on my face, "Honey, I'm depressed! That has been what has been dragging me around since I retired!" She looked at me with her marvelously tender eyes and said, "Yes, my love, I know." It is what she had been trying to help me understand for months. But it had taken someone who had (literally) walked the same path I had to get me to inject this truth into my psyche. There is not a specific name for what was troubling me. It was a combination of a severe displacement in my life: no longer being a part of something or a group of someones that strive to accomplish a common goal, the camaraderie of my fellow letter carriers, missing the daily encounters with my precious customers—well, basically nearly everything you have just spent 300-plus pages reading about.

And one other thing. You can't tell anyone. But just between us, I was afraid of being forgotten. I poured 27 years of my life into route 0655 and I didn't want to be a statistic. An asterisk in the folks' hearts of "that-mailman-we-used-to-have-what-was-his-name?" I did not want to become that shadowy memory for them that my mailman when I was a boy had become to me.

Since that time I have continued to work through the emotions of NOT being a mailman. It is a process. I am not by nature a patient man and I truly wish I could have snapped my fingers and been, well, myself again. But I walked as a mailman for 30 years, so it is only natural it will take some time to walk OUT of being a mailman.

Another sweet moment came after a chance meeting one evening as I was driving through that neighborhood on my way to a meeting at the church I attend. I saw my friend Curt, the gentleman who briefly spoke at my retirement party about missing me and who had called the television station about me. He and I chatted a moment and he told me the neighborhood had a social media page and invited me to join it. After I did, he wrote these terribly gracious words about me:

September 27, 2018

For those of you who don't know our newest addition to the group, it is our retired mail carrier (Merrit Hearing) who walked these streets for [27 years]. He was a member of our little neighborhood and knew everyone. He looked out after us and watched the kids grow up. We actually had a parade for him in the neighborhood on the last day he walked these streets. His retirement party was packed as a testament to his dedication to the folks he served. We miss seeing you bringing our mail, Merrit, but after seeing you the other day it looks like retirement is working well for you.

About the statement of driving through the neighborhood of my old route. I've been doing that going back to when I first became the mailman on route 0655. In the early years it was just a sense of "Hey, cool, this is where I deliver the mail." In later years it was more to see who might be out and about that I could stop and have a chat with, especially if my family might be with me. If I was on vacation or recovering from one of my many injuries, I might drive through the area checking to see if they were receiving good mail service during my time off. Now that I'm retired I will take any excuse to drive through the different 'hoods of my route on the chance I might see an old customer and catch up on each others lives. I still get a kick out of this and every time I do it a little flutter goes through my being.

⸎

One day a few months later I decided to try to find someone else. Danny-Jo worked at one of the businesses on my route for several years. But she had eventually transferred out to another branch a considerable distance from my house. But one windy Thursday afternoon I was sort of in the area where she worked and decided to drop in and surprise her with a visit. It had been a long, long time and I was not entirely sure if she would remember be. It turned out to be an inspired idea and a glorious visit.

January 17, 2019

What a supreme delight to find this dear lady after EIGHTEEN years! Danny-Jo was one of my fave customers at one of my favorite businesses on my mail route. She transferred to the west side and I lost touch with her. We laughed and shared stories and hugged about seven times and chatted up a storm for a good half hour. I was very touched that not only did she remember me, but also with the same fondness that I remembered her. And that's why I liked being a mailman.

But I didn't always seek these people out. Sometimes they literally came right through my front door.

January 19, 2019

And the connections just keep coming. My father-in-law brought someone from his church to look at our kitchen for some minor carpentry work. As the man walked in, I could not see his face but I thought I recognized his voice, but I could not place how I knew it. Imagine my surprise when the man looked up at me and I realized it was somebody who had a shop on my route for many, many, many years. He knew that he knew me but he also could not place where. Context, you know. After I told him who I was we embraced and had a lovely visit with each other.

Six days later it happened again. And although the connection was not as in-depth, for reasons I will share after the post, it gave me more . . . hmmm . . . comfort.

January 25, 2019

Annnnd it happened again. Ran into this man and his daughter at Costco. I was his mailman from age 10 (um, his age, not mine). I had not seen him in several years and was very touched that he remembered me. It was a delightful encounter and brought many years of memories. I can distinctly remember dozens of times over my career his father coming out to greet me with his European accent saying, "Hey, buddy, how are you doing today?" Dang, this mailman stuff was pretty cool, wasn't it?

The reason this encounter touched me so deeply even though I would not describe this young man as one of my closer acquaintances, was for precisely that reason. He was NOT one of my closer relationships . . . and yet, he remembered me. Maybe I won't be forgotten after all.

There were aftershocks of my career. I attended our postal Christmas party the first two years after I retired and had a fabulous time. Everyone was delighted to see me and I them. Lots of laughs and stories. And a bit of melancholy on my part. But thoroughly enjoyable. But the third one? I looked around the establishment where the party was held. Good grief, who WERE these people? Fully a third of the attendees were strangers to me. And I can only imagine what I looked like to them. I felt out of place. Out of time. Not unwelcome. Not at all. But these were no longer my people. Creston was no longer my post office. An even newer generation of letter carriers was invading the postal service. And old, broken-down, grumpy, EX-mailmen are not needed. And that is okay. It's how it should be.

One thing that did not change was my identification of being a mailman. People still sent me their jokes and still asked the questions. And because I was no longer doing the deed on a daily basis, sometimes those moments caught me hilariously off guard.

One day on Facebook someone had posted the question, "What was the craziest thing you ever did for money?" If you are familiar with this social media, this is the silly type of question that will be put up from time to time and then will make the rounds through several people's "pages." I was trolling one day and came across this particular one.

I scrolled down the page to see some of the answers and lost my mind at a picture that someone had posted to answer the question. It was a photo of a very cold and snowy winter day . . . with a mailman trudging through the snow making his rounds. I started laughing and couldn't stop and finally got to the point where I was coughing from laughing so hard. I replied to the question" "Yep, that would be my answer."

———

I still have terrible circulation in my knees, ankles, and feet. Despite the improvement after I retired, the myriad of miles has had a lasting impact on my knees and I have to lather them up with a deep heating ointment two or three nights a week to keep from having spasms of pain while I try to sleep. (By the way, it is best not to confuse this ointment with your toothpaste. Another story for another book.) My right heel is stone cold all the time, a consequence of 75 million steps on that heel. Year round I sleep with flannel pajamas, flannel sheets, a blanket, an electric blanket, and a comforter on top, thick flannel socks on my feet, plus a crocheted afghan folded in quarters placed over my feet. I have to keep my legs that warm to sleep. You have already read much on my knees. My right ankle has become so weak from being sprained so many times that if I am not paying attention I tend to walk on the outside of my right foot to feel balanced. Walking fully planted on that foot makes me feel as if my ankle will fold inside underneath me. But walking on the edge of my foot obviously brings its own problems. When I started I had the highest arches you ever saw. Now I am nearly flat-footed.(By the way, did you know there is an unofficial correlation between the height of your foot arch and the height of the arch of the roof of your mouth? If one is high, they probably both are.) My fingers also have very poor circulation from gripping and fingering letters for 30 years and my knuckle joints almost always feel tender and cold. If I am not using my hands they are often balled up in a fist or tucked in a pocket to keep warm.

But carrying a mailbag over your right shoulder also took its toll.

January 19, 2014

Woke up last Monday morning with a very sore shoulder. I figured I just slept on it wrong. But it got progressively worse through the week. Yesterday delivering the mail (with mailbag on that shoulder), it was very painful all day. I have played this game before. I remember this pain from about 12 years ago. Missed a week of work. Yeah, just what I need right now. Went to urgent care today. Tendinitis. Got cortisone shot. Should be good to go by Tuesday, which is when I work next. Whew!

Loved those C-zone shots. They got me through two bouts of what the doctor called a "dead shoulder." On the other hand, although my knees and right shoulder are worn out and neither are very good to be used for any significant length of time, they also don't simply hurt all the time and are fully functional.

From the fall I took evading the pit bull, my hip causes me some problems from time to time, but all these are issues I can deal with and are typical for a man my age who did what I did. I try to hit the track a couple times a week and walk three miles or so. My doctor says I am the healthiest post-60-year-old she knows because my heart rate and blood pressure and all the other internal stuff is fantastic. So I really cannot complain. And on the other side of things, because I received lots of good advice about lathering on the sun screen, I have no skin problems at all.

Probably what belabors me the most is my dreaming. I found out that I am not alone in this. The other retirees have told me they sometimes dream of the Post Office as well. We all tend to have the same type of postal dream. Some variation of: it's getting dark or at least late in the day; we have most or all of our route to still do; we have lost our keys; we can't find our car; we lost the mail, etc. You get the idea.

I have actually "invented" a neighborhood in my dream state. It does not exist in reality, only in my sleeping. I have visited it several times. I have entered this neighborhood from all directions. With each newly discovered entrance I think I will finally be able to escape what invariably happens. And it always ends the same way. I get stuck at the same spot inside this neighborhood, and from this spot there is no escape. I can't find my car, there are loose dogs and spiders everywhere and it is getting seriously dark. I have had this same dream many, many times. It never ends well. I wake up in the morning and tell Jill, "Well, I visited my neighborhood again last night." We can kind of laugh about it now. Sort of.

—— ⚯ ——

Retrospection. That seems like it might be too big of a word for a book like this. But I suppose this is what this whole tome has been about. In some ways writing these stories and memories down for all to see and enjoy has been cathartic for me.

I hope you have been able in some way to step into my old mailman shoes and catch a glimpse of what I did for 30 years. Mostly, my interactions with the folks, inside my postal station and out. That is what I miss. How cool of a job is it to be able to have dozens of chats on a daily basis with folks who genuinely care about you and appreciate the service you bring to them. Most of those chats were somewhat superficial, but they were still for real with real people discussing real life.

If you did not see them for a time—either because you were off the job or because they were unavailable for some reason—there was a definite sense of missing them, and they you. Beyond price is that.

And within the walls of Creston Station existed what for me is summed up in the phrase "esprit de corps." We were in it together. If the weather, or the mail, or the management, was unpleasant, we shared the wet or heat or cold and difficulty as a unit, with knowing glances between us of a communal experience.

Of the many aspects of being a mailman that I miss, this is the most painful for me to no longer experience on a regular basis. Gosh, what an amazing clan of folks I worked with. Hard work. Camaraderie. And, oh, so much laughter. Irreplaceable, both the people and the experiential feelings that went with them.

Remember at the beginning I said it was all about people? Hopefully this has been made abundantly clear. Have I romanticized my profession? I hope not. It was tough. Really tough. And there were scads of dreary days. But I choose to focus and bring to light the greater aspects of what I did for three decades. As I counted down the days to my retirement day, I was flooded with so many heavy emotions. Let me please share with you now what I posted on social media the night before my last day. It truly encapsulates so much of what I felt and still feel about carrying the mail for the Post Office for 30 years. In some way, you could say this post is a crammed exclamation of what you have been reading on all these pages. My final social media post, before my final day as a city letter carrier of route 0655 and my final day as an employee of the United States Postal Service.

April 29, 2015

So we are down to O N E day left. Whew. A postal retiree from a few years ago put it best: "the days drag, but the years fly." I remember with great clarity my interview, my first day, my first day delivering solo, my first day on my route. I started at the Post Office in my very late 20s; I leave two months shy of 60.

From the time I began my career I have been blessed with three more children in addition to the one I already had. I have gone through full beards, goatees, mustaches, and clean-shaven. I have lived in six different locations. I have worked with about four or five generations of mail carriers. We have shared each other's joys, and cried with one another over our sorrows.

When I lost my son, my coworkers held me up with their love, encouragement, a gazillion hugs, and precious memories. They have seen me win contests for concert tickets and laughed at my over-the-top excitement. I have been blessed with hundreds of amazing customers (28 for the last 27 years). Those customers have allowed me to walk through their lives, and we have shared those lives between us. Again, when my son died, many of those customers came to his memorial, and dozens of them asked me for many months after how I was holding up. YOU CANNOT PUT A PRICE ON THAT, MY FRIENDS!!

And many of them shared with me the joy at my marriage to Jill 3 1/2 years ago. And incredibly, many of those dear customers allowed me to step into their lives as more than just the mailman, but as a friend. They have given me the privilege to know, chat with, and learn from their fabulous kids. Yes, my job has been difficult. Like other mail carriers, I have grumbled through distressing weather, dealt with scary dogs (and one out-of-control rabbit!), and wondered some days if I would ever get to my last stop.

Well, tomorrow, I will get to my VERY LAST STOP for the VERY LAST TIME.

To my coworkers: thank you for your support as we worked side by side.

To my customers: thank you for the supreme privilege to walk through your lives. Tonight, I feel a most fortunate man. Dang, I have been blessed. I was a mailman.

Chapter 35

POSTSCRIPT

Two things. I offer this advice every year on social media just as the hot summer weather hits. Not just to my custo . . . EX-customers, but to all who receive mail. You can have this one for free. Pay attention. It's important.

Hey, kids. Here is some advice from a retired 30-year vet of delivering the mail. Here are some DON'Ts and DO's on how to treat your letter carrier on days like this.

DON'T under any circumstances say "Is it hot enough for ya?" That is annoying beyond words.

DON'T, if you are one of those who like this hot weather, say "Wow, what a great day to have your job!"

DON'T, if your mailman walks his route, yell out for him when he is three houses past yours, "Oh, can you come back and take my letter?"

DO offer him a cool NON-ALCOHOLIC beverage.

DO ask him if he needs some more sunscreen. (uh, if you have some)

DO if your mail receptacle is near bushes, keep it clear of bees, spiderwebs, etc.

MOST IMPORTANTLY:

DO keep your dog secure. The hot weather can make them more aggressive and protective of the little ones playing outside. If your dog is in the house, MAKE SURE your door is shut tight and that the dog cannot even accidentally get out if it is unlatched or a kid opens the door. These can be extremely miserable days to deliver mail. PLEASE DON'T MAKE THEM WORSE BY NOT USING COMMON SENSE.

I mentioned that I attended the Creston Post Office Christmas party in December of 2017. At one point in the evening, Alex—the man who took over my route after I retired—came up to me to talk. At this point he had been the regular mailman on MY (it always will be to me) route for over two years.

"Merrit, I just have to thank you. I love your route. Man, those people out there are great. They treat me so well! They really spoil me. You must have really taken good care of them for all of those years."

Yes, Alex, I did. I really, really did. And they took care of me.

ACKNOWLEDGMENTS

Although this book has obviously not been primarily about my faith, it would be neglectful in the utmost if I did not mention and thank my Lord Jesus Christ for allowing me to have and savor my career. Everything good in my life ultimately comes from Him, and my relationship TO Him supersedes everything else in my life.

In that vein, I wish to thank four individuals who "prayed my way" into my postal job. From the time of my initial exam these four regularly brought before God my desire to become an employee of the United States Postal Service. I will always be grateful to them for their faithfulness in continuing to pray about my situation. Cynthia Elliott (my former wife), Keith and Valerie Sjodin, and Kathi Baker. Thank you, my friends.

And thank you to:

Those nameless postal workers partaking of lunch 40 years ago at Plush Pippin who first suggested to Cynthia I look into a postal career.

My supervisors and managers who treated me fairly and with respect I say thank you for making that aspect of the job enjoyable, when you certainly didn't have to. You know who you are.

Editor Sue Miholer of Picky, Picky Ink, who helped me "write it right." But her friendship is more important to me than her skill. Thanks, my friend.

Anneli worked her magic again, bringing fresh images of my profession to the cover and weaving an attractive view of my words on the pages. She took an image from either my memory or my imagination (I'll never be certain which one) and fabulously reproduced it into a spectacular cover. Only she and I will know the difficulties we faced. One of us was always upbeat about those difficulties. It wasn't me, folks.

My Benefactor. You know who you are and you know what you did. I will always be terribly grateful for your belief in me.

Shelbi, thank you for your encouragement and promotional ideas that were outside the box.

Andrea Cook, thank you for the initial push all those years ago to write my first book, which led to this one, which led to.....We will see what kind of monster you created.

Jim Ferretti, who did a flattering, but accurate, interview with and about me. And thank you for your friendship.

Bruce Porter. Who would have guessed my finances would lead me to the person who would bestow upon me such a brilliant idea for the title of this book. A moment of genius.

Mr. Kenneth Keyn, who gave my book a first run-through read and offered many comments and suggestions that tightened up the stories a tad where they needed it.

Ginger Wright, Billy Gans, Marsha Tate, Jim Ferretti, Buffy Rhoades, & Jerry Fitzsimmons for your incredibly kind words.

A delicious thank you to all the folks at Speedboat Coffee over the years. I thank you 1,103 times from the bottom of my taste buds. For your friendships, I raise my humble cup of hot chocolate. Thanks especially to owner Don, and to those at the end who made it such a celebration of friendship and joy: Andy, Moosh, and Dow-Dow.

To all the employees of All Classical Portland, 89.9 F M, particularly Robert McBride and extra-particularly my dear friend, the effervescent Christa Wessel. A lot of long days my last eight years were made hugely more pleasurable due to your fabulous music and winning personalities. You enhanced my life beyond what I can express.

To the seemingly myriad of medical practitioners who patched, taped, stapled, medicated, operated, exercised, encouraged, and physical-therapied me through my 30 years, especially the last ones when I was consistently falling apart, falling down, and falling onto my couch. My two occupational doctors, Dr. Yoshinaga and Dr. Chang. My chiropractor, Dr. Ashton, who graciously suggested she could do no more for me and recommended back surgery. The late Dr. Z. and his assistant, Mr. Oliver, who fixed by back better than I could have ever imagined possible. Dr. Ann, who possibly saved my life by demanding I get to the hospital to get care for my blood clot when no one else believed I had one. My two P.T.s, Bertie and Anna, who knew just how hard to push me to get my hip and ankle and knee working properly again. Shirley, my counselor who allowed me to blather on about my fears and gave me workable tools to deal with my pit bull attack. Most of all, my affection and deepest thanks to my primary care physician, Dr. Karin Jacobson. She has taken care of me with tender and tough care for more than a dozen years. She has also become my friend and honored me with her presence at my retirement party. Forget about that old ex-basketball player. She is the REAL Dr. J.

Deep thanks to my customers, those who lived on my route for a short time, and especially those who were with me for decades. I hope you were able to recognize yourself in my stories and pick up on my gratitude for them and for you. If you didn't read about yourself, it was not for lack of appreciation. But a 617-page book just was not on the radar, so I couldn't include all of you. But, believe me, you are all included in my heart of memories. And a double ditto for those of you who shared your kids with me. Oh, how I did learn from those little precious treasures.

My coworkers were the best. How do I know? Because they put up with me for YEARS! I wish I had a way to list every single one. All of you impacted my life. An extra-deep gratitude to those who were part of "Aisle 4" and worked in close proximity to me. "Thank you" seems like a pitiful way to express that.

By the way, I wish so much that I could have included photos of all these fabulous folks: the customers who filled me with these delightful stories (especially the fabulous tots) and my coworkers who were so much a part of this adventure you have read about. But it would have required pages upon pages of permission and would have raised the price of this book to $68. So you will just have to imagine.

And one final time, I sincerely wish I could have included every single person I worked with and every single customer I had the privilege of delivering mail to. But obviously, it was not practical. But I thank ALL of you for ALL of it. Those who still live on "my" route, those who moved off, and those who "moved on." On a side note, writing this book led me to a personal project of making up a "route 55" notebook with every address, every person, every memory I can think of jotted down for my memory banks. I don't want to forget any of it.

Thank you to Jill's extended family, who came along during my final years but celebrated my career as if we had been together for the entire journey.

Deep love sent to Jill's daughter Jael, who has become as my own.

I am grateful for a sister who loves me, believes in me, and respects me. I hold her close to my heart. Thank you, Sharon.

I adore my two sons-in-love, Rigo and Ben. Thank you for loving my girls even more than I do. And that's saying something.

To my three fabulous children, Maria, Faitha, and Valeena. What a delight it was to be your mailman daddy all those years. You always treated my profession as important and shared it with pride to your friends. One of my most enduring and endearing memories will be the picture of the three of you along with your brother Elliott bounding out of the house with shrieks of "Daddy's home!" as you flew down the driveway and piled into Mailman Mike's little red pick-up.

And to their mom, Cynthia, I send my sincerest gratitude. Thank you for pointing the way to my profession, your patience with all the aches, pains, and injuries I incurred along the way, and for being a partner for the first half of this journey. (So would that be about 35,000 miles?)

To ALL of you who for year after year as you read my Facebook posts suggested and urged and begged me to compile a book, thanks for the inspiration. I can only hope this book is what you had in mind. If you have caught a deeper glimpse beyond those meager posts of how this job affected me, then count me successful.

Finally, what do I say about and to my delightful song, my Angel Eyes, my tenderhearted wife Jill? You came into the game at the time I was virtually and frequently and literally stumbling through my job. Thanks for the physical care of my knees and shoulder, and the care of my heart as I made my way to the finish line. And thank you for your talent in balancing my sentimental old foolish self with my broken-down, old, grumpy self. You are my sparkle.

And to you the reader I simply say: It's time for you to turn in your keys and slip off your shoes. I hope you enjoyed the ride . . . er . . . walk. Thanks for your time.

*Even at an early age my parents were training
me to deal with those canines.*

ABOUT THE AUTHOR

Merrit Hearing is a retired walking mailman of 30 years, the last 27 of which were on the same route. He is an incurable list maker, loves to eat popcorn, watches Major League baseball as often as he can, and delves into his eclectic collection of music CDs on a daily basis. He has a passion for reigniting old friendships and planning reunions. After trekking 70,000 miles during his career, he hung up his mailbag and resides with his wife of eight years, Jill, in the Portland metropolitan area.

This book is available on:
www.amazon.com

Made in the USA
San Bernardino, CA
02 November 2019